Dancing
With Siva

A Hindu Catechism

Sivaya
Subramuniyaswami

Published by
Himalayan Academy
California • Hawaii

Third Edition

**Copyright © 1990
by Sivaya Subramuniyaswami**

Published by
Himalayan Academy
California • Hawaii

PRINTED IN USA

Dedication

This *Hindu Catechism* is dedicated to the great Satguru, Siva Yogaswami, of Sri Lanka, disciple of Chellappaswami, master of Sivaya Subramuniyaswami, perfect siddha yogi and illumined soul who knew the Unknowable and held Truth in the palm of his hand. He taught all to seek within, to know the Self and to see God Siva everywhere and in everyone. Among his great sayings:

Know thy Self by thyself.

Siva is doing it all.

All is Siva.

Be still.

Siva's Cosmic Dance

I am the dancer, the audience,
  the stage and the show.
I dance divinely. I watch it. I know.

You are dance.
You are all the movements of the universe,
  galaxies complete, planets and suns.
In the dance we will meet,
  and you'll say, "We are One."

Contents

Every gesture in Siva's cosmic dance is rich in mystic symbolism.

Author's Foreword

IT IS NO ACCIDENT THAT WE HAVE MET, THAT YOU HAVE FOUND THIS BOOK AND THE TREA-SURES IT CONTAINS. IT'S ALL PART OF THE DIVINE dance. The treasure is divine knowledge, knowledge about you and God, knowledge about how to live a spiritual life, knowledge about what Hindus teach and believe. All of this and more awaits you in the chapters that follow.

We are all dancing with Siva, and He with us. Ultimately, we are Siva dancing. All motion we see in this external world starts in Siva. The whole universe is engaged in endless motion and activity, a whirling flow of change. Modern physicists have found Siva's cosmic dance to be the most appropriate metaphor to describe their scientific discoveries. In *The Tao of Physics* Fritjof Capra writes, "Indian artists of the tenth and twelfth centuries have represented Siva's cosmic dance in magnificent bronze sculptures of dancing figures with four arms whose superbly balanced and yet dynamic gestures express the rhythm and unity of Life. Modern physics has thus revealed that every subatomic particle not only performs an energy dance, but also *is* an energy dance, a pulsating process of creation and destruction."

Similarly, our friend in Costa Rica, David Carli, inspired by his meditation on a single seed of an extraordinary ginger plant called Siam, wrote: "When you look into the structure of things, you find mostly space, with a smattering of atoms. When you look into the structure of the atom, you find 100 billion times more space than you do electrons and protons. When you look into the structure of electrons and protons, you find an even larger percentage of space. If we could look into the structures of these incredibly small particles, I venture to say it would also consist mostly of space. Ultimately, down and down, smaller and smaller, the last particle is not solid matter at all but a force or energy. For lack of a better name, I call this energy God—a simple force that could also be called existence."

The Symbolism of the Cosmic Dancer

As Nataraja, the King of Dance, Siva is Creator, Preserver and Destroyer of the manifest world. Siva is neither male nor female, but both. Siva is the perfect balance of the masculine-feminine energies, symbolized by the female earring in His left ear and the masculine earring in His right ear. Each symbol of Lord Nataraja is full of meaning. The circle of fire around Him represents the cosmos and, most especially, consciousness. In one hand He holds the drum, from which creation issues forth. A second hand is raised in a gesture of blessing, giving duration to His creation, betokening preservation. A third hand holds a flame, which is destruction, the dissolution of form. One leg stands upon a person, symbol of the ignorance of the ego and the bondage of the human soul before it matures into perfection; thus, this leg is obscuring grace. The uplifted leg is revealing grace, which releases the mature soul from bondage. Siva's fourth hand gestures toward the Holy Foot in assurance that His grace is the refuge for everyone, the way to Liberation. The face looming above Nataraja in the ring of fire is Mahakala, "great time," which devours all. The cobra around His waist is kundalini sakti, the cosmic force and power of consciousness resident within all, for this dance is not just a beautiful symbol, it is a reality taking place within each of us this very moment.

The vast complexity of Siva's cosmic dance is traditionally represented in 108 poses. Over twenty centuries ago, Maharishi Tirumular of the Kailasa Paramparai praised Siva's never-ending dance with loving eloquence: "In all worlds He is, the Holy Lord. In darkness He is, light He is. In sun He is, in moon He is, everywhere He is. The Lord is in all creation. None knows His coming and going. He is distant. He is near. Water, earth, sky, fire and wind, the spark within the body—all these He is. Multiple He is; One He is. Deathless He is."

The Eternal Truths

It is imperative at this time in our history, when the world, our earth, is on the brink of a space age, that we value and learn from ancient Hindu wisdom. Long ago, great sages of India unfolded these eternal truths from within themselves and recorded them as written scripture to be sung out through the voices of their representatives today. So great was their insight, so great was their Hindu wisdom. Truly, this eternal wisdom lives now and will live on into the next generation, the next and the next.

There are billions of souls in physical bodies on this planet today. Among them are Eastern souls in Western bodies and Western souls in Eastern bodies. Hindu souls are scattered throughout the world. Hindus all over the world— be they Eastern souls in Western bodies or Eastern souls in Eastern bodies—may take heed that this book preserves the ageless truths for this technological age. We have left the agricultural era. Closely knit village communities are dispersing. Before the youth run rampant and are seduced by alien ways, let us band together and be strong, gain knowledge and sever ourselves from adharmic ways. If you are a seeker on the path and a free soul on this planet, having never been exposed to religion or to religionists, you may well be enthralled by the investigation into these Vedic-Agamic truths that were realized and spoken so many thousands of years ago. You may discover them to be the most illumined and applicable of all teachings for your life in the world today.

Spiritual unfoldment on this inner path comes through meditation and through deep inquiry into oneself. But traditional Hindu patterns for daily living, worshiping and philosophy are its foundation, its bedrock, for total success. Theoretically, the area of meditation should not be divided from religion or simply practiced as an intellectual exercise. Meditation is the culmination of Hinduism in action in one's life. True, "Truth is one, and paths are many." But one of these paths must be chosen and followed toward the one Truth that it outlines, because methods vary and techniques differ from teacher to teacher. Therefore, all seekers must find the method and the teacher which they intuit are best for them. Once that path has been chosen, they must follow and fulfill it most conscientiously.

This book is the outgrowth of over thirty years of research, slowly developed and taught. We include here permission for others to use this text freely in teaching their young, or within their society, organization or school as a text. We believe that religion, God's law, will work for us in solving the problems, healing the wounds, giving solace to others in these times of stress and strain as man adjusts to humankind's inventions in an age of population explosion, an age of famine and great fortune. We believe Sanatana Dharma holds answers for mankind in a technological age where information is merchandise, and time has a price.

As we proceed through *Dancing with Siva*, you will come to see that it contains a new presentation of very ancient knowledge. You will soon realize that, somewhere within you, you already know these truths. You will find yourself traveling back in your memory, perhaps for several lives, and remembering that you have studied this before in the same way that you are studying it now. I say again, it is no accident that we have met.

A new breed of souls is even now coming up in the world. They are fearless because they are strong. They do not fear death, ill-health or lack of knowledge. Their only qualification is that they love Lord Siva, worship God Siva and the Gods. They have no magic formula. They are selling nothing. They need nothing. They are who they are. This book gives an organized approach as to what to say to the youth and the adults of our religion. This book also gives truth-seekers who have stumbled on the mystical realities a coherent and complete philosophical context through which they can understand and continue to pursue these often unbidden experiences. It validates their inner realizations and gives them the confidence to persevere.

The gurus of the Kailasa Paramparai of the Natha Sampradaya performed great tapas, burned in the fire of spiritual purification. That accumulative tapas made their message heard worldwide. We who succeed these great siddha yogis contemplate their commands and meditate upon their inner findings and conclusions. My Satguru, Siva Yogaswami, once said, "Know thy Self by thyself." This book has been created to make that one goal possible in this very life, to offer the tools, the knowledge and the encouragement when the path seems too difficult to follow, to offer a philosophical and cultural basis on which to practice and unfold spiritually while pursuing one's inmost depths through daily sadhana and meditation.

Proceed with confidence. Success is assured. You cannot fail if bhakti is integrated with jnana, Siddhanta with Vedanta, Vedas with Agamas, and Saivism with everyday life. This is Saiva Siddhanta. This is the secure path leading to knowledge, experience and recognition of your Divine Self.

Sivaya Subramuniyaswami
Kauai Aadheenam, Hawaii
Vijaya Dasami, September 28, 1990

Ardhanarisvara is Lord Siva as the androgynous God in whom all apparent opposites are reconciled in perfect balance.

Introduction

HINDUISM'S GREAT GOD SIVA IS AMONG THE MOST MYSTERIOUS, COMPLEX, PROFOUND AND COMPASSIONATE CONCEPTIONS OF THE one Supreme Being found in the religions of humankind. He is Creator, Preserver and Destroyer of all existence. He is pure love, light, energy and consciousness. He is the timeless, formless and spaceless Absolute Reality. Those who worship the Great God Siva are Saivites, and their religion is called Saivite Hinduism.

Truth seekers on the path in this 20th century know that the first and foremost objective of life is to grow in spiritual maturity and to know God, first in His immanent perfection as Satchidananda, all-pervasive bliss consciousness, and ultimately in His timeless, formless, spaceless perfection as Parasivam, Truth Absolute, the Self God within all souls. Seekers of truth may be individual pathfinders or from any of the many schools of mystical or metaphysical thought, both motivated to look within themselves for deeper realities.

Pilgrims on the path toward enlightenment, seekers of the Divine Mind within themselves, seeing Divinity within all others, transcending the norm through their command of the inner forces and through positive thinking, will take profoundly to this timeless study. Serious aspirants will find here many answers to lingering questions about the world's oldest religion which their search for Truth may not yet have revealed.

There are many advanced schools of metaphysical and philosophical thought in the world today, each elucidating in its own way the three questions: Who am I? Where did I come from? and Where am I going? Inquiry into these penetrating matters will reveal that man is not his body, not his mind or emotions. He is, in truth, the Truth he seeks—and religion is his path to that realization. Through our study of this book we will come to know how the ancients, living in an era before recorded history, answered these questions. If in your study of Dancing with Siva you gain a few new ideas and an appreciable knowledge of the world's most ancient religion, that is reward enough in itself. If you are drawn personally deeper within the superconscious depths of your being, closer to God and to the Gods, awakening love and wisdom from within, then the truest purpose of this book will have been fulfilled.

Perhaps you are among the many souls who were born into the Hindu religion but have been influenced by Western education and values. If that is the case, there may be some concepts herein which conflict with what you have previously learned. Looking closely, you will see that the Vedic-Agamic truths of the Sanatana Dharma shine through and are well preserved. Teach Dancing with Siva to your children. Share it with your friends. Let the wisdom of the oldest religion in the world, the religion of your parents and their parents, flourish in your life and on into the next generation. Let strength come into your mind and love into your heart as you proudly proclaim Saivism as your faith and religion.

The philosophical basis for Dancing with Siva is Natha Sage Tirumular's Vedic-Agamic Saiva Siddhanta theology, which encompasses both Vedanta and Siddhanta. The spiritual authority rests in the Kailasa Paramparai of the Natha Sampradaya. Its advice is standard knowledge among most Saivite communities throughout the world, though that knowledge is usually part of an oral and not a written tradition. In Dancing with Siva we do not attempt to cover all the intricacies of philosophy and practice, or to make comparisons between Siddhanta and Vedanta or to offer yoga techniques or advice for personal unfoldment on the path. Dancing with Siva is a simple summary and guideline. It is not scripture, though it does not conflict with scripture and strictly follows orthodox tenets.

The effort was neither one of exacting scholarship nor of all-inclusiveness. Rather, the effort was to present a complex religion in a simple way for hundreds of millions of truth seekers. There is a Hindu allegory in which the milk from 1,000 cows is churned into rich cream. That cream is further churned into butter. That butter is then clarified into a small amount of precious ghee. In a like manner, this book of Hindu wisdom is the distilled essence of a thousand texts.

∼ Part One ∼
The Catechism

What do Saivite Hindus believe about God and the soul? About goodness and evil? About marriage and asceticism? About saints and worship? Here is perhaps the first complete Hindu catechism, with questions and answers about all the major aspects of the world's oldest living religion. Though the questions and answers speak of Siva, most Hindus will find their spiritual philosophy reflected in this catechism, even if they call the Supreme One by other names—whether Krishna, Brahman, Vishnu, Ayyappan or Sakti.

What is the purpose of a catechism and creed? Historically, catechisms and creeds have developed when a religion is transmitted from one culture to another. Until then, the beliefs are fully contained in the culture and taught to the children as a natural part of growing up. But when the religion migrates to lands where other faiths predominate, as when an Indian Hindu family moves to Africa or North America, then the need for written teachings arises. A catechism and creed is meant to summarize the specific teachings and articles of faith, to imbed and thus ensure their transmission from generation to generation. Creeds, most especially, because of their brevity, aid in maintaining continuity and identity of original verbal doctrines. Both are invaluable in providing guidelines for individuals seeking to understand the meaning and purpose of life and striving to realize their highest destiny on the planet. We know that you will enjoy this catechism for Saivite Hinduism. Freely teach it to your children and share it with friends.

The Siva Lingam, "Mark of Siva," is a simple and most ancient symbol of Siva as Parasivam, God beyond all forms and qualities.

Chapter 1

Our Great God Siva

WE BEGIN OUR STUDY AT THE BEGINNING OF
ALL THINGS, SIVA, EXPLORING GOD'S NATURE
AND CREATIVE POWER. GOD IS WORSHIPED IN
MANY WAYS, BUT TRADITION OFFERS THREE
ESPECIALLY MEANINGFUL FORMS.

What is the nature of God Siva?
Truly, God Siva is All and in all, the One without a second,
the Supreme Being and only Absolute Reality. He is Pati, our
Lord, both immanent and transcendent.

God Siva is a one Being, yet we understand Him in three
perfections: Absolute Reality, Pure Consciousness and the
Primal Soul. As Absolute Reality, He is unmanifest, unchanging and transcendent, the Self God which is timeless,
formless and spaceless. As Pure Consciousness, He is the
manifest Primal Substance or Pure Love and Light flowing
through all form and existing everywhere in time and space
simultaneously as Infinite Intelligence and Power. As the Primal Soul, He manifests in three aspects: Brahma, the Creator; Vishnu, the Preserver; and Rudra, the Destroyer. This
Primal Soul is our personal Lord, source of all three worlds
and the laws therein, our Divine Father-Mother who protects, nurtures, guards and guides us, veiling His Truth as we
evolve and revealing Himself when we are mature enough to
receive His Bountiful Grace. We know God Siva as All and in
all, great beyond our conception, a sacred mystery that can
be known in direct communion but cannot be adequately
described or explained. When He is known, all is known.

Did God Siva create the world?
Yes, God created the world and all things in the world. He creates and sustains from moment to moment every atom of the seen physical and unseen spiritual universe.

God Siva created us. He created the earth and all things upon it, animate and inanimate. He created the sea and all things within it. He created time and the vast spaces and the uncounted stars. He created night and day, joy and sorrow, love and hate, birth and death. He created the gross and the subtle, this world and the other worlds. All things without exception are His creation, perpetuated by Him and to a lesser degree through his co-workers in the creative act: man and the great inner plane devas and Mahadevas. Creator of all, God Siva Himself is uncreated. He has no beginning, but is eternal. He abides within His creation, ruling from within and not above. God Siva is All-Knowing, All-Powerful and All-Encompassing. He is good, holy, merciful, true, just and compassionate. There is only one Supreme God; He is called by many names. The One Great God animates all life and is worshiped in all religions. Paramaguru Siva Yogaswami taught us, "Who bids the sun to move? Who makes the moon resplendent? Who illumines the eye to see? Who tends the blooms to blossom? Ponder deeply and you will discern that Siva's Will reigns supreme. He is all-pervasive; from Him emanates everything."

Does God Siva have form or is He formless?
God Siva has form and is formless. He is the immanent Pure Consciousness or pure form; He is the Personal Lord manifesting as innumerable forms; and He is the impersonal, transcendent Absolute beyond all form.

We know Siva in His three perfections, two of form and one formless. First, we worship His manifest form as Pure Love and Consciousness. Second, we worship Him as our Personal Lord, the Primal Soul, who tenderly loves and cares for His devotees—a Being whose resplendent body may be seen in mystic vision. In our daily lives we love, honor, worship and serve God in these manifest perfections. Ultimately, in perfectly simple yet awesomely austere Nirvikalpa Samadhi, we realize Him as the formless Parasivam, sought for and known only by yogis and jnanis. We cannot speak of His Absolute Reality, which is beyond qualities and description, yet knowable to the fully matured soul who seeks God within through yoga under the guidance of a Satguru. Gurudeva has taught us the Affirmation of Faith: "God Siva is immanent Love and transcendent Reality."

That part of Him which belongs to darkness is
He who is called Rudra. That part of him which
belongs to obscurity is He who is called Brahma.
That part of Him which belongs to goodness is
He who is called Vishnu.

MAITRAYANA UPANISHAD

In what forms do we worship God Siva?
Truly, all forms are God Siva's forms. But our worship is directed primarily toward three murthis from the ancient tradition: Siva Lingam, Ardhanarisvara and Nataraja.

We contemplate God Siva as Parasivam when we worship the Siva Lingam. Its simple shape speaks silently of His unspeakable Absolute Being. We invoke Him as Satchidananda, Pure Love and Consciousness, when we worship Ardhanarisvara, Siva-Sakti, in whom all apparent opposites are reconciled. We exalt Him as Mahesvara, Primal Soul, when we worship Nataraja, the Divine Dancer whose five potent acts of creation, preservation, destruction, veiling grace and revealing grace animate the universe. Thus we worship the three perfections of our God Siva in three murthis or forms: Siva Lingam is Parasivam, Absolute Reality; Ardhanarisvara is Satchidananda, Pure Consciousness;

and Nataraja is Mahesvara, the Primal Soul. But we cannot limit our God to these forms alone. He is also Dakshina-murthi, the Silent Teacher, Guru of Gurus and Great Yogi. He is all this and more, our God Siva.

Do the other Gods exist apart from Siva?

Siva has created the Gods and given them distinct existence and powers, and yet He pervades them wholly. They are separate but inseparable. At the deepest level, nothing exists apart from Him. He alone prevails everywhere. Not an atom moves except by His will.

Ganesha, Muruga, Indra, Agni and all the thirty-three million Gods of Saivism are beings just as we are, created by Siva and destined to enjoy union with Him. The Gods are souls as we are souls, but of a high evolution. They are very old and mature souls, mighty beings who are neither male nor female, though they may be popularly depicted as Gods and Goddesses. We understand the spiritual domain as the abode of God, Gods and devas. God Siva is the Supreme Being, the One without a second, the Lord of Lords. Amongst His creation are the Gods or Mahadevas who also live in the Third World. The devas are angels, celestial beings abiding in the Second World and usually subject to rebirth. They help guide evolution from their world between births. There are billions of devas. We worship God Siva and the Gods Muruga and Ganesha, which we also call Mahadevas. We do not worship the devas. Gods Muruga and Ganesha and all the devas worship God Siva. Paramaguru Siva Yogaswami taught us that "It is clear that there is nothing apart from the Supreme One. His Will prevails from everlasting to everlasting."

What is our relationship with God Siva?

In truth, we are not essentially different from God Siva. The Vedas proclaim, *Tat tvam asi*. As Parasivam, we are *That*. As

Satchidananda, pure superconsciousness, He abides within us as us this very moment. As Mahesvara, He is our Supreme Master and Beloved. God Siva has never been apart from us. He is the Life of our life, the Breath of our breath.

Our relationship with God Siva evolves as we evolve, as our understanding deepens. Before we enter religious life, we look upon Him as a stranger, unknown to us and seemingly unknowable. Later we find the spiritual path and relate to Him as a servant to a master, through fear and obedience. Later we relate to God as a son to his father, through love and duty. Still later we come to know God as an intimate friend in fellowship and fidelity. Finally, our relationship is one of lover and Beloved. When that love matures and the two become one, we realize God Siva as our deepest Self. Paramaguru Siva Yogaswami taught us, "Believe in God. Believe in Him with perfect trust. Consider Him as sweeter than the sweetest of earthly joys. Reflect on His glory night and day and at all times. Cherish the Lord in the recesses of your heart. We are the servants of God Siva. Our duty is to serve the Lord. It is the fundamental goal of our life in this world."

> *From Him are born the many Deities.*
> *From Him are born the angelic beings, man*
> *and the beasts and birds, and the rice and corn,*
> *and the very air we breath.*
>
> MUNDAKA UPANISHAD

Our individual soul body, a subtle body of self-effulgent light.

Chapter 2

Our Immortal Soul

KNOWING OURSELF STARTS
BY UNDERSTANDING THE SOUL,
HOW IT IS DIFFERENT FROM GOD
AND HOW IT IS THE SAME.

What is the nature of our soul?
Our individual soul is the immortal and spiritual body of
light that animates life and reincarnates again and again until all necessary karmas are created and resolved and its
essential unity with God is realized.

Our individual soul is the creation of God Siva and the
source of all our higher functions, including knowledge, will
and love. The soul is neither male nor female. It is that which
never dies, even when the four outer sheaths or bodies—
physical, pranic, astral and mental—change form and per-
ish, as they naturally do. The soul body is the fifth and
innermost body. We are not the physical body, mind or
emotions. We are the immortal soul, called *pasu*. Paramaguru Siva Yogaswami taught us that "We are the soul, *atma*.
You must become thoroughly convinced of this."

How is the soul different from God Siva?
Our individual soul body was created in the image and like-
ness of the Primal Soul, God Siva, but is different from the
Primal Soul in its maturity.

For the sake of understanding the mysteries of the soul,
we distinguish between the soul body and its essence. As a
soul body, we are individual and unique, different from all
others. Our soul is a self-effulgent body of light which
evolves and matures through an evolutionary process. This

soul body is of the nature of God Siva, but is different from Him in that it is less resplendent than the Primal Soul and still evolving, while He is unevolutionary Perfection. We may liken the soul body to an acorn, which contains the mighty oak but is a small seed yet to develop. The soul body matures through experience, evolving through many lives into the likeness of God Siva and merging with Him totally. Even when God-Realization is attained, the soul body continues to evolve in this and other worlds until it merges with the Primal Soul as a drop of water merges with its source, the ocean. This is the destiny of all souls without exception.

How is the soul identical with God Siva?

The essence of our soul, which was never created, is immanent Love and transcendent Reality and is eternally identical with God Siva.

At the core of the subtle soul body is Satchidananda, or immanent Love; and at the core of that is Parasivam, or transcendent Reality. At this depth of our being there exists no separate identity or difference—all are One. Thus, deep within our soul we are identical with God this very moment, for within us are the unmanifest Parasivam and the manifest Satchidananda. These are not aspects of the evolving soul, but the nucleus of the soul which does not change or evolve. They are eternally perfect and one with God Siva. From an absolute perspective, our soul is already in non-dual union with God in His two perfections of Satchidananda and Parasivam, but to be realized to be known. Satchidananda is the superconscious mind of the soul body—the mind of God Siva. Parasivam is the inmost core of the soul. We are That. We do not become That. There exists no relation between Satchidananda, which is pure form and consciousness, and Parasivam which is without form. Paramaguru Siva Yogaswami taught us, "You are Siva. I am Siva. All are Siva. Even as Siva is immortal, so too are we."

*Pure Consciousness, taking form as Knowledge
and Action, is present in the soul everywhere and
always,...for the soul is universal in its
unfettered state.*

MRGENDRA AGAMA

If we are identical to God Siva, why don't we have omniscience also?

The three bonds of anava, karma and maya veil our sight.
This is God Siva's purposeful limiting of awareness which
allows us to have individual identity and to evolve. In the
superconscious depths of our soul, we share God's all-know-
ingness.

Just as a child is kept from knowing all about adult life
until it has matured into understanding, so too is the soul's
knowledge limited. We learn what we need to know, and we
understand what we have experienced. Only this narrowing
of our awareness, coupled with a sense of individualized ego,
allows us to look upon the world and our part in it from a
practical, human point of view. The three bonds of *pasam—
anava,* which is ignorance; *karma,* which is the conse-
quences of thought and deed; and *maya,* which is the principle of matter—are given by Lord Siva to help and protect us
as we unfold. Yet, God Siva's all-knowing Divine Mind may
be experienced for brief periods by the meditator who turns
within to his own essence, which is none other than Satchidananda.

Why are some souls apparently more advanced than others?

Souls were not created all at once. Lord Siva is continually
creating souls. Souls created a long time ago are old souls.
Souls created not so long ago are young souls.

Lord Siva, Architect of the Universe, is constantly creating souls in His image and likeness. It is His nature to do so,

as it is the nature of a fruit tree to bear fruit and of the sun to radiate energy. Souls are created in the Third World. They evolve in the Second and First Worlds and ultimately return to the Third World. We recognize an old soul as being refined, selfless, compassionate, virtuous, controlled in body, mind and emotions, radiating goodness in thought, word and deed. We recognize a young soul by his strong instinctive nature, selfishness, lack of understanding and absence of physical, mental and emotional refinement. At any given time there are souls of every level of evolution. Paramaguru Siva Yogaswami taught us that "The world is a training school. Some are in kindergarten. Some are in the BA class."

What happens to our soul when we die?
Our soul never dies; only the physical body dies. After death, the soul body continues to evolve in unbroken continuity in the inner plane worlds, then again enters into birth.

Death comes to all, but it is not the end of our existence. When the lessons of this life have been learned and karmas reach a point, the soul leaves the physical body which then dies and returns its elements to the earth. The awareness, the will, the memory and the intelligence which we think of as ourselves continue to exist in the soul body. This process is like walking through a door, leaving one room and entering another. Death is a most natural experience, not to be feared. It is a quick transition from one state to another. After this transition, we are in the Second World where we continue to have experiences until we are prepared for yet another physical birth. Because certain seed karmas can only be resolved in the First World, our soul must enter another physical body in order to continue its spiritual evolution. When our soul has sufficiently evolved and undergone all necessary karmas in this physical universe and God-Realization has been attained, it will not return to the First World. All the worlds rejoice when an old soul is freed from samsara, the cycle of birth, death and rebirth.

Does God Siva punish souls who think and act wrongfully or who do not believe in Him?

No. God Siva is Perfect Goodness, Love and Truth. He is not a wrathful or a vengeful being.

Jealousy, vengefulness and vanity are qualities of man's instinctive feelings and nature, not of God. There is no reason to ever fear God Siva. He is with us always, even when we are unaware of His presence. He *is* His creation. It is an extension of Himself; and He is never apart from it nor limited by it. When we act wrongly, we create karma for ourselves, and we must then live through experiences of pleasure and suffering to fulfill the law of karma. Such karmas may be very painful, but they were generated from our own thoughts and deeds. God never punishes us, even if we do not believe in Him. It is through worship of and meditation on Him that our self-created sufferings are softened and assuaged. He is the God of all—of the believers within all religions, not just our own, and of the nonbelievers, too. God Siva does not destroy the wicked and redeem the righteous. He grants the precious gift of Liberation to all souls.

> *The three impurities are: anava, maya and the one caused by actions.*
>
> SUPRABHEDA AGAMA

The physical cosmos, created by God Siva, in which souls evolve.

Chapter 3

The World We Live In

BY UNDERSTANDING THIS WONDERFUL
WORLD, WE CAN FACE ITS PAINS AND JOYS
WITH COURAGE AND INSIGHT. OUR RELIGION
DOES NOT BELIEVE IN ETERNAL
HELL OR IN ORIGINAL SIN.

Where did this world come from? Is it real?
Lord Siva created this and numberless other worlds of relative reality for souls to inhabit as they evolve.

This world, and indeed all of existence, is maya, the
principle of matter. While God is absolutely real, the world is
relatively real. That does not mean that the world is illusory
or non-existent, but that it is impermanent and subject to
change. It is an error to say that the world is unreal, for it is
entirely real when experienced in ordinary consciousness,
and its existence is required to lead us to God. Therefore, we
call it relatively real to distinguish it from the unchanging
Reality—God Siva. *Pasam,* the soul's triple bondage, is com-
prised of maya, karma and anava. Without the world of
maya, the soul could not evolve through experience. Karma
is the law of cause and effect, action and reaction governing
maya. Anava is ignorance, the sense of separateness and of
ego. Maya is the classroom, karma the teacher and anava the
student's ignorance. As individual souls, we experience the
profound reality of the world as God's sovereign purpose at
work. Paramaguru Siva Yogaswami taught us that "God Siva
is in the world. The whole world is in God. He exists as
earth, water, fire, air, ether and all else."

Does the world ever end?

The material world exists in endless cycles of creation, preservation and dissolution. The world ends, only to be created again.

In vast sequences of space and time, the physical universe is created by Lord Siva, exists in Him and is absorbed back into Him, to be created again as He repeats the cosmic cycle. Time and space are non-linear, and the universe was not created out of nothing in one point in time to thereafter exist forever. The universe is born, evolves and dissolves in cycles much as the seasons come and go through the year. These cycles are inconceivably immense, ending in Mahapralaya, when the cosmos undergoes universal dissolution. All three worlds—including time and space—dissolve in God Siva at Mahapralaya, which is His ultimate grace, when the evolution of all souls is perfect and complete as they lose individuality and return to Him. Then God Siva exists alone in His three perfections until He again issues forth creation to begin another cycle of cosmic manifestation. Paramaguru Siva Yogaswami taught us that "The world is eternally expanding and contracting. God, soul and world. In the end the world also will become God."

Why is there so much suffering and misery in the world?

The nature of the world is duality. It contains each thing and its opposite: joy and sorrow, goodness and evil, love and hate. Through experience of these, we learn and evolve, finally seeking Truth which transcends all opposites.

There is a divine purpose even in the existence of suffering in the world. Suffering cannot be totally avoided. It is a natural part of human life and the impetus for much spiritual growth for the soul. Just as the intense fire of the furnace purifies gold, so does suffering purify the soul and offer us the important realization that true happiness and freedom cannot be found in the world, for worldly joy is inextricably bound to sorrow and freedom to bondage. Having learned this, the matured soul practices spiritual disciplines, turning to God Siva for refuge and Liberation from the endless cycles of experience in the realm of duality.

> *In fondness for us He created the seven worlds.*
> *In fondness for us He created the several eons.*
> *In fondness for us He created the five elements.*
> *In fondness for us He created this body and breath.*
>
> SAINT TIRUMULAR

If true joy and enlightenment cannot be found in the material world, should we then avoid all involvement in the world?

No. The world is the bountiful creation of our benevolent God Siva. It is meant for us to live positively in it, facing karma and fulfilling dharma. We must not despise or fear the world.

The world is the place where our destiny is shaped, our desires fulfilled and our soul matured. In the world we grow from ignorance into wisdom, from darkness into light and from a consciousness of death to immortality. The whole world is an ashram in which all are doing sadhana. We must love the world, which is God's creation. Gurudeva has taught us that "The world is a glorious place, not to be feared. It is a gracious gift from God Himself, a playground for His children in which to interrelate young souls with the old—the young experiencing their karma while the old hold firmly to their dharma. The young grow; the old know."

Are man and the world sinful by nature?

No. Both man and the world are intrinsically good. There is no inherent sin. Neither is there mortal sin by which the soul is forever lost. Sin does exist, however, as intentional transgression of divine law.

What men term sin, the wise call ignorance. Man's true nature is his soul nature, which may be described as perfect goodness in the image and likeness of God Siva. It is not sullied by sin. Sin is related only to man's outer instinctive-intellectual nature as a transgression of dharma. Still, sin is real and to be avoided, for our wrongful actions return to us as sorrow through the law of karma. Sin is terminable, and the effects of our sins may be compensated for by penance and good deeds which settle the karmic debt. The young soul on the planet, less in tune with his soul nature, is inclined toward sin; the old soul seldom transgresses divine law. Knowledge of God Siva's law brings forth goodness from men, while ignorance induces sinfulness. Gurudeva has taught us that "Sins are the crippling distortions of the intellect bound in emotion. When we sin, we take the energy and distort it to our instinctive favor. When we are unjust and mean, hateful and holding resentments year after year and no one but ourselves knows of our intrigue and corruption, we suffer. As the soul evolves, it eventually feels the great burden of faults and misdeeds and wishes to atone. Penance is performed, and the soul beseeches the grace of the Gods."

Is there a hell where those who transgress God's laws suffer eternally?

No, there is no eternal hell. However, there are hellish states of mind and woeful births for those who think and act wrongfully.

There are three worlds of existence. This physical universe is the First World. The astral, or mental sphere, which exists "within" this world is called the Second World. The spiritual realm is the Third World. These worlds are further divided into *lokas,* or places. This earth is the *Bhuloka.* The devas, or celestial beings, live in the *Devaloka.* The Gods live in the *Sivaloka.* Hell is termed the *Narakaloka.* Gurudeva has taught us that "Hell is often delineated as a place of fire and heat, of anguish and dismay, of confusion, despair and depression. Hell is only to be found as states of confusion, mental conflict and the tormenting moods that plague the mind and lift the fiery forces. This hell can be experienced in the world. We do not have to die to suffer in hellish states of consciousness. When we *do* die in a hellish state of consciousness, with the symbols of our mental hell around us—hatred, remorse, resentment, fear and all the distorted patterns of thought—we arrive in the Second World fully equipped to experience hell."

Is there a Saivite heaven?

Yes, deep within the superconscious mind, in the Second and Third Worlds, exist the celestial spheres, the Devaloka and the Sivaloka, where mature souls continue to evolve even after earthly births have ended.

The spiritual world is the natural refuge of all souls. It is a world of light and of blessedness. Gurudeva has taught us that "Saivite heaven is the abode of Lord Siva as Mahesvara, or the Primal Soul, and His entourage of Mahadevas in the Third World and devas in the Second World. It exists within man himself."

Immanent He is in all of us, like the hidden fire
within withered wood, or butter within milk....
If we draw the strings of devotion, we shall behold
Him, the resplendent light of heaven.

SAINT APPAR

Four dharmas: cosmic law; four stages of life, self dharma, social dharma.

Chapter 4

Dharma

DHARMA EXISTS ON ALL LEVELS OF LIFE,
INCLUDING COSMIC, HUMAN, SOCIAL AND
PERSONAL. FINDING AND FOLLOWING OUR
UNIQUE PATH BRINGS REWARDS OF INNER
PEACE AND FULFILLMENT.

What is dharma?
Dharma is Siva's Divine Law, the law of being. It is the orderly
fulfillment of an inherent nature and destiny.

When God Siva created the world, He endowed it with
order, with laws to govern creation. Dharma is God's Divine
Law prevailing on every level of existence, from the sustaining cosmic order to religious and moral laws which bind us
in harmony with that order. We are maintained by dharma,
held in our most perfect relationship within a complex universe. Every form of life, every group of men, has its dharma,
the law of its being. When we follow dharma, we are in conformity with the truth that inheres and instructs the universe, and we naturally abide in closeness to God Siva.
Adharma is opposition to divine law. When we leave the
path of dharma and indulge in vices such as lust, anger or
covetousness, we find ourselves estranged from God.

Are there different kinds of dharma?
Yes, there are four kinds of dharma which are God Siva's law
at work on four levels of our existence: universal dharma,
human dharma, social dharma and personal dharma.

No single definition can capture the fullness of the
meaning of *dharma*. It is at work in our lives on all planes,
in simple and profound ways, internally and externally as

well. It prevails in the laws of nature and is expressed in our
culture and heritage. It is piety and ethical practice. It is duty
and obligation. It is the path which leads us to knowledge of
God Siva. Universal dharma is known in Sanskrit as *rita
dharma*. Human dharma is known as *ashrama dharma*. Social dharma is called *varnashrama dharma*. Our personal
dharma is *svadharma*. Paramaguru Siva Yogaswami taught
us that "All are engaged in Siva's work. The sun, moon and
stars, devas and asuras and all sentient beings are engaged in
activity in consonance with Siva's Will. Work is worship.
Perform your work, your svadharma."

What is universal dharma?

Universal dharma is cosmic order, God's Law at work throughout the physical province. It is also called rita dharma.

   Rita dharma is the underlying divine principle and universal law regulating nature from the voyage of the stars in
their vast galactic orbits to the flux of infinitesimal subatomic energies. Rita is the Tao. It is destiny and the road to destiny. It is the intelligence at work in nature. It is the sustaining cosmic force. Gurudeva has taught us that "When we are
in tune with universal dharma, with nature, and realize that
man is an integral part of nature and not above it or domi-
nating it, then we are in tune with rita dharma. The Saivite
feels he has responsibilities to nature, which when fulfilled
balance nature's responsibilities to him. The physical body
was gathered from nature and returns to nature. Nature is
exquisitely complex and orderly. The coconut always yields a
coconut tree, not another species. How constant nature is,
and yet how diverse, for in mass producing its creations, no
two ever look exactly alike. Yes, the Saivite knows himself to
be a part of nature and seeks to bring his life into harmony
with the universal path."

*Do not neglect the learning and teaching of the
Veda. Do not neglect the sacrificial works due to the
Gods and Fathers! Let thy mother be to thee like a
God! Let thy father be to thee like a God! Let your
guest be to thee like a God! Do only such actions as
are blameless. Always show reverence to the great.*

TAITTIRIYA UPANISHAD

What is our human dharma?

Our human dharma is the natural expression and growth of
the body, mind and emotions through four stages of life:
student, householder, elder advisor and religious solitaire. It
is also called ashrama dharma.

We are born with our human dharma and fulfill it in a
most natural way through four stages called ashramas. We
may liken these ashramas of our life to the course of a day:
morning, midday, afternoon and evening. As children, we
are nurtured through early training and experience. As
young adults, we enter the first ashrama of life—that of the
student—or brahmachariya. During this stage, roughly
from ages 12 to 24, we undertake the study and skills that will
serve us in later life. As married householders, we enter the
second stage of the grihastha. From 25 to around 48 we work
together as husband and wife to raise the family, gather
wealth and knowledge through our profession and serve
society in many ways, including support of the members of
the other three ashramas. Once the family is raised and we
have retired from our occupations, we enter the third stage
of life, that of the vanaprastha. From 49 to around 72 we are
the respected elder of the community, sharing our experience through counsel, guiding and advising the younger
generation. After age 72 we enter the fourth and last stage of
life, that of the sannyasin (this differs from the renunciate
monastic who takes formal holy orders of sannyas). During
this time of life, as the physical forces wane, we are naturally

withdrawn from concerns of the world and turn our thoughts and efforts toward diligent religious practices including scriptural study, worship, austerities, meditation and the disciplines of yoga. Thus, our human dharma is a natural awakening, expression, maturing and withdrawal from involvement in the world. It is determined not only by age, but by sex and marital status as well. Paramaguru Siva Yogaswami taught us that "By remaining in the *madams* of brahmachariya, grihastha, vanaprastha and sannyasa, we can complete the pilgrimage."

What is our social dharma?

Our social dharma consists of the duties and responsibilities we must fulfill as a member of our nation, our community and our family. It is also called *varnashrama dharma.*

In Hindu agricultural societies of old, caste determined social dharma. Caste was hereditarily determined by skin color and occupation. However, in this technological age when all the world's races are blending, caste is determined by knowledge, skill and occupation. Social dharma is fulfilled in adherence to the laws of our nation, to the responsibilities to our immediate community and the duties and obligations among family and friends. An important aspect of social dharma is religious and moral law. A comprehensive system of duties, morals and religious observances make up God's Law at work in our daily life. Gurudeva has taught us that "The Saivite who seeks to fulfill his social dharma respects and adheres to the laws of the country and of the community in which he abides. He does not try to establish unlawful patterns of his own, but endeavors to uphold God's law in discharging man's law in whichever country, state or city in which he may abide. He finds his place within the whole of humanity, within his country, within his immediate community, and within his family, and he strives to excel in all departments of life in fulfillment of his dharma."

What is our personal dharma?

Our personal dharma is the sum of accumulated seed karmas inherited from this and past lives as they relate to the
collective effect upon us of universal dharma, human dharma and social dharma. It is also called *svadharma.*

Each human being has an individual, personal dharma.
This dharma is determined by two things: the karmas, both
good and bad, from past lives and the three dharmas of this
life—universal, human and social. The key to discovering
and understanding personal dharma is the worship of Lord
Ganesha, the God of memory, time and wisdom, who knows
our past lives and can clarify our most perfect pattern, our
right path in life. When we follow this perfect individual
pattern, we are content and at peace with ourselves and the
world. Gurudeva has taught us that "Dharma is to the individual what its normal development is to a seed—the orderly fulfillment of an inherent nature and destiny."

As thoughts alone cause the round of births,
let a man strive to purify his thoughts.
What a man thinks, that he is;
this is the old secret.

MAITRAYANA-BRAHMANA UPANISHAD

Good conduct includes purity, devotion, humility, charity and love.

Chapter 5

Good Conduct

OUR OWN CONSCIENCE AND VIRTUOUS PEOPLE
ARE OUR TEACHERS IN GOOD CONDUCT, AS ARE
THE YAMAS AND NIYAMAS, AND OUR SACRED
ETHICAL SCRIPTURE, THE TIRUKURAL.

What is good conduct?
Good conduct is right thought, right speech and right action.
It is the performance of virtuous deeds which are in harmony
with divine law and reflect the innate purity of the soul.

Good conduct is the hallmark of purity. When the heart
and mind are freed of baseness, when desires have been tem-
pered and excesses avoided, dharma is known and followed,
and good conduct naturally arises. The Saivite knows humility and shuns arrogance, seeks to assist, never to hinder,
finds good in others and forgets their faults. Gurudeva has
taught us that "Good conduct determines our behavior in
day-to-day life. We should be uplifting to our fellowman,
not critical or injurious. We should be loving and kind, not
hateful or mean. We should express the soul's beautiful qualities of self-control, modesty and honesty. We should be a
good example to others and a joy to be around, not a person
to be avoided. Good conduct is the sum of Saivite living, and
it comes through keeping good company. There is no other
way to be called a good Saivite, a devotee of God, but to conduct ourselves properly within ourselves and among our fellow men." Paramaguru Siva Yogaswami taught us that
"Greater than life itself is good conduct. Those who conduct
themselves with rectitude possess everything that is worth-
while. Even as a man uses a staff to climb a mountain, so
should virtue be used in life."

What happens when we do not follow virtue and good conduct?

When we do not think, speak and act virtuously, we create negative karmas and bring suffering upon ourselves and others. We are happy, serene and stable when we follow good conduct, when we listen to our conscience, which is the knowing voice of the soul. We suffer when we act instinctively and intellectually without guidance from the superconscious mind. The superconscious mind, the mind of our soul, knows and inspires good conduct always. The instinctive-intellectual mind must be guided by the superconscious in matters of morality and virtue. Wrongdoing and evil lead us away from God Siva, deep into the darkness of doubt and despair. Gurudeva has taught us that "When virtue and good conduct are not observed, we are out of harmony with ourselves and our fellow Saivites and must seek companionship elsewhere, be amongst those who are also crude, unmindful, greedy and lacking in self-control. In this company new karma is created as Saiva Dharma cannot be followed. The karma accumulates, blinding us to the religious life we once lived. Penance and throwing ourselves upon the mercy of God and the Gods are the only release for the unvirtuous Saivite who conducts himself poorly. Fortunately, our Gods are compassionate, and God Siva loves His children, His devotees."

What are the four keys to good conduct?

Purity, devotion, humility and charity are the four keys to good conduct. Of these, purity is the cardinal virtue.

Purity is the pristine and natural state of the soul. It is, as Gurudeva has taught us, "an inner glow, not an outer show." We cultivate purity through thinking, speaking and doing only that which is conceived in love. We cultivate purity by refraining from anger and retaliation, by maintaining a clean and healthy body, and by guarding our virginity until marriage. We cultivate purity by seeking the company of good men and women, and by living a disciplined life. Devotion is love of and dedication to God Siva, to the Gods of Saivism, to our guru and the holy men of our religion, to our family, our relatives and friends. We cultivate devotion through being loyal and trustworthy. We cultivate devotion through worship and through selfless service, called *Sivathondu.*

Humility is the state of profound maturity in which the soul, immersed in the depths of understanding and compassion, radiates the qualities of mildness, modesty, reverent obeisance and unpretentiousness. We cultivate humility by taking the experiences of life in understanding and not in reaction, and by seeing God everywhere, in all sentient and insentient forms. We cultivate humility through showing patience with circumstances and forbearance with people. Charity is selfless concern and caring for our fellow man. It is generous giving without thought of reward, always sharing and never hoarding. We cultivate charity through being compassionate toward the hungry, the sick, the homeless, the elderly and the unfortunate.

> *Dispassion is equanimity in pleasure and pain,*
> *among friends and foes, with pebble or with*
> *gold....One who has recoiled from sensual*
> *pleasures and devoted himself to undefiled,*
> *pure wisdom, is sure to achieve everlasting*
> *Moksha, even if he does not consciously seek it.*
> DEVIKALOTTARA AGAMA

From whom should we learn good conduct?
Our conscience is the first teacher in matters of right conduct. To know what is right and what is wrong we can also turn to God, to our Satguru and swamis, to scripture and to

our family and trusted friends.

Divine laws cannot be avoided. They are not ruling us from above, but wrought into our very nature. Even death cannot efface the karma created by evil deeds. Good conduct alone can resolve woeful karmas. Therefore, it is essential that we learn and adhere to good conduct. Good people are the best teachers of good conduct, and should be sought out and heeded when we need help or advice. The great scripture *Tirukural*, or *Holy Kural*, is superior to all other human writings in matters of good conduct and should be read and studied regularly, and its wisdom followed. Gurudeva has taught us that "In this technological age, advice from the wise is all that can be given, and the only rigid rule is our wisdom in using it. Talk with them, the wise ones, and in good judgement be guided accordingly. The loud voice of our soul, ever heard within our conscience, is a worthy guide, for it indicates the impact of an action in accordance with its anticipated reaction. When we grasp the subtle mechanism of karma, we wisely follow the good path."

What are some guidelines for good conduct?
Besides the *Holy Kural*, we follow the yamas and niyamas as general guidelines for a good life. The yamas are restraints; the niyamas are observances.

The yamas and niyamas are the accumulated wisdom of thousands of years of Saivite culture. They are advice and simple guidelines, not commandments. The yamas are the "do not's," those things which we should avoid or refrain from doing, while the niyamas are the "do's," those things which we should observe or strive to fulfill. Memorize the yamas and niyamas and the path of good conduct will be well charted.

Yamas: The Saivite Restraints
1. Ahimsa (Noninjury): Do not harm others by thought, word or deed.

2. Satya (Truthfulness): Refrain from lying and betraying promises.
3. Asteya (Nonstealing): Neither steal nor covet nor enter into debt.
4. Brahmachariya (Sexual Purity): Control lust by remaining celibate when single, and faithful in marriage.
5. Kshama (Patience): Restrain intolerance with people and impatience with circumstances.
6. Dhriti (Steadfastness): Overcome non-perseverance, fear, indecision and changeableness.
7. Daya (Compassion): Conquer callous, cruel and insensitive feelings toward all beings.
8. Arjava (Honesty): Renounce deception & wrongdoing.
9. Mitahara (Moderate Appetite): Neither eat too much, nor consume meat, fish, fowl or eggs.
10. Saucha (Purity): Avoid impurity in body, mind & speech.

Niyamas: The Saivite Observances
1. Hri (Remorse): Be modest & show shame for misdeeds.
2. Santosha (Contentment): Seek joy and serenity in life.
3. Dana (Giving): Tithe and give creatively without thought of reward.
4. Astikya (Faith): Believe firmly in God, Gods, guru and the path to enlightenment.
5. Isvarapujana (Worship): Cultivate devotion through daily worship and meditation.
6. Siddhanta Sravana (Scriptural Listening): Study the teachings and listen to the wise of your lineage.
7. Mati (Cognition): Develop a spiritual will and intellect with a guru's guidance.
8. Vrata (Sacred Vows): Fulfill religious vows, rules and observances faithfully.
9. Japa (Recitation): Chant holy mantrams daily.
10. Tapaha (Austerity): Perform sadhana, penance, tapas and sacrifice.

Are there other guidelines for religious life?

The Pancha nitya karmas—five constant, or minimal, duties—are the treasure of all Hindus, constituting an amalgam of the ethical counsel of the Vedas, Agamas and other Hindu scriptures to guide one's conduct through life.

The Pancha Nitya Karmas

1. Virtuous Living (Dharma): Proper conduct follows the laws of dharma and includes observing the teachings of a favorite ethical scripture, remaining celibate until marriage, obeying sthree dharma for women and purusha dharma for men. It is goodness in thought, word and deed.

2. Worship (Upasana): Personal worship in the home shrine includes performance of puja, japa, sadhana and religious study. Regular devotions in the home and temple bring forth love of God and prepare the mind for the practices of meditation.

3. Holy Days (Utsava): The observance of Hindu festivals in the home and temple, including guru puja days, brings deep communion with God during highly spiritual times of the year. Utsava includes fasting and attending the temple on Friday, the Hindu Holy Day.

4. Pilgrimage (Tirthayatrai): At least once each year, every Hindu must make a pilgrimage to a holy place, near or far. This is a time when all worldly matters are set aside and God becomes the central and singular focus of life.

5. Sacraments (Samskaras): Sacraments are special ceremonies which mark our passages in life and sanctify these cycles of experience. They include the rites of birth, first feeding, learning, marriage, death, monastic vows for monks and more.

Keep the mind free of impurity—
that alone is the practice of virtue.
All else is nothing but empty display....
Virtue yields heaven's honor and earth's wealth.
What is there then that is more fruitful for a man?
                                        SAINT TIRUVALLUVAR

The Siva temple is a most beautiful and spiritually powerful place.

Chapter 6

The Holy Siva Temple

THE TEMPLE HAS SPECIAL SANCTITY AND
PURPOSE. HERE WE EXPLORE HOW IT IS BUILT
AND WHEN WE ATTEND. WE LEARN SOME
IMPORTANT CUSTOMS TO OBSERVE
WHENEVER WE ENTER THE TEMPLE.

What is the significance of the holy Siva temple?
The Siva temple is a most sacred place, for it is the abode of
our God Siva and the precinct in which the three worlds
most consciously commune.

The three pillars of Saivism are the temples, the scriptures and the Satgurus. These we revere, for in them is contained and preserved the ancient wisdom. Siva temples, whether they be small village sanctuaries or towering citadels, are esteemed as God's home and consecrated abode. In the Siva temple we draw close to God Siva and find a refuge from the world. His grace, permeating everywhere, is most easily known within the precincts of the Siva temple. It is in the purified milieu of the temple that the three worlds commune most perfectly, that First-World devotees can establish harmony with Second and Third-World inner plane spiritual beings. Gurudeva has taught us that "Lord Siva has established many temples to communicate His love to His children throughout the world. He has done this deliberately. His children have spread to all corners of the earth and long for His ever-present love. They build temples in His name and install His image, chant His praises and thus invoke His presence. Lord Siva accepts these temples as His own and sends His ray to vivify and vitalize them. When the Sakti—that ray of ever-abiding love flowing through the core of life itself—permeates the sanctum sanctorum and floods out to the world, Saivites know they are in a most holy place where God and the Gods commune with them."

How is a Siva temple founded and built?
Siva temples are founded by God Siva Himself, designated often in a vision or dream of a devout Saivite, then erected by temple craftsmen usually following strict Agamic law.

Because of its holiness, a Siva temple is most often and properly established by God Siva through His devotees and not founded by men. Once the site is known, hereditary temple builders, known as *stapathis,* are commissioned to design and construct the temple. By tradition, every stone is set in place according to the sacred architecture found in the Agamic scriptures. When properly consecrated, the temple becomes a place upon the earth in which the three worlds can communicate for the upliftment of mankind and the fulfillment of Siva's dharmic law. Such communication takes place through a great psychic ray which is established over the *garbagriha,* or sanctum sanctorum, connecting it to the Third World. In such a special and holy place, Holiness Itself can reside.

When should we attend the temple?
We attend the temple whenever we feel a need to commune with God Siva, but especially on Fridays, on festival days and on the most holy day of the year, Maha Sivaratri.

Saivites consider it most important to live near a Siva temple, and we build one wherever we find ourselves in the world. To build a Siva temple is considered a most meritorious act, earning blessings in this life and the next. Saivite religious life centers around the temple. We go to the temple at anytime during the week, though women never go during their monthly period. We attend the temple every Friday and especially during festivals when the Sakti of the Deity is most powerful. Devout Siva bhaktas attend daily puja in the temple. All Saivites, without exception, visit the temple on Siva's most sacred day of the year, Maha Sivaratri. Paramaguru Siva Yogaswami taught us to "Arise with the dawn and wash the feet and hands. Go to the temple and worship Siva's Holy Feet. That is proper conduct. That is a sacred rite."

When worship ceases in Siva's temple,
harm befalls the ruler; scanty the rains;
theft and robbery abound in the land.
Thus did my holy Nandi declare.

SAINT TIRUMULAR

What is a typical visit to a Siva temple like?

Activities within a holy Siva temple vary from the daily round of pujas to the elaborate celebrations on annual festival days. Even amid large crowds, our worship is very personal and individual, not congregational, and follows a specific pattern.

We visit a Siva temple after having bathed, dressed in clean clothes and prepared an offering, which can be as simple as a few flowers or fruits. Inwardly, we bring the mind to the holy feet of the Deity even as preparations are begun, chanting His hymns silently or aloud. After leaving our shoes outside, we enter through the *gopuram,* or temple tower, and seek Lord Ganesha's blessings at a shrine or subtemple. Next we walk around the inner court in a clockwise direction. We wash hands, feet and mouth before entering the inner chambers. Inside we prostrate before the *kodimaram,* or temple flagpole, and then approach the *garbagriha,* or sanctum, where the Deity abides. Men and boys should remove their upper garments before approaching the sanctum. Next we perform *pradakshina,* walking around the sanctum itself an uneven number of times, usually three, returning to the sanctum entrance for puja. During puja, we stand with hands folded or in namaskaram, though at certain points it may be proper to sit and to sing devaram hymns or bhajans, according to the custom of the temple. After the *arati*, or waving of the camphor light before the Deity, we prostrate and rise to receive the *prasadam*, or blessed items, taking them always with the right hand. Before leaving the temple, we sit in quiet meditation on God, even for just a few minutes, and then prostrate, perform pradakshina one final time and take our leave. Generally, there are seven times when pujas are held: at five, six and nine in the morning, at noon, and at six, eight and ten in the evening. Besides the daily round of pujas, many other events take place within the temple: pilgrims offering special vows; weddings; philosophical discourses in the pillared halls; bhajan, especially in the evenings; feedings for the impoverished; and many events associated with the annual ten-day festival held in most Siva temples.

Who are the temple pujaris?
The temple pujaris are married men who care for the temple and conduct its varied rites and rituals.

Every temple has its own staff of priests. Some temples will hire only one, while others have hundreds to take care of the many shrines and elaborate festivals. The temple pujaris are usually from the brahmin caste, though in certain temples they are not. Pujaris are well-trained from early childhood in the intricate liturgy that has been passed down to them from their father, who is almost always a pujari. They must learn hundreds of Sanskrit mantrams and chants which are required in the ritual worship within a Siva temple. Temple pujaris are not counselors or ministers; they do not attend to the personal problems or questions of devotees. They are God's servants, tending His temple home and its related duties. Officiating priests are almost always married men, while their assistants may be unmarried brahmacharis or widowers.

Is temple worship only for beginners, those in the chariya and kriya margas?

No, temple worship is for all men and women at every level of spiritual development. Its meaning and experience deepen as we unfold spiritually.

We never outgrow temple worship. It simply becomes more profound and meaningful as we progress spiritually. During the chariya marga, we attend the temple because we have to, because it is expected of us. During the kriya marga, we attend because we want to; our love of God is the motivation. During the yoga marga, we worship God internally, in the sanctum of the heart; yet even the yogi immersed within the superconscious depths of mind has not outgrown the temple. It is there—God's home on the earth plane—when he returns to normal consciousness. The bhakta and the jnani worship together at God Siva's sanctum, each drawing from the source of spiritual power and insight according to his maturity. Paramaguru Siva Yogaswami taught us that "It is devotion to God, *Sivabhakti*, alone that makes a man blessed. Everything else is useless. Therefore, without break, practice *Sivadhyana*. By ceaselessly meditating and contemplating in this way, let us eliminate baser qualities and attain the higher Divine Reality."

> *May we know the Lord of lords, most brilliant of*
> *the Deities, Master of the masters, the highest one.*
> *May we know Thee, the most adorable God,*
> *Lord of the Universe.*
>
> SVETASVATARA UPANISHAD

A pujari waves camphor flame before Ganesha during puja.

Chapter 7

Puja, Our Sacred Worship

WE LEARN HOW WORSHIP IS AN
INNER PRACTICE, AND HOW WE PREPARE
OURSELVES FOR THESE RITES. OUR WORSHIP
IS OFFERED IN THE TEMPLE AND
IN THE HOME SHRINE.

What is the significance of puja?

Puja is a sanctified act of the highest importance for the Saivite, the invoking of God Siva and the Gods and the solemn expression of our love and devotion.

Puja is a most blessed ritual, for it is the invoking of the grace of the Deity. Puja is our holy communion, a sanctified act, full of wonder and tender affections. It is that part of our day which we share most closely and consciously with our beloved Deity; and thus it is for Saivites the axis of religious life. Our worship through puja may be demonstrated by festive celebration of important events in life, by adoration and thanksgiving, by penance and confession, by prayerful supplication and requests, or by contemplation at the deepest levels of superconsciousness. Puja may be conducted on highly auspicious days in a most elaborate, orthodox and strict manner by the temple pujaris, or it may be offered in the simplest form each morning and evening in the home shrine by any devotee, called *atmartha puja*, or personal worship. Paramaguru Siva Yogaswami taught us that "Even the unlearned will attain salvation if with songs and flowers they offer worship to the Almighty's Holy Feet. Morning, noon and evening offer up your praise."

During puja do we worship the sculpted image?
No. We worship only God Siva and the Gods who by their infinite powers indwell within the image.

We commune with God Siva and the Mahadevas through the ritual act of puja in which the Deity is spiritually present within the holy image. The image, or *murthi*, is not merely a symbol of the Deity; it is the form through which His love, power and blessings flood forth into this world. We may liken this mystery to our ability to communicate with others through the telephone. We do not talk to the telephone; rather we use a telephone as a means of communication with another person who is perhaps thousands of miles away. Without the telephone, we could not converse across such distances; and without the sanctified murthi we cannot easily commune with the Deity. His vibration and presence can be felt in the image, and He can use the image as a temporary physical-plane body or channel. As we progress in our worship, we begin to adore the image as the Deity's physical body, for we know that He is actually present and conscious in it during puja, aware of our thoughts and feelings and sensing even our touch on the metal or stone.

What preparations do we make before puja worship?
We prepare ourselves for worship by bathing, dressing in clean clothes, quieting the mind and gathering offerings for the Deity.

Our worship is only as meaningful and effective as we make it through proper preparations and performance. Before we attend or conduct a puja, we should carefully bathe the body, rinse the mouth and dress in fresh clothing—saris for women and white verthis and shawls for men where this is the custom. Throughout these preparations we may sing hymns or chant mantrams or God's holy names silently or aloud, taking care to keep the mind free from worldly matters. We then gather offerings for the Deity. If mealtime is near, we eat only after puja has been concluded. Paramaguru Siva Yogaswami taught us, "Let your thoughts embrace the whole. Do not give up prayers and puja. As food is necessary for life, so is prayer necessary for the realization of Truth. Prayer is an aid, and not the end. When you worship God, you must not ask for anything. You must worship for the sake of love. Afterwards you can ask for your requirements."

> *What has learning profited a man, if it has*
> *not lead him to worship the Good Feet of*
> *Him who is pure knowledge itself?*
>
> SAINT TIRUVALLUVAR

What does the temple pujari do during puja?

The temple pujari is trained in the complex arts of worship. During the puja, through mantrams, mudras and esoteric ritual, he invokes the presence of the Deity.

Only a trained and qualified pujari may perform puja in the consecrated temple. No one else may enter the inner sanctum or touch the Deity. All practices and observances for puja are precisely detailed in the Agamas; every act, every intoned syllable is rich in esoteric meaning. The pujari prepares himself by performing strict ablutions and disciplines in order to purify himself for his sacred duty. Before the puja, he ritually purifies the atmosphere. As the puja begins, the pujari meditates on Lord Ganesha, praying that all obstacles to the success of the puja may be removed. He then beseeches the Deity to indwell in the image, to accept the offerings and the love of His votaries, to hear the prayers of devotees and to shower His blessings and love on all. Calling the name of the Deity and chanting Sanskrit mantrams and hymns from the Vedas, the pujari makes offerings of unbroken rice, burning camphor, incense, vibhuti, water, kumkum, tumeric, flowers and food. Sometimes offerings of milk, rosewater, sandalwood paste and yogurt are poured over the Deity as an oblation in the ceremony called *abhishekam*. During the puja, temple bells are loudly rung, conch shells are sounded, and musicians may play the temple drum and woodwind, or *nagasvaram*. The pujari treats the Deity with utmost honor and care, attending to Him in every way, as the King of kings. When the puja has ended, the pujari passes the sanctified offerings to those present.

What is the difference between puja and archana?
Puja is adoration of the Deity, while archana is a particular form of puja in which the name of a devotee is intoned before the Deity to invoke special, individual blessings.

   If we wish to receive the Deity's blessing for something special that is happening in our life, we may request an archana. This is arranged within the temple itself, normally after the main puja. A basket or tray is usually given to the pujari upon which have been placed certain articles to be offered to the Deity: fresh flowers and fruits (carefully washed and not even breathed upon), vibhuti, kumkum, incense, camphor, rosewater, sandalwood paste and a contribution for the pujari. The pujari asks for our name, which we tell him aloud and which he then intones before the Deity along with a Sanskrit verse. He then asks for our *nakshatra,* or birthstar. If we know the lunar asterism under which we were born, this is spoken to him; if not, then we tell him the sign of the zodiac under which we were born, such as Capricorn. Finally, he asks for our *gotra*. This is the name of the rishi with which our family is associated. Church members who have no other gotra should say, "Subramuniya Gotra." A brief puja is then performed specifically on our behalf, and special blessings received. At the end, the pujari will return most of the offerings and the tray. Gurudeva has taught us that "Invoking the Deity through having our name, nakshatra and gotra spoken before the sanctum identifies us and beseeches Him to peruse our karmas, past and future, making necessary adjustments so our petition may manifest properly. These are, in a sense, our credentials."

What is the significance of the home shrine?

Every Saivite maintains a shrine in the home. It is the most important room in the house, an extension of the temple and abode for the Deity and our guardian devas.

Every Saivite home centers around the home shrine, a special room set aside and maintained to create a temple-like atmosphere in which we conduct puja, read scripture, perform sadhana, meditate, chant bhajan and do japa. In the rarefied vibration of the well-kept home shrine the Deity's presence is always felt, and we remember Him throughout the day, especially morning and evening and before meals, when the food is ceremonially offered to Him before we partake. Worship in the home shrine traditionally begins before dawn, with the simple act of dedication for the coming day. After a bath, morning puja is performed which includes the repetition of the Gayatri Mantram by those duly initiated. Another puja may take place anytime after sunrise which includes offerings of flowers, incense and food. The day's devotionals end with evening puja, after which our meal may be taken. The form of a home puja is simple: the Deity—usually Lord Ganesha—is invoked and asked to abide in the murthi; offerings are made and He is asked to accept them along with our love; after the final arati, or offering of the light, we supplicate the Deity to bestow His grace on us, our family and all devotees.

Let us adore the Lord, the Luminous One.
SVETASVATARA UPANISHAD

Our scriptures are the repository of the Sanatana Dharma.

Chapter 8

Sacred Scriptures

HINDUISM'S MOST ANCIENT SCRIPTURES ARE
THE VEDAS, UPANISHADS AND AGAMAS. FOR
SAIVITES, OTHER HOLY BOOKS INCLUDE THE
TIRUMANTIRAM, TIRUKURAL, DEVARAMS AND
THE TEACHINGS OF ONE'S PARAMPARAI.

What are our most ancient Saivite scriptures?
The Vedas are our most ancient scriptures, written over
6,000 years ago. There are four Vedas: the *Rig, Sama, Yajur*
and *Atharva.*

The Vedas are revealed scripture, called *sruti* in Sanskrit.
They are of divine origin, being revealed to man directly by
God and the Gods. The Vedas are written in an ancient form
of the Sanskrit language and are the oldest scripture on our
planet. Paramaguru Siva Yogaswami taught us that "You can
go to the top by climbing step by step. But exceptionally
there are some who, with the help of the revealed scriptures,
sruti, the guru and their own understanding and experience,
can fly like birds."

What do the Vedas contain?
The Vedas contain two different types of scriptural writings.
First are the many hymns of praise, supplication and invocation to the Gods which are chanted by priests while performing different Vedic ceremonies. Second are the dia-
logues of great rishis sharing their spiritual realizations with
their disciples.

Each Veda has four sections: the *Samhitas, Brahmanas,
Aranyakas* and *Upanishads.* The first three sections contain
the hymns, instructions on how to properly chant them and

descriptions of the many Vedic ceremonies and their mystical significance. The Vedas are a composite of many religious
traditions. Thus, not just God Siva and His sons Lord Ganesha and Lord Muruga are worshiped, but many other Gods
as well. The fourth section, the Upanishads, is the philosophical section. The word *upanishad* means "sitting near
devotedly," which refers to disciples' sitting around their
guru while he expounds his realizations and answers their
philosophical queries. These great rishis spoke out their
inner experiences, profound insights into the true nature of
God, soul and world.

**What scripture contains the authoritative declaration
of Saivism?**
The *Saiva Agamas* are the authoritative explanation of Saivism. Like the Vedas, they are revealed scripture, written over
2,000 years ago in the Sanskrit language.

In all there are 28 Saiva Agamas. Within them is contained a complete exposition of all aspects of the Saivite
Hindu religion. Each of the Agamas is divided into four sections—*chariya, kriya, yoga* and *jnana*. The chariya section
explains in detail the daily religious observances and conduct that a devout Saivite should follow. The kriya section
describes all aspects of temple worship, from the protocol of
attending and conducting a puja to the detailed descriptions
of how to build a temple, install the Deities and conduct festivals. The yoga section contains a complete description of
the eight-limbed yoga of yama, niyama, asana, pranayama,
pratyahara, dharana, dhyana and samadhi, from the basic
practices to the most advanced. The jnana section contains a
thorough explanation of the philosophy of Saivism, ex-
pounding the nature of Pati, pasu and pasam—God, soul
and world—and their relationships. Truly, all aspects of the
Saivite religion are contained in the sacred Agamas.

I walk with those who go after God,
I live with those who sing His praise.
The Lord blesses those who seek Him;
with them I consort; their feet I seek....
Where Siva jnanis flourish, misfortunes will not
be. New ways of prosperity dawn, and all good
things befall. A veritable heaven that land will be.

SAINT TIRUMULAR

Among Saivite scripture, what is the unique position of the *Tirumantiram* of Saint Tirumular?

The uniqueness of the *Tirumantiram* lies in the fact that the essential teachings of all the 28 Saiva Agamas are found within this one scripture. It is the confluence of Siddhanta and Vedanta.

Saint Tirumular was first and foremost a great yogi, a man of profound spiritual realization. In the *Tirumantiram,* he recorded the tenets of Saivism in concise and precise verse form, drawing upon his own realizations and the Saiva Agamas. His work is not an intellectual construction, and it is not strictly a devotional canon either. It is based in yoga; it exalts and explains yoga as the kingly science leading man to knowledge of himself, and it lays the foundation for sadhana and tapas for those on the sadhana marga. Saint Tirumular wrote in the language of the people of South India—Tamil—rather than in the traditional scriptural language of Sanskrit. Thus, his work was an attempt to make more available to everyone the great teachings of our heritage as found in the 28 Saiva Agamas. For this reason the Tirumantiram is called the "Tamil Agama." *Tirumantiram* is part of *The Holy Bible of the Saivite Hindu Religion.*

What is the importance of the *Tirukural* of Saint Tiruvalluvar?

The *Tirukural,* or *Holy Kural,* is the world's greatest ethical scripture, considered the Tamil Dharma Shastra.

   Saint Tiruvalluvar lived over 2,000 years ago. His work, the *Tirukural*, provides guidelines for living a good and virtuous life. Its lyrical couplets, ranging widely through all departments of life, are easy to memorize and beautiful to hear. The *Holy Kural* consists of 133 chapters, each elucidating a different aspect of human virtue or human fault. In each chapter there are ten couplets—like facets of a gem, all reflecting the light of his understanding slightly differently and adding to the richness of our comprehension. As such, the *Holy Kural* gives a thorough exposition of the chariya marga and can well be considered the scripture of chariya. Besides being an important religious scripture, it is admired as the greatest classic work of the Tamil language. The *Tirukural* is part of *The Holy Bible of the Saivite Hindu Religion*. Paramaguru Siva Yogaswami taught us that "You must know yourself. There is no necessity for you to study. But even study is yoga. Study well the *Tirukural*."

What other scriptures are frequently used in our daily devotional practices?
Besides the philosophical and ethical scriptures, the sacred written teachings of our Guru Paramparai are used in our daily worship, as well as important devotional scriptures containing the sacred hymns of the four Samaya Achariyas: Saints Sambandar, Appar, Sundarar and Manikkavasagar.

   These four great saints all lived in the 7th to 9th centuries during the time of a great Saivite renaissance. They were all great bhaktas, lovers of God, who pilgrimaged throughout the Tamil land singing in praise of the murthis of God Siva enshrined in each temple they visited. By their exemplary lives and powerful devotional songs, they captured the hearts of Saivites all over the land. Saivism is not a fixed revelation, but a living and growing tradition, and we consider the written and oral teachings of our Siva Yoga-

swami Guru Paramparai as authoritative scripture—including the *Natchintanai,* or "Good Thoughts," of Siva Yogaswami and the written teachings of Gurudeva, Sivaya Subramuniyaswami.

What is the path prescribed by Siva Yogaswami in *Natchintanai?*

Our Paramaguru prescribed service and meditation, *Sivathondu* and *Sivadhyanam.*

Belief in God is most necessary, but that alone will not
bring Liberation. In *Natchintanai* and through personal instruction, Siva Yogaswami taught the sadhana marga. Work,
discipline, personal unfoldment, purification and inner
transformation are required. Our sadhana marga includes
study of the *Holy Kural* and remaining *summa,* still, in silent
contemplation. Paramaguru Siva Yogaswami taught us,
"Know thy Self by thyself. Concentration of mind is required
for this. Practice the ceaseless and constant remembrance of
Siva. See God everywhere. Contemplate on Him and do His
bidding. Do everything as *Sivathondu.* Give up 'I' and 'mine.'
Everything else will come if you do *Sivadhyanam.*"

> *To share in Siva's nature follows from*
> *communion with Siva and contiguity with Siva.*
> SUPRABHEDA AGAMA

The holy men of Saivism commune with God Siva within.

Chapter 9

Saints, Sages and Satgurus

AS A GUIDE LEADS A CLIMBER
TO THE MOUNTAIN PEAK, SO DO
ENLIGHTENED SOULS LEAD US
TO KNOW TRUTH.

Who are the holy men and women of the Saivite religion?
The saints, sages and Satgurus who commune with God and
the Gods through devotion and meditation are the holy men
and women of Saivism.

There are and have always been many holy men and women in the Saivite religion. They are considered holy because of their great love of God Siva and of the Gods, their
dedication to our faith, and their profound realizations. It is
very difficult to be so disciplined and devoted, and so we
honor and love those who have attained Siva's Grace. We do
not worship or invoke them as we do the Gods, but we do
offer our reverent homage and strive to follow their example and their words of wisdom. There are saints, sages and
Satgurus in the Saivite Hindu religion.

**What is the difference between a saint, a sage and a
Satguru?**
A saint is one who is devoid of ego and reflects the peace,
humility and purity of a devout life. A sage is inwardly free
and pure, but his outer appearance may be common or
ordinary; he usually does not teach. A Satguru is a fully
matured and realized soul who actively helps us in our religious life and personal unfoldment.

Because of its great diversity and decentralized form of
organization, there is within Saivism no ecclesiastical hierar-

chy. Saints, sages and Satgurus are recognized by their followers and through their works and lives, but they are not officially canonized, for there is no single authority within Saivism to do this. Therefore, each within his own sphere of devotees is the authority on religious matters and is listened to and obeyed as such. Saints are honored as exemplars of our faith, teaching us by their example how to act and how to serve God Siva. The purity of the saint's heart is evident in his actions and words. There are many men in our Saivite religion who are inwardly pure and awakened, but who do not outwardly display their attainment. These are known as sages and often live as secluded munis or wander as homeless mendicants. The Satgurus of our religion are the most honored among holy men, for they are the teachers and guides who bring us into the fullness of spiritual life. The Satguru is always an unmarried man, an initiated swami of a recognized paramparai, or spiritual lineage. The Satguru is the embodiment of Lord Siva, not an incarnation of Siva, but an individual soul in union with Siva. Siva pervades all souls equally, but is most apparent in the form of the illumined Satguru. We worship the divine within the Satguru, not his personality or humanness. Paramaguru Siva Yogaswami taught us that "Transcending all mutations of form and attribute, surpassing all finite measure is the guru, embodiment of the highest wisdom. Gurubhakti is the greatest blessing. Cherish it."

Who are the foremost Saivite Saints?
Among the many holy men who have lived throughout Saivism's long history, we honor six most highly: Saints Tirumular, Tiruvalluvar, Appar, Sundarar, Sambandar and Manikkavasagar.

Four Nayanars, or "devoted servants of Lord Siva"— Saints Appar, Sundarar, Sambandar and Manikkavasagar— are known as the *Samaya Achariyas*, "teachers of the faith," and are revered for their many hymns sung in praise of Siva in His temples throughout South India. Their hymns today form a major portion of our traditional scriptures. We also honor Saint Tiruvalluvar, who wrote the major Saivite ethical scripture, *Tirukural,* and Saint Tirumular, siddhar sage and yogi who composed the mystical scripture, *Tirumantiram.* Besides these six important saints, there are many others from ancient and contemporary times. Paramaguru Siva Yogaswami taught us to "Follow the precepts of the seers in general and the utterances of the four saints. Walk in the footsteps of the great masters."

> *Earnest seekers who worship Enlightened Ones*
> *at sight, with perfume, flowers, water, fruits,*
> *incense, clothing and food, or by word, deed and*
> *thought, are absolved then and there.*
>   DEVIKALOTTARA AGAMA

Who is Paramaguru Siva Yogaswami and what is the Siva Yogaswami Guru Paramparai?

Siva Yogaswami was a siddhar and the Satguru of our Gurudeva Sivaya Subramuniyaswami. He is our Paramaguru. He lived in Northern Sri Lanka from 1872 to 1964.

We derive our spiritual heritage from the line of siddhars from South India and Sri Lanka known today as the Siva Yogaswami Guru Paramparai. The first Satguru of this lineage of which history has preserved knowledge is known simply as the Rishi from the Himalayas. He initiated Kadaitswami who traveled to Sri Lanka. There he lived and spread the Saiva Siddhanta teachings. Kadaitswami initiated Chellappaswami. Chellappaswami initiated Siva Yogaswami in 1910. On a full moon day in May of 1949, the eminent Siva Yogaswami initiated our beloved Gurudeva Sivaya Subramuniyaswami into the siddhar line. Siva Yogaswami attained Mahasamadhi on March 24, 1964, having reigned as spiritual head of Saivism in Sri Lanka for over 50 years. Gurudeva has taught us that "Our Saiva paramparai is most illustrious! Its entire thrust for several hundred years has been to preserve the Sanatana Dharma intact and move it forward from generation to generation in the lives of individuals and through the group mind. Now we see it coming into even greater fulfillment in bringing Saivism into the mass mind in the West as well."

Are there other terms used for holy men and women of our religion?
Yes, there are many terms which describe Saivism's religious aspirants, teachers and awakened souls.

Achariya—A respected teacher. Also called aasaan.

Brahmachari—An unmarried man and spiritual aspirant who practices continence, observes certain disciplines and is often under simple vows.

Brahmacharini—An unmarried woman and spiritual aspirant who practices continence, observes certain disciplines, often relating to devotion, service and teaching children, and who may be under simple vows.

Guru—A teacher. Though it can connote a teacher of any subject, usually describes a spiritual teacher or master.

Ma—A respectful and endearing term for exemplary women in the community.

Muni—One vowed to complete silence or who rarely speaks. Also, one established in stillness of mind, "summa," often living in seclusion.

Pandit—A learned brahmin, usually married, who teaches and decides questions of conduct within the community.

Rishi—An old and venerated sage or seer, often a visionary who sees beyond the present time.

Sadhaka—A serious aspirant who exerts himself in observing spiritual disciplines, or sadhana.

Sadhu—A pious seeker or holy man, usually an ascetic or

mendicant sannyasin who lives simply and wanders home-less.

Sannyasin—A single man who has renounced the world for God-Realization and service to humanity, and who has been formally initiated by a qualified sannyasin into the holy orders of sannyas after proper training and disciplines.

Satguru—A spiritual teacher or master who has attained God-Realization and assumes responsibility for the spiritual life of his sishya, disciples.

Siddhar—A "perfected one," or accomplished yogi, a man of great spiritual attainment or powers.

Sishya—A disciple who has proven himself and has formally accepted a Satguru as his guide in spiritual instruction.

Swami—The same as sannyasin, a single man and Hindu monk. May be used as a title before or after the name or instead of the monk's name.

Tapasvin—An ascetic, one who seeks purification through austerities, penance and rigorous disciplines.

Yogi—One who practices yoga, specifically raja yoga.

The brahmachari moves, strengthening both the worlds, in him the devas meet in concord; he upholds earth and heaven; he satisfies his achariya with the power of tapas....By the tapas of brahmachariya the king protects the state; by the tapas of brahmachariya, the achariya seeks his pupil.

ATHARVA VEDA

Bride and groom circle the homa fire in front of a wedding canopy.

Chapter 10

Marriage

IT IS MARRIAGE WHICH MOST PERFECTLY
EXPRESSES AND HARNESSES THE SEXUAL
ENERGIES, NURTURING A TRULY SPIRITUAL
RELATIONSHIP BETWEEN MAN AND WOMAN.
THERE IS WISDOM IN MARRYING WITHIN
ONE'S RELIGION.

What are the two purposes of marriage?
The two purposes of marriage are: the mutual support, both
spiritual and material, of husband and wife; and bringing
children into the world.

Through marriage a man and a woman each fulfill their
dharma. A man and a woman are physically, emotionally and
spiritually complete in marriage. He needs her tenderness,
companionship and encouragement, while she needs his
strength, love and understanding. Their union results in the
birth of children and the perpetuation of the human race.

Is marriage a spiritual or a civil union?
Marriage is a spiritual sacrament, a mutual contract and a
civil institution.

Marriage is a three-fold state: it is a sacrament, a contract and an institution. As a sacrament, it is a spiritual union
in which man and woman utter certain vows one to another
and thus bind themselves together for life and for their souls'
mutual benefit. As a contract, it is a personal agreement to
live together as man and wife, he to provide shelter, protection, sustenance, and she to care for the home, and bear and
nurture their children. As an institution, marriage is the law-
ful custom in society, bringing stability to the family and the

social order and providing knowledgeable application of society's law. We recognize the civil and spiritual implications of marriage through two ceremonies: one before a judge or magistrate and another in the temple or home.

Must the husband always work and support the family and the wife always remain in the home?

Yes. By their physical, mental and emotional differences the man is suited to work in the world and the woman to bear and raise their children in the home.

The biological differences between man and woman are part of their human dharma. The two together constitute a whole. It is a man's duty, his *purusha dharma,* to protect and provide for his wife and family. He is well-equipped physically and mentally for the stress and demands placed upon him. When he performs his dharma well, the family is materially secure. Still, he is not restricted from participation in household chores, remembering that the home is the wife's domain and she is its mistress. It is a woman's duty, her *sthree dharma,* to bear the children, then to nurse, raise and educate them. Her more intuitive and emotional qualities of gentleness, modesty, kindness and compassion are needed for the child's proper care and development. She is the homemaker, standing proudly beside her husband as the mother and educator of his children and the home's silent leader. They are equal partners in joy and sorrow, companions and helpmates, yet their functions differ. The Saivite home and family are the fortress of the religion; the wife and mother are duty-bound to maintain them and thus to perpetuate the faith. As long as the husband is capable of supporting the family, a woman should not leave the home to work in the world. The spiritual loss suffered and the karma accrued from having a wife and mother work is never offset by the financial gain. It is the man's duty to see that his wife never has to work in the world.

What is the purpose of sexual intercourse?

The purpose of sexual union is to express and foster love's beautiful intimacy and to draw husband and wife together for procreation.

Sexual intercourse is a natural reproductive function, a part of man's instinctive nature, and its pleasures draw man and woman together that a child may be conceived. It also serves through its intimacy to both express and nurture love. It is love which endows sexual intercourse with its higher qualities, transforming it from an animal function to a human fulfillment.

> *May there be cows giving plentiful milk,*
> *the good draught-bull, and the swift horse.*
> *May the woman be at home with husband and*
> *children....May Parjanya shower rains according*
> *to our needs; may our trees bear ripe fruit,*
> *may our exertion and rest prosper.*
>
> YAJUR VEDA

Should only a husband and wife have sexual intercourse?

Yes, wisdom and experience demand that the intimacies of sexual intercourse be confined to marriage.

Sexual intercourse before marriage is not advisable. When a young virgin man and woman marry and share physical intimacy with each other, their union is very strong and their marriage stable. This is due to the subtle, psychic forces of the human nerve system. Their psychic forces, or *nadis,* grow together and they form a one body and a one mind. This is the truest marriage and the strongest, seldom ending in separation or divorce. Conversely, if the man or woman have had intercourse before the marriage, the emotional-psychic closeness of the marriage will suffer, and this in proportion to the extent of promiscuity. For a marriage to succeed not only as a partnership but as a spiritual partnership, sexual intercourse must be preserved for husband and wife, for in that context love may mature through the years. Each should grow to understand the other's needs and take care to neither deny intercourse to the married partner nor make excessive demands. A healthy, unrepressed attitude should be kept regarding sexual matters. Boys and girls must be taught to value and protect their chastity as a treasure, and to save the special gift of intimacy for their spouse. They should be taught the importance of loyalty in marriage and to avoid even the thought of adultery.

Must one marry within one's own religion?
It is not mandatory that a Saivite man or woman marry another Saivite, but to marry a partner of the same religion is wise and should be earnestly sought for.

The mutual spiritual unfoldment of man and wife is a central purpose of marriage. When we marry outside of our Saivite religion, we unnecessarily create problems of disharmony and conflict, for ourselves as well as for the children. Such a marriage draws us away from our religion instead of deeper into its fulfillment. For marriage to serve its spiritual purpose to the highest, husband and wife should hold the same beliefs and share the same religious practices. Their harmony of minds and mutual self-respect will be reflected in the children who will grow up as strong members of the Saivite Hindu religion. Should a Saivite marry a non-Saivite, it must be with the clear understanding that each spouse may freely practice his or her faith and that the children will be raised fully in the Saivite religion with no conflicting beliefs or customs.

What is the law pertaining to abortion, birth control, sterilization, divorce, remarriage, masturbation, homosexuality, petting and polygamy?
These are neither condoned nor condemned. Our religion does not arbitrate all matters of sexuality for its members. The only rigid rule is wisdom, guided by tradition and virtue.
    The intensely personal matters of sex as it affects the family or individual are not legislated by our religion, but left to the judgement of those involved, limited by the laws and customs within the community. Saivism does not exclude or draw harsh conclusions against any part of life. Advice in such matters should be sought from our elders, ministers and spiritual leaders.

> *The foremost duty of the householder is to duly serve these five: ancestors, God, guests, kindred and himself. When family life possesses love and virtue, that is both its essence and fruition. A worthy wife is the blessing of a home, and good children are its precious adornment. Among those who strive for Liberation, the foremost are they who live the blessed state of family life as it should be lived.*
> SAINT TIRUVALLUVAR

The Saivite home is the family's serene sanctuary for a spiritual life.

Chapter 11

Children and Family Life

PARENTS AND CHILDREN ALIKE HAVE THEIR
DUTIES, THE FULFILLMENT OF WHICH BRINGS
JOY TO A FAMILY. CREATING A STRONG, HAPPY
HOME REQUIRES EVERYONE'S BEST AND
CONSTANT EFFORTS.

What is the greatest source of happiness in marriage?
Children are the greatest source of happiness in marriage.

Marriage is made rich and complete when children are born, at which time the marriage becomes a family. Large families are more cohesive, more stable, and are encouraged within the limits of the family's ability to care for them. Gurudeva has taught us that "The fulfillment of the grihastha dharma is children. The birth of the first child cements the family together. At the birth itself the Second-World community of guardian devas of the husband, wife and child are eminently present. Their collective vibration showers blessings upon the home, making of it a full place, a warm place. It is the duty of the husband and wife to become father and mother. Raising several children rewards the parents and their offspring as well."

What are the duties of the parents toward their children?
The fundamental duty is to provide food, shelter and clothing and to keep the child safe and healthy. The secondary duty is to provide an education, including instruction in morality and religious life.

Assuring the health and well-being of the children is the most essential duty of parents to their children, never to be neglected. Beyond this, parents should provide a good example to their children, being certain that they are taught the religion along with good values, ethics, strength of character and discipline. Children should worship regularly at puja with the parents, and the Saiva samskaras should all be provided. Education in all matters is the duty of the parents, including teaching them frankly about sex, its sacredness and the necessity to remain chaste until marriage. Children must learn to respect and observe civil law and to honor and obey their elders. Parents must love their children dearly, and teach the children to love. The best way to teach is by example: by their own life, parents teach their children how to live. Paramaguru Siva Yogaswami taught us that "Because of worldliness, the light in the faces of the young has become less bright nowadays."

How strictly should parents guide their children's lives?
Parents should be most diligent in guiding their children toward virtue, protecting them from all bad company and influences, being strict yet allowing them prudent freedom in which to grow.

Children are constantly learning, and that learning must be guided carefully by the parents, taking care not to be overly restrictive either. A child's faults if not corrected will be carried into adult life. Children need and seek guidance, and only the parents can truly provide it. The young's education, recreation and companions should be supervised. They should be taught the *Holy Kural* and other scriptures. Their religious education is almost always in the hands of the parents. All girls and most boys should be prepared for married life; girls especially schooled in household culture and the arts. In general, it is the mother who always provides love and encouragement, while the father corrects and disciplines. Gurudeva has taught us that "Children, be they young or old, have a karma and a dharma of their own. Their parents have a debt to pay them; and they have a debt to return later in life. The karma balances out and the community goes on when every action is followed by a transaction that is agreeable to all as the karmas are erased in action performed. Pleasant times will be the blessing of the father and mother with their children who are only theirs until puberty."

> *Let son be loyal to father and of one mind*
> *with his mother; let wife speak to husband words*
> *that are honey-sweet and gentle. Let not a brother*
> *hate a brother, nor a sister hate a sister;*
> *but unanimous, united in aims, speak words with*
> *friendliness....Let a man think well of wealth and*
> *try to win it by the path of law and by worship.*
>   ATHARVA AND RIG VEDA

Should all children be encouraged to marry?

All who do not enter the monastic path should be encouraged to marry. Young boys wishing to be monastics should be helped and trained in the home.

Generally, children should be taught to follow and prepare themselves for one of the two traditional paths: householder or monastic. Most will choose married life, and they should be schooled—the boys in technical skills and education and the girls in household arts and culture. If a young boy expresses a desire to become a monastic, the parents should not discourage that inclination. It is a great blessing for the family to have a son become a Saivite monastic. Gurudeva has taught us that "Saivite families should encourage their young men to devote two years of their life serving the religion as a missionary or in a Saivite monastery prior to entering the grihastha community."

What are some ways to create and sustain a happy marriage and family life?

A happy marriage is based first and foremost on a mature love, not a romantic ideal of love. It requires selflessness and constant attention. A successful marriage is one which both partners work at making successful.

First of all, it is important to marry for mature reasons and not too young: men after 21, women after 18. There is a certain wisdom in arranged marriages, which have always been an important part of Saivite culture. Their success lies in the judgement of the family to base a marriage on pragmatic matters which will outlast the sweetest infatuation and endure through the years. Mature love includes accepting obligations, duties and even difficulties. Still, not all marriages must be arranged. Be prepared to work toward the success of your marriage, not expecting it to take care of itself. It is good for both bride and groom to write out a contract by hand, each pledging to fulfill certain duties. Approach the marriage as holy, destined to advance both partners spiritually. Marry a suitable partner, one who is serious about raising children in the Saivite way, who is dependable and chaste, and then worship and meditate together. Make the home strong, the center of activity and creativity, kept beautiful and clean, a sanctuary for the whole family, a holy environment in which all members may progress spiritually. Strive to conceive high-souled children by living purely. Do things together and with the children. Keep a healthy attitude toward sex, never offering it as reward or withholding it as punishment—though celibacy, or brahmachariya, may be observed at times with mutual consent. Never lose respect for your partner, but seek new depths of love and understanding. Don't fight or argue. Be patient with each other's faults. Don't criticize each other, even mentally, for that erodes the marriage most quickly. Always control your emotions, or you and the family will be controlled by them.

Learn to discuss problems with each other freely and constructively. Do not be jealous or overly protective; have trust in one another and live up to that trust. Except for blood relatives, limit guests in the house to no more than three nights. Plan activities, bring the family close through shared experiences. Strive for abundance, but be content with what you have; live within your means. Study the *Holy Kural* and follow its wisdom. Seek and follow the advice of family, elders and spiritual leaders in times of difficulty or hardship. Gurudeva has taught us that "A good marriage requires that the masculine and feminine forces be balanced. The husband who does not take the lead is not fulfilling his duty. The wife who takes an aggressive lead in the marriage makes her husband weak. She must be shy to make him bold. The wife who tries to dominate her husband through guiding his mind 'for his own good' to perpetuate her material security is disciplined by nature with feelings of anguish, fear and guilt. Her difficulties end when she realizes that it is his dharma to accept gentle suggestions made by her, whether taken or not by him, and to listen to her thoughts, though not necessarily to follow them."

The father's duty to his son is to make him worthy of precedence in the assembly of the wise. The son's duty to his father is to make the world ask, "By what great austerities did he merit such a son?"
                                                    SAINT TIRUVALLUVAR

Monastic life centers around service and meditation.

Chapter 12

Monastic Life

HINDUISM PROVIDES A NOBLE MONASTIC
PATH. HINDU MONKS MUST MEET MANY
QUALIFICATIONS, FOR THEIR VOWS ARE
STRICT AND DEMANDING. LIVED WELL, THEIR
SELFLESS LIFE LEADS IN STAGES TO THE
ULTIMATE SPIRITUAL GOALS.

In general, what is the path of the Saivite monk?
In the Saivite tradition there have always existed among men
a few for whom the world held no attraction and karmas
were on the wane. Such men are by nature inclined toward
knowledge of God and disinclined toward desires of family,
wealth and property. Some among them are *sadhus* dressed
in white. They are anchorites living in the seclusion of distant caves and remote forests or wandering as homeless mendicants, itinerant pilgrims to the holy sanctuaries of Saivism.
Others dwell as cenobites assembled with their brothers,
often in the ashram, *aadheenam* or *math* of their Satguru.
These devotees, when initiated into the order of sannyas, don
the saffron robes and thereby bind themselves to a universal
body of Hindu renunciates whose existence has never ceased.
    Scriptural doctrine states that the two paths—house-
holder and renunciate—are distinct in their dharmas and
attainments, affirming that true renunciation may not be
achieved by those in the world even by virtue of a genuine
attitude of detachment.
    The sannyasin balances within himself both the male
and female energies. Complete unto himself, he is whole and
independent. There arises within him a pure energy, neither
positive nor negative. This is the sushumna current coming

into power through which he gains control of the kundalini force and eventually, after years of careful guidance, attains Nirvikalpa Samadhi.

Eventually, in one life or another, all will turn to the renunciate path. It is inevitable. However, it would be equally improper for a renunciate-minded soul to enter family life as for a householder to seek to be a sannyasin.

What are the two fundamental objectives of renunciate monastic life in Saivism?

The two fundamental objectives of sannyas are to promote the spiritual progress of the individual, bringing him into God-Realization, and to protect and perpetuate the religion. Renunciation and asceticism have been an integral component of Saivite culture from the earliest days, the most highly esteemed path of the Hindu Dharma. Monastic life has both an individual and a universal objective. At the individual level, it is a life of selflessness in which the monastic has made the supreme sacrifice of renouncing all personal ambition, all involvement in worldly matters, that he might direct his consciousness and energies fully toward God Siva. Guided by the Satguru along the *sadhana marga,* the initiated sannyasin unfolds through the years into deeper and deeper realizations. Ultimately, if he persists, he comes into direct knowing of Parasivam, transcendent Reality. At the universal level, Saivite monasticism fosters the religion by preserving the truths of the Sanatana Dharma. Competent swamis are the teachers, the theologians, the exemplars of their faith, the torchbearers lighting the way for all. Paramaguru Siva Yogaswami taught us, "Hail, O sannyasin, thou who know'st no guile! Establish in thy heart and worship there the Taintless One—Panchakshara's inmost core. Thou that regard'st all others as thyself—who in this world can be compared with thee?"

Who is eligible to become a Saiva sannyasin, and who is authorized to give sannyas diksha?

Young, unmarried men who are members of the Saivite Hindu religion may qualify for sannyas. Any legitimate sannyasin may initiate a candidate into sannyas, but the most valued and spiritually potent initiation comes from a Satguru.

Saivite monasticism is restricted to unmarried men. In our Order, if a candidate enters monastic training before age 25 and meets other qualifications, he may, generally after a minimum of 12 years of preparation and training, take the sannyasin's lifetime vows, called holy orders of sannyas. Only a swami or sannyasin can bring another into the ancient order of sannyas. However, since the purpose is God-Realization, most candidates seek initiation from a spiritually advanced knower of God who can bring them into realization. Initiation is called *sannyas diksha.* It is given in simple or most formal ways—the formal rites including the shaving of the novitiate's head, conveyance of certain esoteric teachings, abjuration of the worldly life and dharma, administration of monastic vows, and the giving of the kavi vestments. Gurudeva has taught us, "A word of warning. Be hesitant to accept promises of great kundalini awakenings. Spiritual rewards from severe practices given to the unprepared by representatives of yoga who do not teach, preach of or initiate members into the Saivite Hindu religion should be cautiously considered. Those entering into the serious life of the sannyasin must be prepared to follow the traditional path of unrewarded sadhana through the years, apart from dear family and friends. Such is the way to reach the truth of yoga, and the earned jnana proclaims them unrefuted knowers and teachers of the faith. It takes many, many years for the soul to thus ripen and mature."

There are five ways to follow: purification,
serenity, asceticism, study and devotion to the
Lord. For success, the three-fold mastery of breath
must first be attained:...exhaling, retaining and
inhaling. When the particular form of the subject
of concentration has been elaborated,
one is in meditation.

                                        SUPRABHEDA AGAMA

What vows does the Saiva sannyasin pledge himself to uphold?

Sannyasins take lifetime vows of poverty, obedience and chastity.

Like the vows of matrimony taken between husband and wife, the solemn vows of the sannyasin are for life, never to be relinquished or rescinded. He takes three vows. The first is known in Tamil as *ahatturavu*—the sacred vow of renunciation. It is the surrendering of the limited identity of the ego that the soul may soar to the depths of impersonal Being. It is a repudiation of worldly involvement and dharma, and thus includes poverty and simplicity. The sannyasin owns nothing in this world, not even the robes he is given to wear. The second vow is *tallvu ennum tanmai*—the sacred vow of obedience. It is a pledge to follow the traditional ways of the Sanatana Dharma and the specific directions of his Satguru. It embraces obedience to his own conscience, to scripture, to God and the Gods and to the teachings of his illustrious guru paramparai. The third vow is *tirikaranna-sutti*—the sacred vow of purity. As defined in this vow, purity is of mind, speech and body—thought, word and deed. It is a vow to remain continent throughout life, to protect the mind from all lower instincts, from deceit, hatred, fear, jealousy, anger, pride, covetousness and so forth. This vow includes a pledge to observe *ahimsa,* or non-violence, even in thought, to speak truthfully and to eat a vegetarian diet.

In our order, called the Saiva Siddhanta Yoga Order, two additional vows are given upon acceptance: *pannivu,* or humility, and *rahasiyam,* or confidence.

How does the sannyas monk relate to his guru?

The guru-disciple relationship is the crux of Saivite monasticism. In entering the order of sannyas, the sannyasin enters into the mature stages of the guru-disciple relationship. The sannyasin should strive to perceive the Satguru as his higher self, not different, not external to himself. In many ways he and the guru have become one, and that oneness will blossom forth through the years. Theirs is a one mind, a one energy, a one mission. The sannyasin must foster and protect this relationship, working daily to bring his mind ever deeper into harmony with that of his Satguru. He should consider this his first and foremost monastic duty.

> *With the earnest effort hold the senses in check.*
> *Controlling the breath, regulate the vital activities.*
> *As a charioteer holds back his restive horses, so*
> *does a persevering aspirant hold back his mind.*
> SVETASVATARA UPANISHAD

Saivism's inner truths never change, but its outer practices do evolve.

Chapter 13

Our Religion Today

THE SANATANA DHARMA IS ALIVE
AND WELL IN A CONTEMPORARY WORLD.
WE EXPLORE HOW SAIVISM RELATES TO
OTHER HINDU SECTS AND TO OTHER
RELIGIONS, THEN LEARN WHERE AND
HOW SAIVITE HINDUS LIVE TODAY.

How old is Saivism?
Saivism is ancient, truly ageless, for it has no beginning. It is
the oldest religion in the world, the "eternal faith," or
Sanatana Dharma.

Saivism was not founded by anyone or created at any
point in history, but endures as the innate spirituality within every man and woman. There never was a time when
people on the planet did not practice Saivism and worship
Siva, the Auspicious One. Knowledge of man's evolution
from God and back to God, of communion with greater beings in other realms through temple worship, of the soul's
ever-expanding unfoldment and awakening guided by enlightened sages, of karma, reincarnation and dharma—all
this is not knowledge assembled in one era to be dispelled in
another. Knowledge of Truth and the path to it are ever-existent, true for all time, past and future.

**What tradition today preserves the entire Sanatana
Dharma?**
The Sanatana Dharma is completely embodied in Saiva Siddhanta as expounded by Saint Tirumular. It is a theology
that encompasses both Vedic and Agamic traditions.

All religions on the earth are the offspring of the Sanatana Dharma and contain elements of its teachings; Saivism preserves the whole of the eternal religion. The Sanatana Dharma is fully embodied in Saivite Hinduism—called *Agamic Saivism.* Within Saivism there are six main sub-sects. Of these six, the original Saiva Siddhanta—as delineated by Saint Tirumular over 2,000 years ago in his treatise, the *Tirumantiram*—most faithfully carries forward the complete and pristine Sanatana Dharma found in the Vedic Upanishads and in the Agamas.

What do we call the theology of Saivism?

Saivism is a most unique religion in which God is both manifest and unmanifest, dual and non-dual. Our theology would be known as monistic theism.

Saivism is not pantheistic, polytheistic or monotheistic. It could best be described as monistic theism. Monism is the opposite of dualism. It is the doctrine that Reality is a one whole or existence without independent parts. Theism is belief in God and the Gods, both immanent and transcendent. Saivism is monistic in that it believes in a one Reality and in the advaitic or non-dual identity of man with that Reality. Saivism is theistic in its belief in God as personal Lord, immanent in the world, and in the Gods, or Mahadevas. Thus, Saivism encompasses the non-dual and the dual, both advaitic Vedanta and dvaitic Siddhanta. This unified doctrine is also known as Suddha Saiva Siddhanta. Paramaguru Siva Yogaswami taught us, "Thus shall Sivathondan light the way with love: His sound expositions of truth shall reveal that Vedanta and Siddhanta are not separate paths, but are essential facets of the Luminous One."

How does Saivism relate to the rest of Hinduism?

Within the Sanatana Dharma, known today as Hinduism, there are three main sects—Saivism, Vaishnavism & Saktism. Long ago the Sanatana Dharma was none other than Sai-

vism. Over the centuries these other sects have evolved until
today they are known collectively by the world as Hinduism.

Saivism is the precursor of the many-faceted religion
now termed Hinduism. There was a time when there were
no sectarian divisions; there was only Saivism. Today three
sects do exist as important components of the Hindu faith.
Saivism, Vaishnavism and Saktism hold such divergent beliefs that they are virtually complete and independent religions. Though autonomous, they share in common a vast
heritage, a belief in karma, reincarnation and the Deities,
and a reliance upon the Vedas as scriptural authority.

> *As smoke and sparks arise from fire,...*
> *even so, Maitreyi, has all knowledge,*
> *all wisdom been breathed forth from the Eternal.*
> *The Rig Veda, the Yajur Veda and the rest*
> *are the breath of the Eternal.*
>
> BRIHADARANYAKA UPANISHAD

How does Saivism relate to and look at other religions?
Though the beliefs of Saivism and of other religions are
diverse and different, the Saivite respects and encourages all
who worship God and the Gods.

Since the inner intent of all religious practice is to bind
man back to God, Saivites seek not to interfere with anyone's
faith or practice. We believe that all religions are God Siva's
Divine Law at work in the world, that there is no exclusive
path, no one way for all. While all paths are valid, we realize
that all religions are not the same and consider ours the
greatest religion in the world, the primal religion. Gurudeva
has taught us that "Saivites all over the world mix and min-
gle freely with those of other religions without being undu-
ly influenced by any of their basic beliefs. Peoples all over the
world are now acquainted with the laws of karma and reincarnation. They recognize the Saivite as a worshiper of God

Siva. The Saivite proceeds contentedly with his practices, with his sadhana, not by drawing a square to keep others out, but a circle of love to take them in. He profoundly knows that God Siva is the same God peoples of all religions and faiths draw near to in worship and in whom all of mankind finds solace, comfort and bliss."

Where are Saivites living in the world today?

There are nearly 400,000,000 Saivites living all over the world, mostly in India.

Most Saivites live in India—the Holy land and stronghold of Saivism over the past 5,000 years. But there are Saivites in every nation in the world, with larger communities in Nepal, Sri Lanka, Burma, Bali, Malaysia and other parts of Indonesia, Australia, Africa, England, Europe, Trinidad and Tobago, Canada, the United States of America and several Arabian nations. Saivism possesses vast facilities and institutions, including universities, colleges, hospitals, presses, ashrams, aadheenams, pilgrimage sites and more. Today we find Siva temples not only in India and Sri Lanka but in many other countries to which Saivites have immigrated. Besides its many institutions, Saivism possesses a wealth of art and architecture, and a storehouse of philosophy and scholarship. All these and more make Saivism the most well-endowed religion in the world.

How does Saivism adapt to the technological age?

Inner truths never change, but the outer forms of practice and observance do evolve. Saivism seeks to preserve its religious tradition while simultaneously adapting to the cultural, social and economic changes of our technological age.

Saivism is an orthodox religion, conservative in its ways and yet pliant and understanding. It is simultaneously the most demanding spiritual path and the most forgiving. Gurudeva has taught us that "Saivism and Saivites have per-

sisted through many ages in the course of time through suc-
cessfully adapting work, service and skills according to the
times while internalizing worship and holding firmly to the
eternal values. The outer form of service or occupation does
not change the spiritual search. Be he a skilled farmer, dairy-
man, factory worker, a village merchant, computer pro-
grammer or corporate executive, the Saivite's religion serves
him well. God Siva, transcendent and yet immanent, has all
of the facilities for the education of man back to the Source.
The technological age brings different facilities, new ways of
working, planning, communicating, manufacturing, traveling and producing food. Yet, it is not all that different now
than in the ancient days. The technological age does not at
all reflect a difference upon the Saivite's relationship with his
older brother, sister, father, mother, kulam guru, teacher,
Satguru, Gods or God in his daily practice of worship and
living the Saiva Dharma. The Saiva Dharma: it is now as it
always was."

*He is the Ancient One. He created the beings of
earth and heaven in days of yore in Order Divine.
The six faiths seek but the Feet of the One Primal
Peerless God; and He pervades them all
in measure appropriate.*

                                    SAINT TIRUMULAR

In every Hindu home there is a sacred oil lamp, symbol of consciousness and of the radiance of God's presence in our life.

Chapter 14

Sacred Symbols of Saivism

VAST KNOWLEDGE IS STORED IN SYMBOLS,
WHICH PROVIDE A CONCENTRATED, NON-
VERBAL FORM OF COMMUNICATION,
EVOKING MEANING ON MANY LEVELS
OF CONSCIOUSNESS.

Pranava Aum
The Pranava Aum denotes Nada, the
Primal Sound, or Soundless Sound,
from which creation issues forth. The
Pranava Aum is associated with
Ganesha. The abbreviated Pranava
symbol is always placed at the top of
written pages in remembrance of
Him.

Swastika
A swastika is the symbol of
auspiciousness and good fortune.
The word means "It is well." A square
cross + represents materiality, the
macrocosm, which can be grasped
and reduced to understanding
through direct reason. The right-
angled arms of the swastika denote
the indirect way in which divinity is
apprehended, by intuition and
not by intellect.

Siva Lingam

The most ancient symbol of God Siva, the Siva Lingam, is the stone pillar of indefinite mold, a formless form betokening Parasivam, That which cannot be described or portrayed. The Lingam itself is Siva as unmanifest Reality; the Yoni, or base, is His manifest Sakti.

Tripundra and Pottu

The tripundra is the most renowned Saivite symbol—three stripes of gleaming vibhuti across the brow. Vibhuti connotes purity, and the three lines signify the burning away of the triple bondage of anava, karma and maya. The pottu, or dot, placed midway on the lowest stripe or between the eyebrows at the point of the third eye, stimulates our discrimination and spiritual insight.

Ankusa

The ankusa, or goad, usually held in Ganesha's right hand, is used to remove obstacles from our path when He judges that proper in relation to our karma and dharma. The goad may be seen as the force of fear, by which all things are repelled from us. With the goad Lord Ganesha spurs the dullard onward.

Tiruvadi

Tiruvadi, or the holy feet, are symbolized by the sandals worn by the Satguru. The holy feet are the source of Sakti or grace of the Satguru. We prostrate before him, obey him explicitly, and worship the holy feet for release from worldliness. Truly, grace resides in Tiruvadi.

Naga

A symbol of the kundalini slumbering on the petals of the muladhara, the naga, or cobra, inspires each Saivite to proceed with personal unfoldment, to lift the serpent power within to the heights of God-Realization. The cobra's royal hood betokens the regal destiny of every Saiva soul.

Nandi

Nandi is Lord Siva's mount, or vahana. Nandi, whose name means "the joyful," is a huge white bull with a black tail. Nandi's meanings are rich: the ideal devotee or liberated soul in constant communion with God Siva; the embodiment of dharma; the joy of Saivism; the symbol of purity, wisdom and steady devotion; the very image of strength. None but Siva may ride upon his back.

Vel

The Vel, Lord Muruga's lance, is wide, long and sharp, signifying incisive discrimination and spiritual knowledge which must be broad, deep and penetrating. The Sakti Vel is the deadly foe to the arrogant lower nature; yet to the awakened soul it offers strength and refuge in adversity.

Kalasa

Lord Ganesha can be represented by a kalasa, a husked coconut on a pot, circled by five mango leaves. Coconuts are sacred to Lord Ganesha. The breaking of a coconut before His shrine represents the shattering of the human ego—the pride, prejudices and apprehensions that conceal the sweet fruit of a spiritual nature.

Vata

The vata, or banyan tree, is an ancient symbol of Saivism, Sanatana Dharma, which branches out in all directions, draws from many roots, spreads its cool shade far and wide, yet stems from a single great trunk. It is associated with Lord Siva as Dakshinamurthi, the Silent Sage who sits beneath it to teach the ancient wisdom.

Mayil

The elegant Mayil, or peacock, is the vahana of Lord Muruga. Mayil, the slayer of serpents, is swift like Muruga Himself whose grace subdues the bonds of our lower nature. Lord Muruga is a most royal and beautiful God, carried on a most regal mount which also symbolizes His conquest over ego, vanity and pride.

Rudraksha

Saivites prize rudraksha seeds as the compassionate tears Lord Siva shed for the suffering of mankind and wear them always as a symbol of His love. All devout Saivites repeat the Panchakshara Mantram, "Aum Namasivaya," and wear tripundra and rudrakshas.

Seval

Vanquished in combat with Lord Muruga, Surapadman was cut in half by the Sakti Vel. One part became the beautiful mayil, the other the seval, or fighting rooster. Large and red, he crows from the War God's battle flag to herald the dawn of wisdom.

Trisula
Trisula, Lord Siva's trident, is the royal scepter of the Saiva Dharma. Wielded in all three worlds, it signifies desire, action and wisdom—Iccha, Kriya and Jnana Saktis—by which God Siva administers His divine laws of dharma.

Mushika
Mushika is Lord Ganesha's vahana, the mouse, traditionally associated with abundance. The mouse carries Lord Ganesha's grace into every nook and cranny of the mind. Moving silently under cover of darkness, seldom visible yet always at work, Mushika is likened to the unseen grace which influences our lives.

Kamandalu
The kamandalu, or water vessel, is carried by the sannyasin. It symbolizes his simple, self-contained life, his holy orders of sannyas and his oath to seek God-Realization. The only other object he carries is the danda, or walking staff, which reminds him of his constant sadhana and tapas.

Trikonam

The trikonam, or triangle, is a symbol of God Siva which, like the Siva Lingam, denotes His Absolute Being. It represents the element fire and thus portrays the process of spiritual ascent and Liberation.

Bilva

The bilva, or bael, tree's fruit, flowers and leaves are all sacred to Siva, who wears a wreath of bilva flowers in His hair. To plant bilva trees around our home or a temple is highly meritorious and sanctifying. The Siva Lingam is traditionally worshiped with bilva leaves and water.

Shadkonam

The shadkonam, or six-pointed star, found in Lord Muruga's yantra, is formed by two interlocking triangles: the upper one stands for Siva and fire while the lower one represents Sakti and water. Their union gives birth to the Divine Child Muruga whose sacred number is six.

Konrai
Konrai, or Golden Shower, tree blossoms are the flowering symbol of Siva's honied Grace, associated from time immemorial with His temples throughout Tamil Nadu and mentioned in many Devaram hymns. A konrai garland adorns Siva's chest.

Homa
The homa, or fire pit, is the symbol of ancient and still existing Vedic rites. It is through the element of fire that we make our special offerings to the Gods, and it is before the homa fire that Saivite marriages are solemnized.

Kuthuvillaku
The standing oil lamp, or kuthuvillaku, burning in the temple, shrine room or home, keeps the inner atmosphere pure and serene. We honor the kuthuvillaku as a symbol of the Divine and never fail to keep the holy light burning in our home.

Mangkolam

The mangkolam, or paisley design, is taken from the mango and associated with Lord Ganesha, who often holds one in His hand. Mangos are the sweetest of fruits, attractive and pleasing to all, symbolizing the happy fulfillment of legitimate worldly desires. Ganesha is the Patron of Arts, and the paisley is among artists' favorite motifs.

On festival days a parade Deity is taken around the temple.

Chapter 15

Holy Days and Festivals

WHETHER IN GREAT RELIGIOUS CENTERS OR
REMOTE VILLAGES, SAIVITES HONOR GOD
SIVA AND THE MAHADEVAS ON SPECIAL DAYS
EACH YEAR, IN SACRED CELEBRATIONS THAT
MAY BE ELABORATE OR SIMPLE.

What is the Hindu Holy Day?
Friday is the Hindu Holy Day, set aside each week for special
fasts, worship and meditation.

We honor Friday as a most auspicious and sacred day, a
day on which we intensify our religious observances and
sadhana. We especially worship Siva-Sakti, or Ardhanarisvara, on this holy day, drawing from the unlimited Sakti, or
power, of our God Siva which gives us the strength and energy to face the challenges of the coming week. On Friday we
visit the temple or hold a special puja in the home, we clean
and decorate the home shrine, observe prayers, japa and study
of the scriptures. Fasting is the most common of all vows,
and we always fast on Friday, taking only fresh fruits, juices
and sweet milk. After the 6:00 PM puja, we break the fast
with our regular evening meal. Most temples conduct special pujas on Fridays, and many devotees request special
archanas to petition the Gods' help. Friday is not a day of
rest, for we carry on our usual work.

How many festival days do we observe?
We faithfully observe nine major Deity festivals, two festivals
that honor the guru and several home observances not related to the Deity or temple.

Saivites observe nine major Deity festival days: Maha

Sivaratri, Ganesha Chaturthi, Navaratri, Skanda Shasti, Sivalaya Deepam, Vinayaga Viratam, Markali Pillaiyar, Tiruvembavai and Thai Pusam. Additionally, we honor the Satguru on his Jayanthi, or birthday, and again on Guru Purnima. Also, the temple in each Saivite community holds an annual festival, usually lasting for ten days, and we attend these celebrations. There are some home observances which are important, too, including: Deepavali, Thai Pongal and Holi.

What is Maha Sivaratri?
Maha Sivaratri, "Siva's Great Night," is the most profound and sacred of all Saivite holy days, honoring Lord Siva, the Source and Self of all that exists.

Maha Sivaratri falls on the 13th day of the dark half of the moon's passage in the month of Maasi (February/March) and is the most sacred day of all for Saivites. We observe it both as a discipline and a festivity, keeping a strict fast all day and night, taking only fruits and milk. As a special discipline of this festival, we keep an all-night vigil while performing japa, meditation and prayer. All through the night we sing in praise of Siva, recount His glories and exploits, chant Sri Rudram and His 1,008 names repeatedly and dedicate ourselves heart and soul to Him. We offer bilva leaves, fresh milk, pure water and other sacraments over the Siva Lingam and garland it with rudrakshas and flowers. At 4:00 AM we end the festivity by breaking our fast.

What is Ganesha Chaturthi?
Ganesha Chaturthi is the festival day celebrating the birth of Lord Ganesha.

Lord Ganesha's birthday is celebrated on the chaturthi, or "fourth day," after the new moon in the month of Avani —August/September. We decorate the temple and home shrine with banana leaves, sugarcane and strings of mango leaves, making it look like a small forest. We bring baskets of fruits and sweets, especially modaka balls, and place them before the sanctum of Lord Ganesha. He receives special pujas throughout the day and often a festival parade. Each year we obtain a small or large soft clay image of Ganapati, and use it for worship at home for two to ten days prior to Ganesha Chaturthi. Then in the evening of this day, the image is taken to a nearby river, temple tank, lake or sea-shore and ceremoniously dissolved in the water. This is a day for rejoicing and for seeking the blessings of the Lord of Obstacles to bring wealth and success into our life.

> *Offerings of perfumed substances, flowers, incense, lamps and fresh fruits—these are the five elements of the traditional puja which culminates with the offering of the lamps.*
>
> KAMIKA AGAMA

What is Navaratri?

Navaratri is one of the most sacred of Saivite Hindu festivals, second only to Maha Sivaratri. On Navaratri we worship God Siva as Parasakti.

Navaratri is celebrated during the nine nights following the new moon in the month of Puttathi—September/Octo- (PURATTATHI) ber. During Navaratri, which literally means "nine nights," we worship Siva as Parasakti, the Universal Mother, through prayers, pujas and bhajans. Just as we worship the unmanifest Parasivam on Sivaratri, so do we worship the manifest Sakti during Navaratri. Sakti is the manifested energy of God Siva and inseparable from Him, the feminine half of Divinity. Without Siva, the active and potent Sakti has no existence. Without Sakti, Siva remains transcendent, silent and unmanifest. Siva and Sakti are one in mystical alliance. At Navaratri we worship Parasakti in three aspects. Just as Brahma, Vishnu and Rudra are aspects of our one God, so are Sarasvati, Lakshmi and Durga aspects of God Siva. The first three days are devoted to Durga, and prayers are offered to Her invoking strength, health and eradication of impurities. The second three days we worship Lakshmi and offer prayers for wealth, beauty and peace. The last three days are devoted to Sarasvati, and devotees petition for the refinements of art, culture and learning. The tenth day is known as Vijaya Dasami, a day of rejoicing in the triumph of righteousness and truth. This final day is most auspicious for beginning any new enterprise or field of learning.

What is Skanda Shasti?
Skanda Shasti is a temple festival honoring Lord Skanda's victory over Surapadman, the conquest of good over evil.

Shasti means "six," and Skanda Shasti occurs the first six days following the new moon of Aipasi—October/November. Joining in the festival processions and pujas at His temples, we observe each of the six days with worship and prayers to Lord Muruga as Skanda, the Divine Warrior, invoking His protection and grace. Skanda fought the demon Surapadman for six days, and on the evening of the sixth day killed him. Thus, the festival ends in a crescendo of activity on the sixth day, a victory celebration of light over darkness, good triumphing over evil. Often we can watch mock battles fought between large figures of Skanda and Surapadman, which end in setting fire to the asura. On Skanda Shasti we intensify our meditative sadhana and seek Lord Muruga's blessings in removing selfishness, pride and vanity from our life.

What is Sivalaya Deepam?
Sivalaya Deepam is a joyous one-day festival on which we worship God Siva as the Divine Light, self-effulgent and unknowably vast.

Sivalaya Deepam, also called Karttikai Deepam, falls on the full moon night of Karttikai—November/December. We honor God Siva's appearance as an infinite Lingam of light which Brahma and Vishnu could not fathom. When the sun sets, we light many candles and lamps, setting them in window sills and every room of the house, then observe special Siva puja, japa and bhajan.

What is Vinayaga Viratam?

Vinayaga Viratam is a 21-day festival honoring Lord Ganesha.

Vinayaga Viratam begins on the full moon day in the month of Karttikai—November/December. During these days, Vinayaga Purana or stories are recited in the temples and special pujas are conducted at every Ganesha temple. Many devotees observe the vow—*virata* means "vow"—of attending daily puja at a Ganesha temple and taking only one meal a day, and that in the evening.

> *You are the Heavens and the devas;*
> *You are the essence of the Vedas and the hymns;*
> *You are the letters and the numbers;*
> *You are the seven seas; You are our God;*
> *You are the eyes that see You;*
> *You are the earth, the light and the darkness.*
>
> SAINT APPAR

What is Markali Pillaiyar?

Markali Pillaiyar is a month-long home religious festival held in honor of Lord Ganesha. For untold thousands of years, winter festivities and ceremonies have been held in honor of Lord Ganesha. During the month of Markali—from the middle of December to the middle of January—we worship Lord Pillaiyar, the Noble Child, with special devotion, prayers and japa of His names. This month is the most spiritual time of the year, and we meditate diligently, especially between four and six in the morning. Traditionally, all worship, prayer, spiritual disciplines, or sadhanas, are commenced during the month of Markali, and the home is cleaned each day.

What is Tiruvembavai?
Tiruvembavai is a ten-day festival honoring Siva Nataraja. The ten-day Tiruvembavai festival ends on the full moon day in the month of Markali—December/January. All Siva temples celebrate this most important of Siva Nataraja festivals with special pujas and abhishekams. Each morning at 4:00AM, the famed and mystically rich songs of Saint Manikkavasagar, called "Tiruvembavai," are sung or recited in the home shrine. On all or at least the final day of the festival, young unmarried virgins go together in small groups to the temple to pray for unfailing rains, for the welfare of the land and especially for their own wish to be blessed to have undying love for Siva and to marry a fine, dedicated Siva bhakta.

What are Jayanthi and Guru Purnima?
Jayanthi is the day we celebrate the birthday of our Gurudeva. Guru Purnima is a day honoring all the great spiritual teachers, especially our Satguru.

We celebrate Jayanthi each year on the birthday of our guru with a week of festivities. On Jayanthi day a special guru puja is conducted with abhishekam to our Satguru's feet. We bring offerings of garlands, fruits, cloth and funds to support the publications he gives away as prasadam, placing our gifts on Gurudeva's seat to show our love and gratitude for his guidance in our spiritual life. During the guru puja the pujaris bathe the Satguru's feet with precious offerings such as milk, yogurt, honey and rosewater. If he is not physically present, the Tiruvadi, or sacred sandals, which represent him receive our love and veneration. We honor the Sat guru in a similar way on Guru Purnima which falls on the *purnima,* or full moon day, in Adi—July/August.

What is Thai Pusam?
Thai Pusam is a festival held to commemorate the day Lord Muruga received the Sakti Vel.

Thai Pusam is held on the full moon day in the month of Thai—January/February. It is a most colorful celebration in remembrance of Lord Muruga's receiving the Vel from Parvati. It is also a day on which Siva Nataraja performed a blessed dance for the benefit of and witnessed by the Gods, by Saint Vyagrapadar, Saint Patanjali and the 3,000 brahmin priests at Chidambaram. Thai Pusam is celebrated at both Siva and Muruga temples.

> *Oh Infinite Effulgence, praise be to thee.*
> *Hail!…Thou who is water, fire, wind, ether too!*
> *Hail thou who creates all souls but is Himself*
> *uncreated. Hail thou the culmination of all souls,*
> *hail!…To the one who embodies within Himself*
> *the Vedic hymns and Vedic sacrifice, truth and*
> *untruth, light and darkness, joy and sorrow, the*
> *divided and undivided, the attachment and*
> *release, the beginning and ultimate end—*
> *to Him our songs of praise we sing.*
>   SAINT MANIKKAVASAGAR

A lady feeds a deer, practices ahimsa, noninjury in thought or deed.

Chapter 16

Ahimsa,
The Ethic of Nonviolence

WE EXPLORE NONINJURY
AS A WAY TO ACHIEVE HARMONY
WITH OUR ENVIRONMENT, PEACE BETWEEN
PEOPLES AND COMPASSION
WITHIN OURSELVES.

What is the basis for Hinduism's ethic of noninjury?
Many are the sources of Hindu thought which inspire men
and women to live the ideals of compassion and nonviolence. The rishis who revealed the principles of dharma, or
divine law, in Hindu scripture knew full well the potential
for human suffering and the path which could avert it. To
them a one spiritual power flowed in and through all things
in this universe, animate and inanimate, conferring existence by its presence. To them life was a coherent process
leading all souls without exception to enlightenment, and no
violence could be carried to the higher reaches of that ascent.

These rishis were mystics whose revelation disclosed a
cosmos in which all beings exist in interlaced dependence.
The whole was contained in the part, and the part in the
whole. Based on this cognition, they taught a philosophy of
non-difference of self and other, asserting that in the final
analysis we are not separate from the world and its manifest
forms nor from the Divine which shines forth in all things
and all peoples. From this understanding of oneness arose
the philosophical basis for the practice of noninjury and
Hinduism's ancient commitment to it.

We all know that Hindus, who are one-sixth of the

human race today, believe in the existence of God everywhere, as an all-pervasive, self-effulgent energy and consciousness. This basic belief creates the attitude of sublime tolerance and acceptance toward others. Even tolerance is insufficient to describe the compassion and reverence the Hindu holds for the intrinsic sacredness within all things. Therefore, the actions of all Hindus are rendered benign, or *ahimsa*. One would not want to hurt something which one revered.

How does Hinduism define ahimsa?

In Sanskrit *himsa* is doing harm or causing injury. The *a* placed before the word negates it. Very simply, *ahimsa* is abstaining from causing hurt or harm. It is gentleness and noninjury, whether physical, mental or emotional.

The Hindu looks at nothing as intrinsically evil. To him the ground is sacred. The sky is sacred. The sun is sacred. His wife is a Goddess. Her husband is a God. Their children are devas. Their home is a shrine. Life is a pilgrimage to Mukti, or Liberation from rebirth, which once attained is the end to reincarnation in a physical body. When on a holy pilgrimage, one would not want to hurt anyone along the way, knowing full well the experiences on this path are of one's own creation, though may be acted out through others.

It is good to know that nonviolence speaks only to the most extreme forms of wrongdoing, while ahimsa (which includes not killing) goes much deeper to prohibit the subtle abuse and the simple hurt. Patanjali (*circa* 100 BCE), the sagely codifier of ashtanga yoga, regards ahimsa as the yogi's *mahavrata*, the great vow and foremost spiritual discipline which those seeking Truth must follow strictly and without fail. This was not meant merely to condemn killing, but extended to harm caused by one's thoughts, words and deeds of all kinds—including injury to the natural environment. Even the intent to injure, even violence committed in a dream, is a violation of the principle of ahimsa.

How do beliefs and attitudes produce peace or violence?
Every belief creates certain attitudes. Those attitudes govern
our actions. Our actions can thus be traced to our inmost
beliefs about ourself and about the world around us. If those
beliefs are erroneous, our actions will not be in tune with
the universal dharma.

For instance, the belief in the existence of an all-pervasive Divinity throughout the universe creates an attitude of
reverence, benevolence and compassion for all animate and
inanimate beings. This equals ahimsa, non-hurtfulness. The
belief in the duality of heaven and hell, the white forces and
the dark forces, creates the attitude that we must be on our
guard, and that we are justified in giving injury, physically
and emotionally, to others whom we judge to be bad, pagan
or unworthy for other reasons. Such thinking leads to ratio-
nalizing so-called righteous wars and conflicts.

> *Ahimsa is not causing pain to any living being*
> *at any time through the actions of one's mind,*
> *speech or body.*
>
> SANDILYA UPANISHAD

What are the reasons Hindus oppose killing?
Hindus oppose killing for several reasons. Belief in karma
and reincarnation are strong forces at work in the Hindu
mind. They full well know that any thought, feeling or action sent out from themselves to another will return to them
through yet another in equal or amplified velocity. What we
have done to others will be done to us, if not in this life then
in another. The Hindu is thoroughly convinced that violence
which he commits will return to him by a cosmic process
that is unerring. Two thousand years ago, South India's weaver saint Tiruvalluvar said it so simply, "All suffering recoils

on the wrongdoer himself. Therefore, those who desire not to suffer refrain from causing others pain." A similar view can be found in the Jain scripture Acaranga Sutra: "To do harm to others is to do harm to oneself. You are he whom you intend to kill. You are he whom you intend to dominate. We corrupt ourselves as soon as we intend to corrupt others. We kill ourselves as soon as we intend to kill others."

Because of the knowledge of reincarnation, the Hindu knows that he may one day be in the same position of anyone he might be inclined to harm or persecute. The Hindu who is consciously aware within his soul knows that he is the time traveller and may incarnate, take a body of flesh in the society he most opposed, in order to equalize his hates and fears into a greater understanding which would result in the release of ignorance.

How do higher and lower consciousness relate to ahimsa?
Peace is a reflection of spiritual consciousness, and violence is a reflection of unevolved or base consciousness. The Hindu knows that at this time on this planet those of the lower nature, unevolved people, are society's antagonists. Being unevolved, they are of the lower nature, self-assertive, confused and protective of their immediate environment. All others are their enemies. They are jealous, angry, fearful. Many take sport in killing for the sake of killing, thieving for the sake of theft, even if they do not need or use the spoils. This is the lower nature, and is equally distributed among the peoples of the world in every nation, society and neighborhood. Those of the higher nature—ten, fifteen or twenty percent of the population—live in protective environments. Their occupation is research, memory, education, which is reason; moving the world's goods here and there, which is will. Those of yet a higher nature delve into the mysteries of the universe, and others work for universal peace and love on earth, as groups and individuals. The Hindu knows that

those of the lower nature will slowly, over an experiential period of time, come into the higher nature, and that those of the higher nature, who have worked so hard to get there, will avoid the lower nature and not allow themselves to be caught up in it. Hindus believe in the progress of humanity, from an old age into a new age, from darkness into a consciousness of divine light.

> *Many are the lovely flowers of worship offered to*
> *the guru, but none lovelier than non-killing.*
> *Respect for life is the highest worship, the bright*
> *lamp, the sweet garland and unwavering devotion.*
> TIRUMANTIRAM

What is the best way to teach peace to the world?

The best way is to teach families to be peaceful within their own home, to settle all arguments and contention before they sleep at night, even if they stay up for three days, so the children can see that peace can be attained and then maintained through the use of intelligence. Humans do not have horns or claws, nor do they have sharp teeth. Their weapon is their intelligence. Children must be taught through the example of parents and by learning the undeniable facts of life, the basic tenets—that an all-pervasive force holds this universe together, that we create with this force every minute, every hour, every day, and because time is a circle, what we create comes back to us. It is up to the parents to create the peacemakers of the future. Remember, we teach children in only one way—by our own example.

Parents must teach children to appreciate those who are different, those who believe differently. Teach them the openness that they need to live in a pluralistic world where others have their unique ways, their life and culture. Teach them the value of human diversity and the narrow-mindedness of a provincial outlook. Give them the tools to live in a world of differences without feeling threatened, without forcing their ways or their will on others. Teach them that it never helps to hurt another.

On a personal level, how can we cultivate ahimsa?

An individual can find total peace within himself, not through meditation alone—for peaceful actions must follow introspection—not through drugs, not through psychology or psychiatry, but through control. Peace is the natural state of the mind. It is there, inside, to be discovered in meditation and then radiated out to others.

Vegetarianism is a natural and obvious way to live with a minimum of hurt to other beings. Those who minister among Hindus have learned that vegetarian families have far fewer problems than those who are not vegetarian. The abhorrence of killing of any kind leads quite naturally to a vegetarian diet. If you think about it, the meat-eater is participating indirectly in a violent act against the animal kingdom. His desire for meat drives another man to kill and provide that meat. The act of the butcher begins with the desire of the consumer. When his consciousness lifts and expands, he will abhor violence and not be able to even digest the meat, fish and eggs he was formerly consuming. The opposite of causing injury to others is compassion and love for all beings. The *Tirukural* puts it nicely: "How can he practice true compassion who eats the flesh of an animal to fatten his own flesh?"

If children are raised as vegetarians, every day they are exposed to noninjury as a principle of peace and compassion. Every day they are growing up, they are remembering and being reminded not to kill. They won't even kill another creature to feed themselves. And if you won't kill another creature to feed yourself, then when you grow up you will be much less likely to injure people.

What can we do to responsibly promote noninjury?
Make a list of all the things you have purchased in the last six months which bring harm to humans, animals, fish, fowl and other sentient beings. Read the labels on simple things like glue or soap and scratch off the list all the things that contribute to violent acts or aid in the destruction of the planet. Then find the willpower to not, for convenience sake, fall back into purchasing these things again. Don't buy endangered plants, animals or products from exploited species such as furs, ivory, reptile skin and tortoise shell.

Talk about peaceful means of dealing with problems, not allowing even your words to promote injury and harm. Volunteer your time to help groups who are sincerely working for a peaceful world. Learn more about other cultures and philosophies, so your appreciation of them is genuine and deep. Work to strengthen your community and the people near you. Reduce stress in your life. Be joyful.

> *Do not injure the beings living on the earth,*
> *in the air and in the water. May all beings look at*
> *me with a friendly eye. May I do likewise, and*
> *may we all look on each other with*
> *the eyes of a friend.*
>
> YAJUR VEDA

❧ Part Two ❧
The Creed

I n part two, the questions and answers change from cultural and religious to theological. A creed is an authoritative formulation of the beliefs of a religion, of religious
communities and their individuals. Every religion has a
creed of one form or another. A creed may be a detailed declaration of beliefs—such as found on the following page—or
it may be a simple statement, called an affirmation of faith,
like the triratna, or "three jewels" of Hinayana Buddhism: "I
take refuge in the Buddha. I take refuge in the dharma. I take
refuge in the sanga." Our own Saivite affirmation of faith
summarizes this entire book in just eight words: "God Siva
is immanent Love and transcendent Reality."

In Saivism, such doctrines have not always been specifically articulated, although even the ancient Gayatri Mantram
is a profession of faith, as are the mahavakiam, or "great sayings," from the Upanishads. But in our technological age in
which village integrity is being replaced by worldwide mobil-
ity, the importance of a creed becomes apparent if religious
identity is to be preserved. We need two kinds of strength—
that which is found in diversity and individual freedom to in-
quire and that which derives from a union of minds in up-
holding the universal principles of our faith. It incorporates
only the convictions of the monistic theism of Saiva Siddhanta as postulated by the Natha rishi, Tirumular, in his
Tirumantiram over 2,000 years ago—a philosophy sometimes called Advaita Siddhanta or Suddha Saiva Siddhanta.
On the following two pages the twelve essential beliefs of the
Saivite Creed appear. In part two, we examine them in detail.

A Creed for Saivite Hindus

GOD SIVA IS IMMANENT LOVE AND
TRANSCENDENT REALITY

1. REGARDING GOD'S UNMANIFEST REALITY
I believe Lord Siva is God, whose Absolute Being, Parasivam, transcends time, form and space.

2. REGARDING GOD'S MANIFEST NATURE OF ALL-PERVADING LOVE
I believe Lord Siva is God, whose <u>immanent</u> nature of love is the substratum or Primal Substance and Pure Consciousness flowing through all form.

Inherent

3. REGARDING GOD AS PERSONAL LORD AND CREATOR OF ALL
I believe Lord Siva is God, whose immanent nature is the Primal Soul, Supreme Mahadeva, Siva-Sakti, the Creator, Preserver and Destroyer of all that exists.

4. REGARDING THE SOUL'S CREATION AND ITS IDENTITY WITH GOD
I believe that each individual soul is created (through emanation) by Lord Siva and (its uncreated essence: Pure Consciousness and Absolute Being) is identical to Him, and that this identity can be and will be fully realized by all souls when the triple bondage of anava, karma and maya is removed through His Grace.

5. REGARDING THE GROSS, SUBTLE AND CAUSAL PLANES OF EXISTENCE
I believe in three worlds of existence: the First World (Bhuloka, or gross plane), where souls take on physical bodies; the Second World (Devaloka, or subtle plane), where souls take on astral or mental bodies; and the Third World (Sivaloka, or causal plane), where soul bodies, Mahadevas, exist in their own self-effulgent form.

6. REGARDING THE ELEPHANT-FACED DEITY

I believe in the Mahadeva Lord Ganesha, Son of Siva-Sakti, to whom I must first supplicate before beginning any worship or task.

7. REGARDING THE DEITY SKANDA

I believe in the Mahadeva Lord Muruga, Son of Siva-Sakti, whose Vel of Grace dissolves the bondages of ignorance.

8. REGARDING THE ESOTERIC PURPOSE OF TEMPLE WORSHIP

I believe that religion is the harmonious working together of the three worlds and that this harmony can be created through temple worship, wherein the three worlds become open to one another, and the beings within them able to communicate.

9. REGARDING KARMA, SAMSARA AND LIBERATION FROM REBIRTH

I believe in the law of karma—that one must personally reap the effects of all actions he has caused—and that each soul will continue to reincarnate until all karmas are resolved and Moksha, Liberation, is attained.

10. REGARDING THE GOODNESS OF ALL

I believe that there is no intrinsic evil.

11. REGARDING THE FOUR MARGAS, OR STAGES OF INNER PROGRESS

I believe that the performance of chariya (virtuous and moral living), kriya (temple worship) and yoga (internalized worship and union with Parasivam through grace of the living Satguru) is absolutely necessary to bring forth the state of jnana.

12. REGARDING THE FIVE LETTERS

I believe in the Panchakshara Mantram, the five sacred syllables "Na Ma Si Va Ya," as the foremost and essential mantram of Saivism.

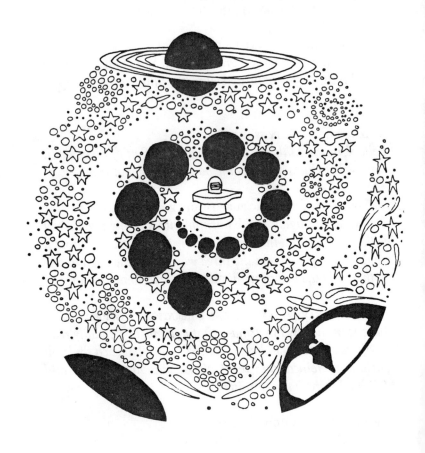

For untold thousands of years, the Siva Lingam has represented God in His unmanifest Reality, termed Nirguna Brahman. The unhewn form of the Lingam alludes subtly to That which is beyond description or portrayal, depicted here as the core of existence—within and above the phenomenal world and its vast galactic contents.

Chapter 17

God's Unmanifest Reality

I BELIEVE LORD SIVA IS GOD,
WHOSE ABSOLUTE BEING, PARASIVAM,
TRANSCENDS TIME, FORM AND SPACE.

Who is Lord Siva?

Lord Siva is God, the uncreated Supreme Being who is ever-existent in His three perfections of Absolute Reality, Pure Consciousness and Primal Soul.

Paramaguru Siva Yogaswami proclaimed: The Universal One is Siva. That without place or name is Siva. The splendor known as Om is Siva. That which has no form is Siva. That which is the Truth is Siva....I saw the Truth of the Godhead transcending the principles of manifestation. Sage Chellappa endowed me with the vision of yogic insight, and I beheld in silence the ever poised essence of Reality. No more sorrows. No more joys. **Gurudeva Sivaya Subramuniyaswami explains:** Lord Siva, God, was never created. He has existed forever and has created all things including everybody's individual soul. Parasivam is His unmanifest first perfection. His second perfection of Satchidananda is all-pervasive, infinite, and is found in every action and particle of His creation. His third perfection, or Primal Soul, is our personal Lord and Ruler of all three worlds. In praying to God Siva, one can visualize His form as Siva Lingam, as Nataraja—the Divine Dancer—or simply see Him as Ardhanarisvara, Siva-Sakti, the Primal Substance permeating all form. It is comforting to know that Lord Siva is the Divine Father-Mother, Creator of our soul. That close to us, that watchful and that loving is God Siva. Such a God is truly God.

Why is God Siva's first perfection, Parasivam, described as Absolute Being?

God Siva is both unmanifest Reality and manifest Reality. Parasivam is the unmanifest Reality or Absolute Being of God, distinguished from His other two perfections, which are manifest and of the nature of form.

Paramaguru Siva Yogaswami proclaimed: "Truth is One. The rest is illusion. Truth is betrayed by the first attempt at articulation. What else can I say? You must realize It yourself. It is wrong even to put it that way. How does one express something changeless and beyond the knowing of the mind? **Gurudeva Sivaya Subramuniyaswami explains:** You see, God Siva is absolute and is Reality Itself. To discover God Siva's ultimate perfection of Reality, the yogi penetrates deep into contemplation. As thoughts arise in his mind, mental concepts of the world or of the God he seeks, he silently repeats, "Neti, neti—It is not this. It is not that." His quieted consciousness expands into Satchidananda. He is everywhere, permeating all form in his blissful state. He remembers his goal which lies beyond bliss and holds firmly to "Neti, neti—this is not That for which I seek." Through mantra, through tantra, wielding an indomitable will, the last forces of form, time and space subside for him as the yogi, deep in Nirvikalpa Samadhi, merges into Parasivam. Such an inscrutable God is our God Siva.

> *This Self is the Lord of all beings, the king*
> *of all beings. As the spokes are held together in the*
> *hub and in the rim of a wheel, just so all beings,*
> *all creatures, all gods, all worlds, all lives,*
> *are held together in the Self.... Therefore should a*
> *sage desire to live with that knowledge*
> *as his only refuge.*
>
> BRIHADARANYAKA UPANISHAD

What is the meaning of the Sanskrit word *Parasivam?*
Para means "supreme." Thus, Parasivam is the highest, final or ultimate state of Siva.

Paramaguru Siva Yogaswami proclaimed: No one can describe the Truth adequately. Even the great Sankara failed to do so....If you say "God exists," that is wrong; and if you say "God does not exist," that is also wrong. **Gurudeva Sivaya Subramuniyaswami explains:** Parasivam is the Self of God Siva, His unmanifest, absolute Self. Only to be realized can God Siva be known, and once realized, can never be explained. Such is the great mystery that yogis, rishis, saints and sages have realized through the ages. Parasivam is the fullness of everything, the absence of nothing. It must be realized to be known, does not exist, yet seems to exist; yet existence itself and all states of mind, being and experiential patterns could not exist but for this ultimate Reality of God Siva. The way to the top of the mountain is outlined through yoga, but once the goal has been reached, one becomes the goal itself and smiles contentedly as the knower of the secret, the sacred secret—Parasivam, the Self God beyond the mind. I once explained, many years ago: "If you visualize nothing....and dissolve yourself into that nothingness, that would be the best way you could explain the realization of the Self. And yet that nothingness is the fullness of everything: the power, the sustaining power, of the existence of what appears to be everything." Such a sovereign God is truly God.

Does God Siva's first perfection, Parasivam, transcend time, form and space in all three worlds?
Yes. The three worlds exist in time and space. Absolute God, however, transcends all three worlds and exists as unmanifest Reality beyond time, form and space.

Paramaguru Siva Yogaswami proclaimed: Siva Peruman is the non-dual Reality. I glory in contemplating that He and I are inseparably linked in Oneness. He is beyond birth and death, transcending time and timelessness. He is eternal and ever unchanging....To realize the formless within one's living form is to reach the basis of all forms. All finite forms of experience are inseparable from the Infinite. **Gurudeva Sivaya Subramuniyaswami explains:** God Siva exists in formlessness, giving permission for form to exist because He exists in this primal state, has always exaltedly existed as unmanifest Reality. Such loftiness cannot be captured by our finite mind or explained by one possessing the most intricate of intellects. The subtlety of the bliss experienced after having realized Parasivam, the Self God, cannot be explained. Can the fire explain itself? Can the water explain the fire? Can a raindrop be separate from a pond once merging into it? Can the yogi speak of his unspeakable experience? No description is adequate to explain That which neither is nor is not. It remains sacred and secret, only known by the knower. Such a lofty God is truly our God Siva.

The transcendent has two aspects.
The one is the Absolute Sound (Sabdhabrahman)
and the other is the Supreme Absolute (Para),
which is the one we name Siva...because of His
Supremacy which derives from His nature,
which transcends speech and mind.

                                                    AJITA AGAMA

As Satchidananda, or Pure Consciousness, God Siva permeates all of existence as its very ground or energy. Some liken this to a cinema screen, which is real but unnoticed as the images of seeming dance upon its surface. Here the natural world, with its groves, mountains and intergalactic spaces, is depicted as the body of Siva. He is in all, and all is in Him.

Chapter 18

God's Manifest Nature Of All-Pervading Love

I BELIEVE LORD SIVA IS GOD, WHOSE IMMANENT
NATURE OF LOVE IS THE SUBSTRATUM OR PRIMAL
SUBSTANCE AND PURE CONSCIOUSNESS
FLOWING THROUGH ALL FORM.

Does Lord Siva's consciousness pervade everything?
Yes, His is a cosmic consciousness that exists everywhere
simultaneously in all three worlds.

Paramaguru Siva Yogaswami proclaimed: You will
know Him if you remain still. God is Love. God is Truth.
God is all things. God is everywhere....God is like the ocean
and the waves. There are all kinds of fish in the ocean. They
cannot exist outside of it. Even a grain of sand is full of God.
No one can ever fathom this ocean. **Gurudeva Sivaya Subramuniyaswami explains:** Consciousness is knowing. Out
of Parasivam ever comes the first manifestation of mind—
superconsciousness, or infinite knowing. God Siva knows in
His infinite, all-abiding, loving superconsciousness. He
knows from deep within all of His creations to their surface.
Infinite is His all-pervasive, superconscious, exalted mind.
His Being is within every animate and inanimate form—
simultaneously, all-at-once, everywhere in this and every
universe. Our finite minds cannot understand such as I have
explained unless chariya has been perfected, kriya mastered
and the heights of yoga attained; then can the yogi but
glimpse in his exalted state for short periods of time into the
constant state of Lord Siva's infinite consciousness. This unbounded Satchidananda has neither beginning nor end. All

is within it. It is within all. Verily, it is the mind of Lord Siva. Such a Lord must truly be God.

Why is Lord Siva's second perfection, Pure Consciousness, called an immanent nature of love?
It is called immanent because it is present throughout the entire universe, near to man and not remote. It is called love for it is the highest of all phenomena, radiating affection, compassion and benevolence.

Paramaguru Siva Yogaswami proclaimed: Love is Kadavul. Love is the world. Love is all things living. Love is everything. It is Love that appears as becoming and as dissolution. Who knows the wonder of Love? **Gurudeva Sivaya Subramuniyaswami explains:** God Siva loves. Pure consciousness, infinite intelligence exists, in the state of "Chit." Pure knowledge knows no second, opposes nothing, communicates with no one, no thing, yet everyone and everything simultaneously. This constant state of knowing is love. It is difficult to understand such a loving God in this second perfection of His Being, but we shall try. Sit quietly and feel the life in your body. It is alive. This life sustains and is loved. If we were to give life an attribute, we could only call it love. God Siva is close to us, closer to us than our life. He loves His devotee, His child. He is the Mother, tenderly kissing our bruises; and He is the Father, sternly harnessing our instinctive-intellectual forces. Such a love can only be God's Love. Such a loving God is truly the infinite and supreme God.

> *Like the touch in wind, like the sweetness in sugar-cane, like the ghee in milk, like the juice in fruit, like the fragrance in flowers is He, our Protector, pervading everywhere.... Visible to your eyes, He rises in your very palm,...as light within your eyes, He guides your way. He is love embodied.*
> SAINT TIRUMULAR

What is the meaning of the term "pure consciousness?"
Pure consciousness refers to that pristine state of Being which is undifferentiated, totally aware of itself without an object of its awareness. It is pure Existence, Knowledge and Bliss, free from all thought and transcending the limitations of ego, radiating as divine light, energy and knowing.

Paramaguru Siva Yogaswami proclaimed: All hail to the Absolute! To Sadasiva all hail! All hail to that Being whose form is consciousness! I have beheld the One that all pervades. All doubts and cares have been removed. It is everywhere—in the universe and in each living creature.

Gurudeva Sivaya Subramuniyaswami explains: Consciousness, in its impure state, or dual state, is limited or limits itself to perceive the other part of itself it limited itself from. God Siva is pure consciousness. All souls that He created are limited in consciousness. They must go through several states of evolution in order to glimpse, even glimpse, the Satchidananda, pure consciousness, which is the consciousness of their God. This is the goal, the evolution, of the soul. The scepter that lifts and proclaims law is the serpent power that lifts, bringing out of dual consciousness into pure consciousness, the holy mind of Siva, as the yogi locked in samadhi returns to his Source. Such is the mystery of our God Siva.

What does "substratum or Primal Substance" mean?
By these terms we describe God Siva's inscrutable presence, which is the ultimate ground and being of all that exists and without which nothing could endure. It is called many names: silence, love, existence, power, consciousness and more.

Paramaguru Siva Yogaswami proclaimed: It cannot be seen by the eye, yet It is the eye within the eye. It cannot be thought by the mind, yet It is the mind within the mind. It is the Primal One without past or future....A jackfruit is large in size, yet it hangs from a slender stalk. Its power to hang lies in the strength of the stalk. In the same way, the whole world depends on an unknowable energy for all its activities. It is all the same whether this energy is called God or given any other name. **Gurudeva Sivaya Subramuniyaswami explains:** All the three worlds relate and interrelate one with another and within themselves through the all-pervasive, manifest Being of God. God is ever-present, present ever in all three worlds. Should God, Siva, by some mystical means unknown even in our Saiva scripture, remove His all-pervasive presence from any one of or all of the three worlds, they would crumble, disintegrate and fade away. Such is the almighty power of God Siva. He is the sustaining power and presence throughout the universe, filling it entirely with His Being. Such a God truly is our God.

> *At the moment of Creation, the Great Lord,*
> *having in mind the fulfillment of man's destinies,*
> *established an Immaculate Consciousness*
> *constituted of His Expansion into the five*
> *directions. Out of this Immaculate*
> *Consciousness He created forth eight*
> *Great Lords whose names were the*
> *sounds inherent in it.*
>
> MRGENDRA AGAMA

From left to right, Brahma, Rudra and Vishnu form the renowned Trimurthi. As Brahma, God Siva is Creator, maker of all things, depicted here as an acorn in spring, an infant and the sun at dawn. As Vishnu, He is preserver during life's summer and high noon. As Rudra, He is Destroyer, drawing His creations back to Himself, completing the natural cycle.

Chapter 19

God as Personal Lord
And Creator of All

I BELIEVE LORD SIVA IS GOD
WHOSE IMMANENT NATURE IS THE PRIMAL
SOUL, SUPREME MAHADEVA, SIVA-SAKTI,
THE CREATOR, PRESERVER AND DESTROYER
OF ALL THAT EXISTS.

Why is God Siva's third perfection described as the "Primal Soul"?
"Primal Soul" means the "original or first soul." Lord Siva is the uncreated, ever-existent Universal Soul who has created all other souls.

Paramaguru Siva Yogaswami proclaimed: As there is one soul in a man's body which makes it walk and eat and sleep, so all movements in the world are simply the play of the Lord....Siva Supreme, You have the power to accomplish everything! You are to me more loving than my mother and father. The Soul of my soul are You indeed. For You there is no end and no beginning. **Gurudeva Sivaya Subramuniyaswami explains:** Lord Siva, God, IS. We need not endeavor to explain or convince others of His IS-ness. When they evolve, they will come to know what you know. To know God is to know God in His three perfections. To know Lord Siva as the Primal Soul, Creator of all souls, is to know Lord Siva as intimately and as fully as the yogi would know Him as he glimpses Pure Consciousness, or as the experienced yoga adept would know Him as the timeless, causeless, spaceless God, Parasivam. You can know God today. You are His image; you are in likeness of Him. To love God is to know God. To know God is to feel His love for you. Such a compassionate God cares for the minutiæ such as we and a universe such as ours. Lord Siva truly is God, the one without a second.

What is the meaning of the term *Siva-Sakti*?
Sakti means "power." Thus, *Siva-Sakti* names Lord Siva as His generative power.

Paramaguru Siva Yogaswami proclaimed: This God is the God of all, and He is also my God. The God that gladly gives His grace to those that have firm faith, who is Knowledge of the Truth that all the sages praise, who is the God of Vedanta and of illustrious Siddhanta. He is the God who bears the name of Siva, the God who abides with Sakti as His other half, the God who supports us as Father and as Mother. **Gurudeva Sivaya Subramuniyaswami explains:** *Si* is the unmanifest Reality of our Lord. *Va* is the manifest power, energy and consciousness of our Lord, His Sakti. Thus, in the name *Siva* is contained both Siva and Sakti—Father-Mother, Siva-Sakti. *Siva* describes our intimate, loving Lord who trains us as we are raised in His infinite love. You are a prince or princess in Lord Siva's royal domain. You are a cherished one, like an obedient child who runs, constantly runs, back to his mother and father. You, the cherished one of Lord Siva, Si-Va, you run into the outstretched arms of love. Such humanness is found in Siva-Sakti. *Eminence, majesty, sovereignty*—such exalted words lose their savor when uttered to describe the brilliance and power of God Siva in all three of His perfections. Siva-Sakti, Author of Knowledge, Architect of Form—can a mortal mind grasp such vastness? Such a God is truly our intimate Lord.

Bright, existing very close, moving in the heart;
great and the support of all; in Him is all the
Universe centered round—all that moves, breathes
and blinks. Know Him who is both with form and
without form, the most adorable, the highest of
beings, the One beyond the ken of the finite mind.
                                   MUNDAKA UPANISHAD

Why is God Siva called the Supreme Mahadeva?

Maha means "great," and *deva* means "shining one." The great shining ones, self-effulgent souls of light, are the Gods who dwell in the Third World. Of them all, Siva is supreme. **Paramaguru Siva Yogaswami proclaimed:** Our Father, who the endless dance performs while yet remaining unknown to Brahma and Vishnu, took me 'neath His rule.... Who is it that exists as Father and Mother? Know that it is the Lord of this world and the world beyond. That Perfect Being, maker of all the world, Lord of the tattvas, playing countless games, master of learning who maintains the whole diversity of art and science—not even for a moment will He be parted from me. Sivayave! **Gurudeva Sivaya Subramuniyaswami explains:** God Siva is the Creator of all the Mahadevas and devas. Living in a physical body, you are a First-World deva. He is the Supreme Mahesvara, greatest of devas in all three worlds, all galaxies. Everything is within Him. He is within everything. So great is our God in His manifest form, King of kings, Superior Monarch, Emperor of all the Universes. So vast is His vastness, so feared is He that men cringe to transgress His will. So loved is He that all have an intimate relationship. So talked of is He that His name is on the lips of everyone—for He is the primal sound. Such a Lord, such a God, can only be described as Aum.

How does God Siva create, preserve and destroy all that exists?

As Supreme Mahadeva, He wills into manifestation all souls and all form. By His will they are preserved, and by His will eventually merge in Him.

Paramaguru Siva Yogaswami proclaimed: Creation, preservation and destruction—all are going on simultaneously....There is one thing that God cannot do. He cannot separate Himself from me. **Gurudeva Sivaya Subramuniyaswami explains:** God Siva: the Creator, the Preserver, the Destroyer. *Brahma, Vishnu* and *Rudra* are His names, naming the functions of His Majesty of all the realms as He performs His office. Would you believe me if I said nothing has ever been destroyed by Lord Siva but that He creates, constantly changes the form of and absorbs back into Himself His creations? For is not the ultimate absorption after eons of time the ultimate destruction of what was once created? This is the goal, is it not, of all in our religion, to merge in Oneness with our God? We are not thus destroyed, but like the water returning to the sea are fulfilled in returning to the Source and relinquishing individuality to become Infinity. Our religion, Saivism, is His law, the law with which He rules throughout all His universes. Such are the great mysteries of our God. Let it be known that Lord Siva reigns supreme. Cry out the message. Let all hear the good news.

> *The bodily form of the Almighty, being constituted of powers, is not comparable to ours. Most conspicuous is the absence of anava. His bodily form, having a head, etc., is composed of five mantras corresponding each to the Five Activities—Isa, Tat Purusha, Aghora, Vama and Aja.*
>
> MRGENDRA AGAMA

God Siva creates the individual soul in much the same way that we create our thoughts, as a natural and effortless extension of ourselves. Here the soul is depicted as a creation of Siva's Divine Mind. The soul evolves, maturing in the fires of experience and ultimately turns within through yoga to realize that it was ever in union with Him.

Chapter 20

The Soul's Creation
And Its Identity with God

I BELIEVE THAT EACH INDIVIDUAL SOUL
IS CREATED THROUGH EMANATION BY LORD
SIVA, AND ITS UNCREATED ESSENCE—PURE
CONSCIOUSNESS AND ABSOLUTE BEING—IS
IDENTICAL TO HIM, AND THAT THIS IDENTITY CAN
BE AND WILL BE FULLY REALIZED BY ALL SOULS
WHEN THE TRIPLE BONDAGE OF ANAVA, KARMA
AND MAYA IS REMOVED THROUGH HIS GRACE.

How is the soul created by God Siva?

At the depth of Satchidananda and Parasivam, the soul is
eternal and uncreated. However, the individual soul body is
created as an extension of God Siva Himself.
Paramaguru Siva Yogaswami proclaimed: The goldsmith melts the gold and fashions from it many ornaments.
Siva, the renowned Goldsmith, takes the molten gold of the
soul and fashions many a jewel for diverse purposes....The
atma is the result of God's Grace. He has become the sun and
moon. He has become the Gods, Indra and all the rest. He
has Himself become the entire universe. This soul and body,
too, has He become. **Gurudeva Sivaya Subramuniyaswami
explains:** Often we are asked, "Why did Lord Siva create
souls?" It is His very nature to create souls, as it is the nature
of your mind to create thoughts. Your thoughts have form,
shape and color in the psychic ethers; and you love your
thoughts, you hate your thoughts. Once created, they evoke
fear in you; and yet they are only thoughts. Our thoughts go
through an evolution of karma until they cycle back to us

and merge into our finite substance and give energy to new thoughts. This energy is Sakti power. Though forever existent and uncreated, Lord Siva ever comes out of Pure Consciousness as the first manifest form. His very nature is to create form, nurse it through its evolution back to His infinite Self. Such is the nature of our Father-Mother, God.

What is the triple bondage of anava, karma and maya?
Anava is the personal ego, karma is the results of our deeds and maya is the world. These three both aid and hinder the soul's realization of God Siva.

Paramaguru Siva Yogaswami proclaimed: You must understand that all these actions that arise from maya are a help to realize the Self. By raising him up and bringing him down again and again, the Lord makes a man gain experience. You must get rid of all illusions. All tests are for the good....Our life on earth is veiled by the power of maya—the illusion of matter and energy. Do not esteem the transient life on earth. We are forever immortal, in timeless eternity. **Gurudeva Sivaya Subramuniyaswami explains:** The brilliance of the milk-white form of the shining body with the red-locked hair can only be seen by the seer who is free from the veiling of anava, karma and maya, but yet is not kept ignorant of God Siva's love for him. Does the child know its mother and father in every aspect of their lives while cradled in their arms? Does the running child know his father and his mother in every aspect of their life while he experiences his running—this mischievous child? He feels their ever-guiding protection lest he fall, and feels their loving kisses upon his bruise when he does. Thus, as infants we know and feel God's presence and love and loving protection of us. Such is the humanness of God Siva, truly the greatest God, first and maker of all Gods.

It is He who bestows soul-force and vigor, whose
guidance all men invoke, the devas invoke, whose
shadow is immortal life, whose shadow is death.
Who is the Deity we shall worship with our
offerings?…The Purusha who is in the sun,
who is here and there, I am He.

RIG AND YAJUR VEDA

What does it mean to say that the individual soul is identical with God Siva?

At the soul's nucleus, we already are That, the uncreated, eternal Truth. The soul body is a body of light which evolves and matures into the likeness of Lord Siva just as the seed of a tree one day becomes a tree.

Paramaguru Siva Yogaswami proclaimed: We are That. It is not a case of becoming That….You will find the attributes of the Divine within man. If you look a little more closely, you will find that man is himself the Divine. You are Truth. You are indestructible. You are eternal. You are the Paramatma….The individual soul merges into the luminous Siva. **Gurudeva Sivaya Subramuniyaswami explains:** One of the symbols of Lord Siva is the sign of infinity, ∞, sign of evolution, sign of life flowing out, experiencing and then returning to its Source. It is the very nature of form to create form. Form cannot exist but that it creates, preserves and destroys, fulfilling the law. Being the first and perfect form, God Siva, in the third perfection of His Being—the Primal Soul, Mahesvara, the Manifest and Personal Lord—naturally creates souls in His image and likeness. We are His creation, His servants. Deeper still, we are as He is. Deep within this physical body, with its turbulent emotions and getting-educated mind, is pure perfection identical to Siva's own perfections of Satchidananda and Parasivam.

How does a soul realize its identity with God Siva?
When the soul has gained enough maturity through experience in the world, it naturally seeks God and eventually receives, from a Satguru, the grace of Siva which grants God-Realization.

Paramaguru Siva Yogaswami proclaimed: Jiva will Siva become for those who offer worship. Will they be born on this earth again? No. It is Siva who creates bondage and Liberation, and it is He who destroys bondage and Liberation. **Gurudeva Sivaya Subramuniyaswami explains:** Lord Siva charts the path when dharma, the accumulated seeds of karma, manifests as a clear pattern. This is to say that, when the manifest soul accumulates enough karma from its experiences to give it material substance, this karma itself forms a one pattern, a course of life, which is called *svadharma.* It is only when dharma clearly identifies itself and begins to be lived life after life that this on-course soul conceives a rising desire to more intimately know God. Thus, a struggle of growth commences, culminating in renunciation of social dharma to take sannyas, to seek God full time under the Satguru. Only we think God Siva is apart from us. Let us give up our ignorance to Divine Knowledge. Let us give up illusion and hold to Truth. Let us fulfill karma and claim our heritage in Param, and in the law of our Lord, the Saiva Dharma. Can there be a greater God than the Lord of Lords?

> *When the two deeds, good and evil, are the same,*
> *the Sakti of sweet grace comes as guru to bestow*
> *the gift of removing the several attributes. With*
> *that knowledge received and actions complete, the*
> *three impurities flee and jiva becomes Siva.*
>
> SAINT TIRUMULAR

The three worlds are planes of existence—gross, subtle and causal—existing one within the other. Here the material world is a lotus-filled mountain lake. Within each lotus—and within every atom of the universe—is the Second World of astral substance. Deep within the Second World is the Third World where Lord Nataraja and the Gods live.

Chapter 21

The Gross, Subtle and Causal Planes of Existence

I BELIEVE IN THREE WORLDS OF EXISTENCE:
THE FIRST WORLD (BHULOKA OR GROSS PLANE),
WHERE SOULS TAKE ON PHYSICAL BODIES; THE
SECOND WORLD (DEVALOKA OR SUBTLE PLANE),
WHERE SOULS TAKE ON ASTRAL OR MENTAL BODIES;
AND THE THIRD WORLD (SIVALOKA OR CAUSAL PLANE),
WHERE SOUL BODIES, MAHADEVAS, EXIST
IN THEIR OWN SELF-EFFULGENT FORM.

What is the First World?
The First World is the physical universe of gross or material substance in which phenomena are perceived by the five senses.

Paramaguru Siva Yogaswami proclaimed: The great Chellappa said, "Pati has become pasu and pasa. No one has ever satisfactorily explained how the Infinite becomes the finite."...Siva looks upon human beings with joy, as blossoms of beauty adorning the garden of His world. Through ignorance we become involved in pleasure and pain. The world changes all the time. God remains unchanged. **Gurudeva Sivaya Subramuniyaswami explains:** It is in the First World of gross matter that we have our experiences, manufacture karma and fulfill the duties of First-World life. It is in the First World that consciousness is limited, that awareness of the other two worlds is not always remembered. The First World can be likened to a room in a home. We have to live in this room day and night, night and day, not remembering that the door can open and through it we can see the other, more beautiful, rooms of the home. These are the limitations of living in the First World. But the freedom from having no apparent direct Second or Third-World authority over us impels the ignorant into temptation and confusion—impels the wise into remembrance of the Overlords. The three worlds have yet another breakdown into fourteen regions, or *lokas*, also called worlds, seven above and seven below.

Where is the Second World and what is it?
The Second World exists "within" this First World. It is the subtle plane of existence where the soul goes during sleep and when the physical body dies.

   Paramaguru Siva Yogaswami proclaimed: "The macrocosm is found within the microcosm within me, and I pay my obeisance—Siva, Siva....One day when I was in the hospital, I saw a different world....Behold the mansion which is within you! You shall have the key from me. Open and enter into its eternal heritage. **Gurudeva Sivaya Subramuniyaswami explains:** The Second World is, for the most part, an exact duplicate of the First World; yet it is more advanced, as beings in the Second World are trained in advanced technology, the arts and increments of culture to take up bodies in the First World, improve and enhance conditions within it. It is here, in the Second World, that new inventions are invented, new chemicals compounded, ecology stabilized, scientists trained and artists taught finesse—all at a later time to appear in the First World. The process is constant. The Second World is often referred to as the astral, or celestial, plane. The astral body is an exact duplicate of the physical body. When we sleep at night, we often leave our physical body and travel in our astral body in the Second World. The astral body is not the soul, for the soul stands within it and is self-existent, apart from the astral body and the physical body.

*As threads come out of the spider, as sparks fly out
of a fire, so all the senses, all the worlds, all the
Gods, yea, all beings issue forth from the Self....
By His divine power He holds dominion over all
the worlds. At the periods of creation and
dissolution of the universe, He alone exists.*
BRIHADARANYAKA AND SVETASVATARA UPANISHADS

Where is the Third World and what is it?

The Third World is deep within the Second World. It is the causal plane of existence where the Gods and highly evolved souls live.

Paramaguru Siva Yogaswami proclaimed: Never forget our Lord's most Holy Feet, which all the seven worlds venerate and praise....Thou Effulgence who illumines heaven and earth, Siva....who in the heavens shines, who rides upon Nandi the bull—those who, having seen, rejoice in seeing Him, will not take birth again. **Gurudeva Sivaya Subramuniyaswami explains:** It is in the Third World that the soul, once matured, lives in its self-effulgent form. The individual soul is a radiant body in which awareness travels. When unshrouded of the physical body's strong instinctive pulls and astral body's harsh intellectual stranglehold, it is free to worship the Gods and God Siva. Through sadhana, japa and regular religious practice, we harness the unruly instinctive forces. Through sadhana and proper religious education, the intellect is purified. Now the soul can see into the Third World through the temple sanctum sanctorum or, with the yoga adept, through the cranial sanctum, the awakened sahasrara chakra, deep in yogic samadhi. Seven are the regions above and seven below, fourteen places of existence, of mind, of consciousness, where awareness, locked in dual states, resides.

What is the soul's journey through these three worlds?
The soul is created in the Third World, evolves by taking on denser and denser bodies until it has a physical body and lives in the First World. Then as it matures, it drops off these denser bodies and returns to the Second and Third Worlds. **Paramaguru Siva Yogaswami proclaimed:** Seeing the world, the microcosm and the macrocosm, to be the form of Siva, do service and gain Liberation. Know those who, having seen, remain enjoying the essential Truth that embraces all three worlds. **Gurudeva Sivaya Subramuniyaswami explains:** Take, for example, a tree. Beginning as a seed, it becomes a sapling, then grows, leafs, fruits and finally dies. Its seeds live on, become other trees, and the species perpetuates itself. So is our species perpetuating itself from the Third World to the Second to the First; and even in the First World, bodies are made in a similar way for Second-World inhabitants to live in. The soul is not created at the moment of conception of a physical body. Each one manufactures a part of the great plan of creation which is ever creating itself. There will be no end to the First World, the Second World, or the Third World, except in the prophecy of the Maha-pralaya. Then the in-breath ends all, but to yield to the out-breath which is a new beginning of the three worlds and the inhabitants therein. Aum Namasivaya! Sivayanama Aum!

> *When there is birth, automatically it is followed by death. And that is life. If there is enmity, there is deceit. My friends, let us reach Edirkolpadi in time, singing the praise of the Lord who besmears Himself with the holy ash, who has a blue throat, who has the Ganges in His matted hair and who rides the bull.*
>
>   SAINT SUNDARAR

Lord Ganesha is the elephant-faced Deity who guides and protects us through His powers to create and remove obstacles from our path. Here a devotee brings a tray of offerings to a small shrine and supplicates His grace before entering the ornate main temple doors. Her earnest prayers have brought Lord Ganesha's radiant blessings.

Chapter 22

The Elephant-Faced Deity

I BELIEVE IN THE MAHADEVA LORD GANESHA,
SON OF SIVA-SAKTI, TO WHOM I MUST FIRST
SUPPLICATE BEFORE BEGINNING
ANY WORSHIP OR TASK.

Who is Lord Ganesha?

Lord Ganesha is a Mahadeva, a Great God, created by Lord
Siva to assist souls in their evolution. He is the elephant-
faced Patron of Art and Science, First Son of Siva.
Paramaguru Siva Yogaswami proclaimed: The God
with the elephant's face I shall never forget—Sankara's Son,
with massive belly and the ring in His ear, the Lord who gave
His grace to Indra, of whom mantra is His very form. **Gurudeva Sivaya Subramuniyaswami explains:** The Sakti, or
"Va," of Lord Siva, the Almighty Power, created heaven and
earth and the God Lord Ganesha to have charge over all the
heavens and all the earths. Lord Ganesha was created as a
ruler by God, an interplanetary, intergalactic ruler over all
the universes, inner and outer worlds. His knowledge is infinite. His rule is supreme in reigning over the heavens, the
earth and the Narakaloka. It is none other than Lord Ganesha and His mighty band of Ganas that gently help souls out
of the abyss of the Narakaloka and adjust them in the Devaloka after due penance has been paid. He, unlike many other
Gods, is intricate of mind, loving pomp and enjoying adulation through constant repetition of His name. Thus it is that
He is acknowledged first. All Mahadevas, devas, minor Gods
and sentient beings must worship Lord Ganesha before any
responsible act of any kind could hope to be successful. Thus,
this Almighty Ruler, Lord of the Universes, is truly a great God.

**Why must we supplicate Lord Ganesha before
beginning any worship or task?**

At the command of God Siva Himself, we supplicate, that is, humbly request, Lord Ganesha to clear obstacles from the path of our endeavor, if it be His will.

Paramaguru Siva Yogaswami proclaimed: May the Supreme Guru, who bestows on me His grace, be my protection! May the elephant-faced God be my protection! May the fair child who wields the shapely lance be my protection! **Gurudeva Sivaya Subramuniyaswami explains:** The father and mother, in a properly conducted home, govern their children and prepare them to be fine citizens when they have homes of their own. The children ask permission from their parents before beginning any new endeavor. The employee asks permission from the employer before beginning any new endeavor. The subjects in a realm ask permission from the monarch before beginning any new endeavor. Why wonder we about asking permission from His Majesty, ruler of this world, head, chieftain of our religion, before beginning any new endeavor? He of intricate mind and power is immediate and aware of any form of sincere prayer and supplication, humble requests to clear obstacles from the path of our endeavors, but only if that be His will. Thus, this God rules our lives, commanding acknowledgement and adulation— a truly great God is He.

> *The yogi, seated in a favorable posture,...first
> salutes the Great Lord, then Uma, Skanda and
> Ganapati....These Lords who, it is said,
> on the Pure Path, attend to various duties deriving
> from a higher realm of maya are at the prow of the
> effects of the higher realm of maya.*
>
> MRGENDRA AGAMA

What is Lord Ganesha's special function?

He is Vighnesvara, Lord of Obstacles. As such, He controls our evolution by preventing or permitting events to happen in our life.

Gurudeva Sivaya Subramuniyaswami explains: Lord Ganesha holds the architect's plans of the divine masterpiece of past and future of this small world and all the universes. They were entrusted to Him when He took office by command of God Siva. His rule is compassionate, His disciplines strong. He is equally feared and loved. His law is just, for justice is His mind. He enjoys adulations, festivity, hearing of His name, for this brings the devotee into His court, into His presence, close to Him. All good comes from Lord Ganesha, and He staves off misfortune for those who performed penance in His name. He is within us and not otherwise, closer than our heartbeat, guiding our karma through the timing of events. This Lord of Obstacles prevents us from hurting ourselves through living under an incomplete concept or making a request unneeded or beginning an endeavor not well-thought-out. He expects us to use all of our intellectual faculties and resources, to wield the knowledge available to us before submitting our petitions to Him. It is for us to try to arrive at the right decision, the one that He Himself would have made in granting the acquisition. Thus, this Mahadeva, wise and all-powerful, truly is a great God.

If an obstacle is encountered despite our sincere supplication of Lord Ganesha, what does it mean?

It may mean that the time, the means or the goal itself is not right for our karma and dharma.

Gurudeva Sivaya Subramuniyaswami explains: The architect presents his finished plans to the engineer. They are rejected for one technical reason or another. The executive presents a completed letter to the president. It is rejected as not being explicit enough in the third paragraph. The architect and the executive were equally sincere in presenting their work. The engineer and the president were performing their duty as well. Lord Ganesha loves us. He is a loving God who guides, governs and controls with speed and accuracy when the plan is perfect, deliberates long and rejects often when the plan needs revision. Take the plan back into your mind. Search your own superconsciousness for the greater ideas and revise your efforts with confidence. Seek for the right timing and proceed with confidence when you know the timing to be right. "When the will rises in command, even the Gods are willing to obey," or to give immediate co-operation, to guide and enhance our efforts. We must work our minds in close cooperation with the mind of Lord Ganesha, and then success is certain. Thus, this God, called *Bhaktavighnavinasana,* He who destroys the obstacles of His devotees, is truly a great creation of God Siva Himself.

> *If you worship the elephant-faced Vinayaga, your life will expand bountifully. If you worship the white-tusked Vinayaga your desires and doubts will flee. Therefore, worship Him with love-offerings of jack, hoppers, plantain and mango fruits and thus mitigate the burden of deeds.*
>
> SAINT AUVAIYAR

Lord Muruga is God Siva's Son, variously depicted as a renunciate, as the King of kings and as Commander in Chief of the celestial armies. Here He is Skanda, the mighty Warrior who fearlessly wields the Vel, the lance of light and spiritual knowledge which overcomes demons and the powers of darkness for devotees who pray to Him.

Chapter 23

The Deity Skanda

I BELIEVE IN THE MAHADEVA
LORD MURUGA, SON OF SIVA-SAKTI, WHOSE
VEL OF GRACE DISSOLVES THE BONDAGES OF
IGNORANCE.

Who is Lord Muruga?

Lord Muruga is a Mahadeva, a Great God, Ganesha's younger brother, created by God Siva to assist souls in their evolution.

Paramaguru Siva Yogaswami proclaimed: God Himself performs all actions. Look at the twelve hands of Lord Subramanya. Each hand performs a different action. He laughs. He weeps. He kills. He protects. Countless and unending are His actions. All this is very difficult to comprehend, and much, much more difficult to communicate. **Gurudeva Sivaya Subramuniyaswami explains:** "Si" created Lord Muruga. "Va" became his Vel. Thus, Lord Muruga is Si-Va in action, flying through the mind's vast substance from planet to planet in this universe. He could well be called the Emancipator, ever available to the call of the needy, those in distress. He is the King of kings, the power in their scepter. Standing behind the temporal majesty, He gives the authority. His Vel empowering the scepter of the rulers, justice prevails, wisdom enriches the minds of citizens, rain is abundant, crops flourish and plenty fills the larders. He is Commander in Chief of the great devonic army, a fine, dynamic soldier within, a fearless Lord fighting for righteousness. Lord Muruga, the first Satguru, reigns over all the religions and faiths of the world. The personified figurehead within all of them is none but He. Verily, God gave Lord Muruga to the world, to the universe and to you. He is a great Mahadeva.

How is Lord Muruga different from Lord Ganesha?

Lord Ganesha slowly and gently guides the soul through its initial evolution. Lord Muruga's dynamic power infuses spiritual knowledge into the soul to propel it onward to the Feet of Lord Siva.

Paramaguru Siva Yogaswami proclaimed: O men of Lanka! Attach yourselves by treading virtue's path to the Holy Feet of Murugan, who pervades all, who is Knowledge of all knowledge and beyond the beyond does stand. Repeatedly prostrate to those Feet, and victory will always be your fruit. **Gurudeva Sivaya Subramuniyaswami explains:** Lord Ganesha, the God of time and memory, the infinite, computerized, reasoning mind, stabilizes all sentient beings while comfortably seated on the muladhara chakra. Lord Muruga, God of will, direct cognition and the purest, child-like divine love, propels us onward—on the righteous way through religion, His Father's law. While comfortably seated on the manipura chakra, this scarlet-hued God blesses mankind and propels us onward when we lift to the inner sky through sadhana and yoga, His realm. The yoga marga begins with the worship of Lord Muruga. The kundalini power is held and controlled by this virginal God, first among renunciates, dear to all sannyasins. Verily, Lord Muruga is the Divine One. He is Divinity emulated in form. A God of great beauty is He.

In the gloom of fear, His six-fold face gleams. In perils unbound, His lance betokens "Fear not." In the heart of those who recount His name, He reveals His gracious feet. Thus He appears to those who chant the hallowed name "Muruga." He stands immanent in all.   SAINT NAKKIRAR

What is the Vel?
The Vel is the lance wielded by Lord Muruga. Embodying incisive discrimination and spiritual knowledge, its tip is wide, long and keen, just as our knowledge must be broad, deep and penetrating.

Paramaguru Siva Yogaswami proclaimed: Convinced that youth is fleeting, clasp the Holy Feet of Him who holds the Vel which immortality bestows, for those Feet will grant everlasting bliss. Know this and lovingly bow down to them in worship. **Gurudeva Sivaya Subramuniyaswami explains:** The Sakti power of the Vel, the eminent, intricate, discriminate power of righteousness over evil, conquers confusion within the realms below where Lord Ganesha sits. Lord Muruga, in His majesty, wields great power through His scepter that, when thrown, always hits its mark and of itself returns to His precious hand. The holy Vel rewards us when righteousness prevails and becomes the serpent's unleashed power that thwarts our every effort with punishing remorse when we transgress dharma's law. Thus, the holy Vel, wielded by the transcendental intelligence of our Lord, is our release from ignorance into knowledge, our release from vanity into modesty, our release from sinfulness into purity through tapas. The Vel inspires us to perform sadhana and uphold the Saiva Dharma most precisely. Verily, the Vel entrusted to this great Mahadeva has power.

How is the bondage of ignorance dissolved?
The bondages of ignorance are darkness, attachment, ego, fear, unhappiness and more. When soul evolution is sufficiently advanced, Lord Muruga destroys the remaining sense of ego, revealing the soul's inherent qualities of spiritual knowledge and universal compassion.

Gurudeva Sivaya Subramuniyaswami explains: In the Second World, the astral plane, energy is personified in form, color and sound. We worry and are concerned, become confused and worry more. This creates around the astral body in the Second World large bubbles of heavy colors, discordant sounds and strange shapes. When these become burdensome to us, playing back through the physical nerve system, we pray to Lord Muruga, "Take me out of my agony. Release me from my anguish." We perform penance and beseech His blessing. This compassionate God of Action, Conqueror of Asuras, hurls His Vel into the Second World, piercing the discordant sounds, colors and shapes, bursting them into freedom away from us, removing the darkness of the mind. We have been blessed, our confusions cleared, our worries ended. Our ego has met its ultimate fate, bursts; and spiritual knowledge is born. The yogi, locked in lotus, venerates Kartikkeya, as his mind becomes as calm and quiet as Saravana, the Lake of Divine Essence. Verily, Lord Muruga is a compassionate God.

> *Why do I not entreat by holy psalms the six-faced One to relieve my confusion caused by lure of worldly possessions? He is the Supreme One who can root out forever the veiled delusion of this enigmatic world....Oh! Lord Shanmukha with the battle-waging Peacock! Oh embodiment of Grace!*
> SAINT ARUNAGIRINATHAR

It is through worship and meditation that we communicate with the superconscious worlds. Here within the temple precincts of the First World, brahmins gather about the homa fire to chant and consciously commune with the Second World devas and the Third World Mahadevas and Gods, shown as Ganesha, Muruga and Siva.

Chapter 24

The Esoteric Purpose
Of Temple Worship

I BELIEVE THAT RELIGION IS
THE HARMONIOUS WORKING TOGETHER OF
THE THREE WORLDS, AND THAT THIS HARMONY
CAN BE CREATED THROUGH TEMPLE WORSHIP,
WHEREIN THE THREE WORLDS BECOME OPEN TO
ONE ANOTHER, AND THE BEINGS WITHIN THEM
ARE ABLE TO COMMUNICATE.

**What does it mean for the three worlds to
harmoniously work together?**
Harmony among the three worlds means that the gross, subtle and causal planes of existence are acting in concert, that
this world is working in conscious conformity with the inner
worlds.

Paramaguru Siva Yogaswami proclaimed: When the
three worlds, gross, subtle and causal, are all understood, the
lady of fragrant tresses, Sakti, will bestow Her lovely grace.
…Arise early and praise His lustrous feet. Worship Him and
don the holy ash. **Gurudeva Sivaya Subramuniyaswami
explains:** There are certain temple rites that can be performed to cause any temple to evoke the sacrament of allowing individuals to communicate directly with the inner
worlds. The most intimate, personal form of communication is the written prayer to the deva, Mahadeva or to God
Himself. Burned in the homa fire, it disintegrates in the First
World and quickly re-forms in the Second World. Its astral
image is received and read by the devas there, given to the
appropriate servant of the God, to be properly dispatched

and answered. When we write a prayer, a wish or confession of our troubles in this ancient way, immediate action is taken. The devas cannot act unless asked. This is the inner law. We have truly been blessed with great facilities in our religion, Saivism, the greatest religion in the world!

What is temple worship?

Temple worship is a ceremony in which the ringing of bells, passing of flames, presenting of offerings and chanting attracts the Second-World devas and Third-World Mahadevas who then come to bless and help us.

Paramaguru Siva Yogaswami explained: Always will I give honor to the holy feet of those who say that it is good each day to worship with fresh flowers Him who forgives my errors, the essence of Panchakshara. By doing bhakti yoga, all the other three yogas will come. **Gurudeva Sivaya Subramuniyaswami explains:** It is not without protocol that one approaches the executive officer of a large corporation, a general in a mighty army, a movie star that has earned great fame, a benevolent monarch, a president or a prime minister to gain their favor. Visiting the home of God Siva or of a God, the temple, is not without its trepidation, protocol and proper conduct, preceded by preparation that we administrate ourselves. This is temple worship. The worship is approaching the God properly, presenting ourselves acceptably. Worship is then to offer our love, our adoration and then to speak out our prayer, our petition. To worship then is to enjoy His presence and not rush away. This would be impolite. We would be expected to stay, to sit awhile, to enjoy the Sakti of the presence of God. Truly, our religion has granted us a voice to extol it as great!

Oh! Siva at Tiruchattimutram! You are the Lord
of the celestials. I am at your mercy. Oh, my Lord,
the five senses have taken possession of my body
and drive me away from your Holy Feet. I am
confused and troubled at heart, like curd which is
being churned. Bestow enlightenment upon me.

SAINT APPAR

What is a temple?

A temple marks an agreed upon meeting place for the three worlds. It is the venerable home of God Siva or of a God, specially sanctified and possessing a ray of spiritual energy connecting it to the Third World.

Paramaguru Siva Yogaswami proclaimed: O Lord! O Primal One, who gives bliss to devotees who have become the embodiment of love. O Supreme Lord! Transcendent One who dwells at Nallur temple, make me to live here like a God....In this world you may acquire a multitude of siddhis, but never stray from bhakti's path, nor disobey the words of bhaktas. **Gurudeva Sivaya Subramuniyaswami explains:** Saivite temples are the most ancient of all temples. They are the homes of the Gods and God. These temples must be approached with great reverence and humility, as the God lives in the temple. Draw near the temple as you would approach a king, a governor, a president of a great realm, anticipating with a little trepidation your audience with him. So it is with the Saiva *koyil*—the temple—the home of the God. The greatest temples are the homes of Lord Siva and within them are private rooms, sanctums, for His two sons and others of His entourage. There is a place for all the thirty-three million Gods in every Siva temple. We have truly been blessed as Saivites with the open access to Siva's homes all over the world. Such is the greatness of our religion!

Where can the three worlds most harmoniously work together?

One can worship God anywhere and be in contact with the inner worlds in the temple, in the home shrine and in the yogi's contemplation. However, it is in the holy Siva temple where the three worlds most perfectly and consciously commune.

Gurudeva Sivaya Subramuniyaswami explains: In the shrine room gather messengers of the Mahadeva being worshiped to hear the prayers of the devotee and carry them to their Master. Gods can be worshiped anywhere when the proper *sankalpam*, preparation, has been performed. God's presence is everywhere, through everything, in everything, for He is the Creator of all things, the Manifestor of time, form and the space between forms. He is worshiped in the mind, in the heart, through the throat, in the head of the yogi locked in yoga. His head is his shrine for the worship of the supreme God, Lord Siva. So great is worship, communion and communication with the centillion devas, that when a little bell is rung, a flame appears in the lamp, the vermilion spot is placed, the flower appears and is offered, God and the Gods are invoked. Contemplating the aftermath of puja or abhishekam, we feel the *sannidhya*, or divine presence, of the Goddess, Mother of Love, permeating to the outer walls around the temple. Truly, the refined facilities of our religion proclaim it great!

> *The Supreme God is the blessed Siva Lingam;*
> *the embodied soul stands as the mighty bull; the*
> *bondage is the holy altar—such things are clear to*
> *those who investigate the Siva temple....*
> *Chariya is basic to salvation, and is the breath of*
> *Suddha Saiva in this world below.*
> SAINT TIRUMULAR

Our individual soul is a body of light which does not die, but takes one body and then another in a succession of births. Here the soul is shown as a stream of light flowing through five of its many lives: a peasant, a soldier, a princess, a businessman and a jnani who has attained enlightenment and will never be born again on the earth.

Chapter 25

Karma, Samsara and Liberation

I BELIEVE IN THE LAW OF KARMA—
THAT ONE MUST PERSONALLY REAP THE
EFFECTS OF ALL ACTIONS HE HAS CAUSED—
AND THAT EACH SOUL WILL CONTINUE TO
REINCARNATE UNTIL ALL KARMAS ARE
RESOLVED AND MOKSHA, LIBERATION,
IS ATTAINED.

What is karma?

Karma is a Sanskrit word which literally means "deed or act," and more broadly describes the principle of cause and effect. It is not fate, for man acts with free will. Esoterically, karma refers to the totality of our actions and their concomitant reactions in this and all previous lives, all of which determines our future. **Paramaguru Siva Yogaswami proclaimed:** Karma is movement in the mind. When the mind remains motionless, there is no karma. Every action has a reaction. If you plant eggplant, you can pluck eggplant. If you sow goodness, you can reap goodness. If you sow evil, you will reap evil. ...You can only reap the fruit of your own actions. You cannot act for another. **Gurudeva Sivaya Subramuniyaswami explains:** Since each action has a corresponding reaction, the effects of karma—action and reaction—can be helpfully invigorating or devastating. The wise, therefore, govern their lives accordingly and in causing an action must necessarily anticipate the reaction. Not all reactions are immediate; they are accumulative in some cases and rebound unexpectedly. Penance is a self-inflicted karma or prepayment of a reaction expected because of an action caused. Penance well performed intercedes between the action and the reaction, counterbalancing and smoothing out the karma.

How do we resolve karma?

By applying religious principles to the experiences encountered in life, we resolve our karma rather than create new karma.

Paramaguru Siva Yogaswami proclaimed: You cannot get rid of evil simply by exposing it. If you try to be good, loving and honest, evil will disappear....Invoke the grace of God and restrain the mind from wandering along the path of the senses. Repeat the Letters Five before your past karmas come and overpower you....Events take place according to prarabdha karma. They do not affect the soul. But man, by mere habit, identifies himself with these events and becomes subject to pain and pleasure. **Gurudeva Sivaya Subramuniyaswami explains:** Religion, the law of Lord Siva, has built within it the actions and interactions to dissolve negative karma, refine positive karma, blending the forces into dharma. When the dharma is set and recognized by ourselves and others in the world, then dharma, duty, is lived and when well performed avoids the extraneous rough edges of karma. Performance of regular sadhana, yearly pilgrimage to holy places, seeing to the needs of others—these invoke the higher energies and direct the mind toward useful thoughts, thus circumventing the creation of burdensome new karmas. Emancipation from karma's heavy bondages is attained through religious observances. Therefore, by performing our dharma, religious position in life, we are free to experience inner worlds of existence while being effectual in the First World.

Like the snake which sloughs its skin, like the bird
which leaves its shell, like forgetting a dream upon
awakening—thus does the soul by Siva's grace go
from birth to birth, reaching its destined place
where it experiences the results of the two karmas,
good and bad.

SAINT TIRUMULAR

What is reincarnation?
Reincarnation is the natural cycle of birth, death and rebirth, called *samsara*. When we die, the soul leaves our First-World physical body and lives for a while in the Second World, returning again to a First-World birth.

Gurudeva Sivaya Subramuniyaswami explains: Reincarnation is many-faceted. Through the ages it has been the great consoling element within our religion, eliminating the inborn fear of death. Saivites do not fear death, nor do they look forward to it. Each one knows his life is eternal. In stepping out of the physical body, consciousness continues in unbroken continuity in the astral body, its exact duplicate. In the Second World, mind continues, emotions continue, associations continue. Just before rebirth, the astral body is sloughed off and the soul in its self-effulgent form soars into the Third World, then enters a new womb in the First. There is no escape from life's experiences. Suicide, for instance, only accelerates the intensity of karma, bringing a series of immediate lesser births and requiring several lives for the soul to return to the exact evolutionary point that existed at the moment of suicide, at which time the still-existing karmic entanglement must again be faced and resolved. Thus turns the slow wheel of samsara. To gain a fine birth, one must live according to the natural laws of dharma and live out the karma in this life positively and fully.

What is Moksha?

Moksha is Liberation from rebirth on this planet. Our soul then continues its evolution in the Second World, eventually in the Third World and finally merges with Lord Siva. **Paramaguru Siva Yogaswami proclaimed:** Man can know his past and future births. By getting rid of desire, he can put an end to birth altogether....In all my births with me He stayed. My present birth He'll terminate. To make me free of future births He gave His grace to me. **Gurudeva Sivaya Subramuniyaswami explains:** Moksha comes when all extraneous karmas have been resolved and dharma has been well performed and God fully realized. This means that before Moksha, the soul must have performed well all the dharmas, the castes, and lived through all the various and varied experiences of life in order to not be pulled back to a First-World birth by a deed left undone. Moksha marks the way station where the liberated soul is free from rebirth. Moksha is sought for and to be attained by every Saivite on the path of personal unfoldment, but not necessarily will it come to every Saivite in this life, even though sought for by him as the ultimate goal. Devotees know this and do not delude themselves that this life is the last. Seeking and attaining profound spiritual realizations, they nevertheless know that there is much to be accomplished on the earth and that only a rare few in each century attain Moksha.

A man acts according to the desires to which he clings. After death he goes to the next world bearing in his mind the subtle impressions of his deeds; and after reaping there the harvest of his deeds, he returns again to this world of action. Thus, he who has desires continues subject to rebirth.

BRIHADARANYAKA UPANISHAD

God Siva created everything and its opposite—joy and sorrow, birth and death, pleasure and pain. Thus, all things are but movements of His Divine Dance. The artist here has used the international symbol of prohibition to illustrate that there is no other force at work in the universe which opposes His will; there is no evil, no eternal hell, no satan or devil.

Chapter 26

The Goodness of All

I BELIEVE THAT THERE IS NO INTRINSIC EVIL. (ஒரு பொருள் எப்படியும் தீது அல)

What is the intrinsic nature of man and the world?
Intrinsic means "inherent, or belonging to the real nature of
a thing." The inherent and real nature of all beings is their
soul, which is perfect goodness. The world, too, is God Siva's
perfect creation.

Paramaguru Siva Yogaswami proclaimed: The great
sage Chellappan used to say there is not a single thing that is
evil. When God is everywhere, how can there be a place for
evil? There are changes, and they sometimes appear evil.
Only God knows what He is doing. There is balance and
order in the universe. **Gurudeva Sivaya Subramuniyaswami explains:** The soul radiates love, is a child of God Siva
going through its evolutionary process of growing up into
the image and likeness of Lord Siva. Goodness and mercy,
compassion and caring are the intrinsic nature of the soul.
Wisdom and pure knowledge, happiness and joy are the
intrinsic nature of the soul. Can we believe the soul is anything but goodness itself, purity and all the refined qualities
found within superconsciousness? The soul is constantly
one with God in its ever-present Satchidananda state at
every point in its evolution. How, then, arises the concept of
evil and suffering? Anava, karma and maya, the play toys of
the soul, are this seeming suffering. Like a child, we play
with the toys of anava in the playground of maya, fall and
are bruised by karma, then run to God Siva for solace and
release into spiritual maturity.

Why, then, are some men evil?

Men act in evil ways when they have lost touch with their soul nature and live totally in their outer instinctive nature.

Paramaguru Siva Yogaswami proclaimed: If the chimney is black with smoke, you cannot see the lantern light. Similarly, maya obscures the soul....There is order in the universe. Even the thief and the trouble-maker are part of this order. **Gurudeva Sivaya Subramuniyaswami explains:** Seemingly, those of lower evolution perform evil deeds, for they are not yet in touch with the ever-present God consciousness of their immortal soul. Those who have been good once and now perform evil actions were not steady in ever-present God consciousness. Children are mischievous, expected to be mischievous, are corrected and adjust to society. Young souls are mischievous, expected to be mischievous, corrected and their karma adjusted to their dharma. Then society holds them in their dharma. Evil is more a concept of the done-to, the onlooker rather than the doer, the experiencer. When we are compassionate, forgiving, we are in this world but not of it. We understand the motives behind action, the intellectual or instinctive impulses behind motive. When we are injured, hurt, we understand that our pain and suffering are but the fulfillment of a karma we once initiated, for which our injurer is but the instrument who, when his karma cycles around, will be the injured. Let us be compassionate, for truly there is no intrinsic evil.

> *That which appears cold and appears hot, good*
> *fortune and bad, pure and sour, love and hatred*
> *toward beings, effort and laziness, the exalted*
> *and the depraved, the rich and the poor, the well-*
> *founded and the ill-founded, all this is Isa*
> *Himself; none other than Him can we know.*
>
> AJITA AGAMA

Who is the source of this instinctive nature?

Lord Siva is the Creator of all things, of the instinctive, intellectual and superconscious dimensions of our being.

Paramaguru Siva Yogaswami proclaimed: Weakness belongs to the body and mind. The soul is always full of strength....There is not even one evil thing. Still, it is good to fear unrighteousness. Those who are unmindful of the good of their souls will go through life confused and disturbed by the pains and pleasures of the world. The wise will rid themselves of "good" and "bad" and "I" and "mine." **Gurudeva Sivaya Subramuniyaswami explains:** Evil has no source, unless the source of evil's seeming be ignorance itself. The ignorant onlooker complains, justifies, fears and criticizes "evil deeds," setting himself apart as a lofty puritan. The ignorant misjudge. Instead of seeing good and evil in the world, observe the nature of man in three interrelated parts: instinctive, intellectual and superconscious. When his instinctive lower nature dominates, man is prone to anger, fear, greed, jealousy, hatred and backbiting. When the intellect is prominent, he is arrogant and analytical. It is when the superconscious soul comes forth that the refined qualities are born—compassion, insight, modesty and the others. All that the Lord has created is in perfect balance. Good and evil do not balance as the same weight one to another in our existence. The sense of evil is only ignorance. Let us be compassionate, for truly there is no intrinsic evil.

Why did Lord Siva create the instinctive nature?

Lord Siva created the instinctive and intellectual natures as dimensions of experience to strengthen our soul and further its spiritual evolution.

Paramaguru Siva Yogaswami proclaimed: If everything were perfect, there would be no need for this birth.... A physician takes various herbs, mixes them together into one medicine with which he cures the disease. Likewise, the

Great All-Knowing Physician, by giving to the soul its body, faculties, the world and all its experiences, cures its disease and establishes it in the bliss of Liberation. **Gurudeva Sivaya Subramuniyaswami explains:** Lord Siva created all souls. Lord Siva created Mahadevas to govern their evolution. Lord Ganesha sees to the young soul in its evolution. Lord Muruga sees to the old soul in its evolution. The animal instincts of the young soul are strong. The intellect, yet to be developed, is nonexistent to control its strong instinctive impulses. When the intellect is developed, the instinctive nature subsides. When the soul unfolds and overshadows the well-developed intellect, its harness is loosened and removed. The animal body is crude and embarrassing to the superconscious soul—its impulses, cravings and fears are so unlike the refined qualities of the soul. That gap of difference narrows as daily religious practice and occasional sadhana are performed. Let us always be compassionate, knowing there is no intrinsic evil.

> *As a man behaves, so does he become.*
> *A man of good deeds becomes good, a man of evil*
> *deeds becomes evil. He becomes pure by pure*
> *deeds, impure by impure deeds....After death he*
> *goes to the next world bearing in his mind*
> *the subtle impressions of his deeds.*
>
> BRIHADARANYAKA UPANISHAD

The four margas are depicted here clockwise from the left. In the chariya marga, we live virtuously and serve, as the lady feeding a mendicant. In the kriya marga, devotion and temple worship are the focus of our life. In the yoga marga, we internalize worship under a Guru's aegis. The jnana marga is the awakened state of the revered holy man.

Chapter 27

The Four Margas, or Stages of Inner Progress

I BELIEVE THAT THE PERFORMANCE OF
CHARIYA (VIRTUOUS AND MORAL LIVING),
KRIYA (TEMPLE WORSHIP) AND YOGA
(INTERNALIZED WORSHIP AND UNION WITH
PARASIVAM THROUGH GRACE OF THE LIVING
SAT GURU) IS ABSOLUTELY NECESSARY
TO BRING FORTH THE STATE OF JNANA.

What is chariya?

Chariya is service and living our everyday life according to traditional religious principles of conduct in order to purify ourselves.

Paramaguru Siva Yogaswami proclaimed: The only path I know is the path of virtue. Everything is that, I can assure. I assure you that it is the easiest path for coming to knowledge of yourself....Doing Sivathondu in this world is chariya. Doing Sivathondu in this world is kriya. Doing Sivathondu in this world is yoga. Doing Sivathondu is having Sivajnana. **Gurudeva Sivaya Subramuniyaswami explains:** A person performs chariya because he has to. Society makes him. Instinctively he may resist and resent, but the benevolence of his parents in their love for him sets the stage for chariya. Chariya is often performed when God is known as existing externally, outside of ourself and apart from us, and thus we may fear Him and worship in respect of our fear. We must go to the temple. We must attend a puja at the home shrine to fulfill the family duty, even though we may feel it a waste of time and rather be doing something else.

Even escaping the religious practices demanded of us, refraining from doing them and doing something else more preferred but still knowing the duties escaped from—this is also chariya. To fulfill the Saiva Dharma, it is absolutely necessary that chariya, karma yoga, be heeded, practiced and made an integral part of one's life. All Saivites are on the path of chariya, kriya, yoga and jnana into Moksha.

What is kriya?
Kriya is the regular practice of temple worship, both internal and external, through which our understanding, closeness and love for God Siva and the Gods deepen.

Paramaguru Siva Yogaswami proclaimed: Work for the sake of work. Love for love's sake. This world is a vast temple to which all kinds of pilgrims come—good, bad and indifferent. Let us concentrate on our own worship, and not find fault with what others do....All of us are performing yoga. Karma yoga is selfless action. Siva yoga is action for the Lord. *Yoga* means concentration of mind. By doing bhakti yoga, all the other yogas will come. **Gurudeva Sivaya Subramuniyaswami explains:** Saiva Dharma demands deep devotion through bhakti yoga on the kriya marga, softening the intellect and solidifying love. As a child, an adolescent, an adult who loves God, he longs to go into His home, the temple. There he waits with hopeful expectation. This soul perfected chariya in a previous birth. He was a mischievous one then, but not now. Kriya is the inbred practice of Saivism, inbred because the cumulative karma of the practice of chariya has naturally evolved to a deeper, well-rounded understanding of God, Gods and devas. This unfolding soul performs temple worship because he wants to, he is pulled there, the temple satisfies his longing. He sings joyfully. He studies the holy scriptures. He is truly deep in kriya and firm on the path to yoga and jnana into Moksha.

He alone is learned, he alone is fortunate and
successful, whose mind is no longer unstable as air
but is held firm. That is the way to Liberation;
that is the highest virtue, that is wisdom, that is
strength, and that is the merit of those who seek.
DEVIKALOTTARA AGAMA

What is yoga?

Yoga is internalized worship which leads to union with God. It is the regular practice of meditation under the guidance of a Satguru through whose grace we attain realization of Parasivam.

Paramaguru Siva Yogaswami proclaimed: Waves rise in the ocean. So do waves of thought arise in the mind. Yoga is the control of thoughts as they arise. The great ones say that *yoga* means union....In order to reach God, the mind must become one-pointed. It is not a simple thing to control the mind. It cannot be done in a day or a year. Through constant effort thoughts come under your control little by little. In this way the uncontrollable mind can finally be brought under control. This is the supreme victory....In yoga samadhi you will comprehend the vanity of enjoyment and the things enjoyed. Thus did my Gurunathan make me to know my Self by myself. **Gurudeva Sivaya Subramuniyaswami explains:** A Satguru is a guru who has realized Sivam and knows the path of chariya, kriya, yoga, and jnana into Moksha. Yoga is the highest practice one can perform in Saivism. Jnana is the by-product of well-perfected yoga. Moksha is the ultimate reward. When yoga is practiced by one perfected in kriya, the Gods receive the yogi into their midst through the fiery fortress of his body. The Gods lift the kundalini fire burning through the Second World into the Third. Truly, a Satguru is needed as a gentle guide.

What is jnana?

Jnana is divine wisdom emanating from the maturity of the awakened soul. It is immersion of the mind in the blessed realization of God, while living out our earthly karma.

Paramaguru Siva Yogaswami proclaimed: To know, as those yogis who do hard tapas know, that the soul is as it has always been, past, present and future, and to live with the mind thus cleared, on earth a Jivanmukta, conforming to the worldly life, deserves high praise....Sivathondu leads to the summation of chariya, kriya and yoga on the earth. It culminates in Sivajnanam—the grand enlightenment. The source of knowledge is mine without learning. The key of existence lies within the palm of my hand. **Gurudeva Sivaya Subramuniyaswami explains:** Jnana is the by-product of yoga. The instinctive mind in the young soul is firm and well-knit together. The intellectual mind in the adolescent soul is complicated, and he sees the First World as his only reality. The subsuperconscious mind in the mystically inclined soul well-perfected in kriya longs for the realization of God Siva's two perfections, Satchidananda and Parasivam. Through the practice of yoga, he bursts into the Lord's superconscious mind, the experience of bliss, all-knowing-ness, perfect silence. His intellect is shattered, and he soars into Parasivam. He now is a Jnani, a knower of the Known, living in a new state of mind, called superconsciousness. The answers now precede his questions.

> *The Self cannot be attained by the weak, nor by the half-hearted, nor by a mere show of detachment. But as strength, stability and inner freedom grow, so does Self-awareness grow....Having realized the Self, the wise find satisfaction. Their evolution complete, at peace and free from longing, they are at one with everything.* MUNDAKA UPANISHAD

The mysteries of the Panchakshara Mantram are deep and many. It is the most holy name of our God Siva. Here an earnest devotee is seated in quiet meditation, silently chanting the sacred Five Letters, Namasivaya, which are depicted in Tamil script as five petals within the lotus of his heart. He is counting on a mala of rudraksha beads.

Chapter 28

The Five Letters

I BELIEVE IN THE PANCHAKSHARA MANTRAM,
THE FIVE SACRED SYLLABLES
"NA MA SI VA YA," AS THE FOREMOST AND
ESSENTIAL MANTRAM OF SAIVISM.

What is the literal meaning of *Namasivaya*?
Namasivaya, literally and exoterically, means "adoration to
God Siva." This mantra, or formula for invocation, is called
the *Panchakshara,* or "Five Letters."

Paramaguru Siva Yogaswami proclaimed: Wear rudraksha beads and repeat the Panchakshara. Let your heart
grow soft and melt. Chant the Letters Five and in love you
will discover His will. Chant so that impurities, anxieties and
doubts are purged. All Hail Namasivaya! **Gurudeva Sivaya
Subramuniyaswami explains:** The Panchakshara Mantram
is the world of God, the name and total essence of God. But,
to chant Namasivaya and to be empowered to chant Namasivaya is likened to the difference between writing a check
without money in the bank and writing a check with money in the bank. The mantram Namasivaya should only be
repeated by the initiated one who is, or whose family is, perfected in chariya. Namasivaya is the gateway to yoga. From
the lips of my Gurunathan I learned Namasivaya, and it has
been the central core of my life, strength and fulfillment of
destiny. To read in a book Namasivaya or be told through
some unauthorized source this mantram is like receiving
unspendable money in a country that does not honor the
currency. The secret of Namasivaya is to hear it from the
right lips at the right time. Then, and only then, is it the
most powerful mantram of Saivism for you.

What is the esoteric meaning of the five sacred syllables?

The symbolism of each of the five letters is: *Si* is Siva; *Va* is His revealing grace, *Ya* is the soul, *Na* is His concealing grace and *Ma* is the world. **Paramaguru Siva Yogaswami proclaimed:** Through the Letters Five the body came to birth. Through the Letters Five the atma shone in splendor. Through the Letters Five bliss came into being. Within the Letters Five was I contained. **Gurudeva Sivaya Subramuniyaswami explains:** Namasivaya is so deeply Saivite, the mere intonation of these syllables reaps its own reward in salvaging the soul from bondages of the treacherous instinctive mind and the steel bands of a perfected externalized intellect. Namasivaya quells the instinct, cuts through the steel bands and turns this intellect within and on itself, making this intelligent intellect face itself and see its ignorance. May we not forget that mantram is life, that mantram is action, that mantram is love and that the repetition of mantram, japa, bursts forth wisdom from within. Japa yoga is the first yoga to be performed toward the goal of jnana. In the temple perform japa. Under the sacred tree perform japa. Seated in a remote cave perform japa. I performed japa all this life as a silent sadhana. It is automatic now. How do you perform japa? "Aum Namasivaya, Aum Namasivaya, Aum Namasivaya, Aum Namasivaya, Aum Namasivaya"—that is how japa is performed.

The hand that holds the drum is "Si."
The hand that sways is "Va." The hand that
offers refuge, "Ya." The hand that holds the blazing
fire, "Na." The lotus foot, firm on anava mala
planted, is "Ma." Thus of the Divine Dance Form
Si Va Ya Na Ma denotes.

SAINT TIRUMULAR

Why is it our foremost and essential mantram?
It is the most holy name of God Siva. All of the essential
knowledge of Saivite philosophy is contained in the esoteric
meaning of these five letters.
Paramaguru Siva Yogaswami proclaimed: Namasivaya
is in truth both Veda and Agama. Namasivaya contains all
mantras and tantras. Namasivaya is our souls, our bodies
and possessions. Namasivaya has become our certain help
and protection. Let Namasivaya be ever on your tongue!
Gurudeva Sivaya Subramuniyaswami explains: Sound has
its counterpart in silence: Na—silence; Ma—silence; Si—
silence; Va—silence; Ya—silence. Is it not the silence in-be-
tween the sounds and the power within these silences that is
the power that the soul hangs onto when the mind is wrapped
in rapture of Namasivaya or Sivayanama? The soul feeds on
sound. The sound of someone's voice can hurt your feelings
or make you happy. The vibrations set up between the syllables nourishes the soul with the sweet fruit and flowers it
needs to have to quickly evolve. The duly initiated audibly
repeats "Namasivaya;" then mentally chants "Sivayanama"
when japa is performed internally, subtly, inaudible to the
ear. There are five ways this mantram can be intoned—each
for a specific purpose. Hail to the Letters Five and to the silence resounding in and between them. Hail to the Saiva
Dharma locked within the Letters Five! Hail Namasivaya!

How is this mantram properly chanted?
Japa of this mantram is performed by repeating verbally or
mentally "Aum Namasivaya," often while counting on a
mala, a strand of rudraksha or sandalwood beads.
Paramaguru Siva Yogaswami proclaimed: That the
Saiva faith may flourish and Truth abound, that the conviction that God *is* may glow within our minds, that more and
more true devotees may multiply and spread, let us chant
"Namasivaya" throughout our span of days....Ah, bliss it is

to chant the primordial mantram that leads to the goal of Liberation. **Gurudeva Sivaya Subramuniyaswami explains:** Aum Namasivaya must be performed on rudraksha beads over and over and over when the sun is setting, when the sun is rising or high noon lights the day. "Aum Namasivaya," the Saivite chants. Aum Namasivaya feeds his soul, brightens his intellect and quells his instinctive mind. Take the holy tears of Siva, the rudraksha beads, into your hands. Push a bead over the middle finger with your thumb and hold as the intonation marks its passage. Chant "Aum Namasivaya." There are many ways to chant this mantram, but perform it as you were initiated to perform it. Unauthorized experimentation is forbidden. Having not been duly initiated, those wishing to do japa may chant "AUM." You inherited Aum at birth. It is a safe and wonderful mantram for any phase of life or stage of evolution. Aum will guide you to the proper lips from which you may receive the great gift of Namasivaya.

> *If, with folded hands, we worship the golden feet*
> *of the Vedic Lord of heavenly light and entrust*
> *ourselves unto Him, His sacred name,*
> *Namasivaya, shall be a raft even when weighted*
> *down and launched into an angry sea.*
>
> SAINT APPAR

அன்பே
சிவமயம்
சத்தியமே
பராசிவம்

Our affirmation of faith is a short and simple summary of the creed, a proclamation of our beliefs which can be used in many ways, as the text explains. The script above presents the affirmation as it is written in the ancient Tamil language, whose spoken sounds are as lovely as their lettered form. It reads "Anbe Sivamayam Satyame Parasivam."

Chapter 29

Our Affirmation of Faith

A SHORT AND SIMPLE SUMMARY OF THE
CREED: GOD SIVA IS IMMANENT LOVE AND
TRANSCENDENT REALITY

What is an affirmation of faith?
An affirmation of faith is a short, simple statement which
summarizes the beliefs and doctrines of a religion. Ours is:
"God Siva is immanent Love and transcendent Reality."

Paramaguru Siva Yogaswami proclaimed: Infinitely
glorious in His transcendence and yet unsurpassing in the
beauty of His immanence, those who see Him thus in gracious forms as their Beloved triumph in eternal bliss....-
Glory to that Grace divine, transcendental yet Primal Cause
of existence. **Gurudeva Sivaya Subramuniyaswami explains:** Come morning, I awaken hearing the voice of my
mind intoning "Anbe Sivamayam Satyame Parasivam" and
feeling the love of God Siva directing my third sight upon
Moksha. "Anbe Sivamayam Satyame Parasivam—God Siva
is immanent Love and transcendent Reality." This is the way
I start my day, by affirming my faith. We must strengthen
our mind with positive affirmations. We must record in the
catacombs of our mind impressions of the distilled and ultimate truths of our religion so that these memories fortify us
in times of distress, worldliness or anxiety. It is we who must
fortify the mind, the instinctive-intellectual mind, with the
eight words in English, reduced to four in Tamil, add "Aum"
to make five, "God Siva is immanent Love and transcendent
Reality—Anbe Sivamayam Satyame Parasivam Aum." Yes,
yes, this is our affirmation of faith. Imprint it deeply and
deeper still.

What do we mean when we say our affirmation of faith?
Intoning the affirmation of faith silently or aloud, we confirm, assert and positively state our conviction that God is both manifest and unmanifest, both permeating the world and transcending it, both personal Divine Love and impersonal Reality. In these eight words is contained the essence of *A Creed for Saivite Hindus.*
   Paramaguru Siva Yogaswami proclaimed: God is here, there and everywhere. He is all of us. He is greater than all His aspects. He cannot be contained....O Siva, who with form and without form stands!...Love is God Siva. Love permeates the world. Life moves to the harmony of Love. He who is transcendent, He becomes immanent, too. He animates all of existence. He is the Self of all selves. Who can know the wonder of His Grace?" **Gurudeva Sivaya Subramuniyaswami explains:** On the lips of every Saivite throughout the world resounds the proclamation "God Siva is immanent Love and transcendent Reality"—the great and grand affirmation of faith of our religion. Before partaking of each meal, we intone this verse. Before parting company one with another, we say it as our departing words. Thus do we remind ourselves that God Siva is immanent Love, that God Siva is transcendent Reality, and that in Him we take refuge and are comforted.

The Supreme Lord of all that moves and
all that stands still, the Inspirer of the spirit,
we call to our help, that He, Pushan,
the defender, the guardian, unfailing,
may increase our wealth and bring us bliss....
Blessings be on us of Pushan, the all-knowing.
                                                    RIG VEDA

How is our affirmation of faith said in Tamil?
In the Tamil language our affirmation is even more succinct and beautiful. It is written:

அன்பே சிவமயம் சத்தியமே பரசிவம்

In English we write it, "Anbe Sivamayam Satyame Parasivam" and pronounce it: "än'bā sē'va mī'yam sät'yamā pä'ra sē'vam."

Gurudeva Sivaya Subramuniyaswami explains: "Anbe Sivamayam Satyame Parasivam!" we repeat prior to sleep, seeing the twenty-four sacred symbols of Saivism in our mind one after another, attempting brief access to the Sivaloka and permanent entrance into the Saivite astral- plane schools in the Second World, the Devaloka. "Anbe Sivamayam Satyame Parasivam!" we say upon awakening out of sleep as we recall the deep truths, the transcendent knowledge gained from the rishis in the schools of the Devaloka attended during our night's sleep. "Anbe Sivamayam Satyame Parasivam!" we say after we bathe and in preparing ourselves to face the day ahead, God Siva's day, reminding us that Umapati, our Father-Mother God, the immanent Love, protects us, guides us, keeps us from harm's way, reminding us, too, of the transcendental Reality which lifts our mind into the arena of useful thoughts, enabling us to fulfill our dharma in winding out our karma without creating undue inhibiting karmas for an unwanted future. In English or in Tamil, silently and aloud, recite the affirmation of faith and let its power bring you closer to His holy feet.

How else is the affirmation of faith important to us?
It is a reminder of our convictions, a verbal reaffirmation of the monistic theism to which we adhere and perhaps the most simple way to express the vast and all-embracing ancient teachings of the eternal path, the Sanatana Dharma.

Gurudeva Sivaya Subramuniyaswami explains: *Anbe Sivamayam Satyame Parasivam!* This affirmation of faith is a powerful, virgin summation of the twelve beliefs for Saivite Hindus found in this Creed. Use it. Meditate upon it. Understand it well. Our Catechism and Creed explain it most perfectly. Well that it is the last page of This *Creed for Saivite Hindus.* Now bring it forward as the ultimate statement of your own belief. Write it 1,008 times in the sacred Tamil script to perform penance—sahasra lekhana. Chant it 1,008 times—sahasra japa—before the holy feet, not as a mantram requiring initiation but as your declaration of faith in standing strong for the Saiva Samayam. Do not relent. Do not cringe or react. Take up the holy Vel and act in His name. *Anbe Sivamayam Satyame Parasivam!* is what you have when you take the milk from the sacred cow of religion, separate out the cream, churn that cream to rich butter and boil that butter into a precious few drops of ghee. *Anbe Sivamayam Satyame Parasivam!* is the sweet ghee of the Saivite Hindu religion.

He is love embodied....transcending all, yet immanent in each He stands. For those bound in the world here below, He is the Great Treasure. The Benefactor of all the worlds, the Supreme Siva, extended His glory.
                                                    SAINT TIRUMULAR

~ Part Three ~
# The Context

Hinduism, more than any other religion, has catego-
rized and encompassed the total spectrum of philosophic positions—and to this day offers living exponents of each. Thus it is that one Hindu teacher will praise
total surrender and devotion to Lord Krishna as the ultimate
path, while another, spurning devotion, says Liberation comes
only upon the shattering of this universe's illusory appearance.

To understand any of Hinduism's ten thousand sects, to
fathom their nuances of philosophy, requires that we plunge
into the history, geography and spiritual lineage which have
molded them. Part three provides such context for the
teachings found in parts one and two. Here we examine the
greater body of Hinduism and discover where Saiva Siddhanta fits into it.

Here we encounter a debate which has been raging for at
least 2,000 years, and which resurfaced in the 1980's in several international conferences and institutions. It is a debate
about God's relationship with the soul and the world, a relationship which two schools of Saiva Siddhanta see very differently. The issues were formally and finally resolved, as you
will see. Here we meet the fascinating sages who realized and
spoke out these truths. Gurudeva Sivaya Subramuniyaswami
is the current Satguru of the Natha Sampradaya's Kailasa
Paramparai. His history and spiritual adventures and those
of his remarkable predecessors are briefly presented in the
last chapter. These were siddhars, men whose magic was to
transform seekers forever.

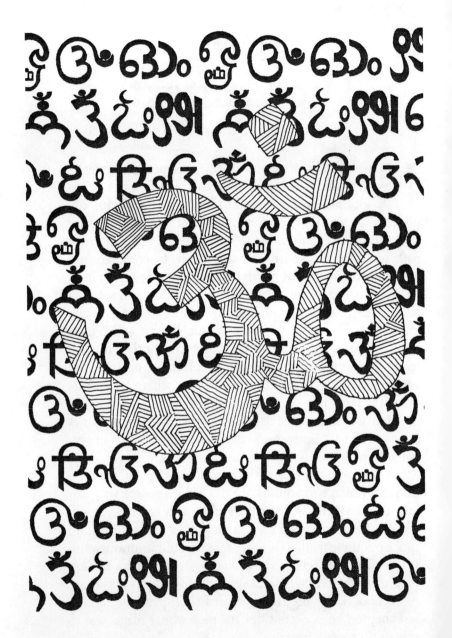

The sacred syllable "Om" in India's diverse languages.

Chapter 30
An Overview of Hinduism

ONE-SIXTH OF THE HUMAN FAMILY
ARE HINDU AND FOLLOW THIS OLDEST
LIVING FAITH, OF WHICH THERE ARE FOUR
PRIMARY DENOMINATIONS.

The soul searches for its Self, slowly ascending the path that leads to Enlightenment and Liberation. It is an arduous, delightful journey through samsara culminating in God-Realization, the direct and personal spiritual experience of Siva, of Self, of Truth. This alone among all things in the cosmos can bring freedom from the bondages of ignorance and desire. This is the highest realization. There is none greater.

Hindus believe that all women and men are on this path and that all will ultimately reach its summit. It is a glorious and encouraging concept—that every single soul will reach Truth, none left to suffer forever for human transgression.

Hinduism is our planet's original and oldest living religion, with no single founder or group of founders. For as long as man has lived and roamed across Earth's land and water masses, the Sanatana Dharma has been a guide of life and soul. One out of every six people belongs to this oldest faith. Shortly into the 21st century, Hindu adherents will number a billion. All of them are Hindus, yes, but they represent a broad range of beliefs, sadhanas and mystic goals. In fact, one way to understand Hinduism is not as a single religion, but as a family of 10,000 independent religions.

Principally, this spectrum of religiousness divides up into the three major sects or denominations of Hinduism: Saivism, Saktism and Vaishnavism. Additionally, there are liberal, non-sectarian forms, most importantly the Smarta Sampradaya.

Hinduism: a Synopsis

Hinduism worships one Supreme Reality (called by many names) and teaches that all souls ultimately realize Truth. There is no eternal hell, no damnation. It accepts all genuine spiritual paths—from pure monism ("God alone exists") to theistic dualism ("When shall I know His Grace?"). Each soul is free to find his own way, whether by devotion, austerity, meditation (yoga) or selfless service. Emphasis is placed on temple worship, scripture and the guru-disciple tradition. Festivals, pilgrimage, chanting of holy hymns and home worship are dynamic practices. Love, nonviolence, good conduct and the law of dharma define the Hindu path. Hinduism explains that the soul reincarnates until all karmas are resolved and God-Realization is attained. The magnificent holy temples, the peaceful piety of the Hindu home, the subtle metaphysics and the science of yoga all play their part. Hinduism is a mystical religion, leading the devotee to experience personally the Truth within, finally reaching the pinnacle of consciousness where man and God are one.

Nine Beliefs of Hinduism

Though Hindus believe many things, there are a few bedrock concepts on which most adherents concur. The following nine beliefs, though not exhaustive, offer a simple summary of Hindu spirituality. They comprise, in a sense, another creed, broader and more generalized than the one presented in part two.

1. *Hindus believe in a one, all-pervasive Supreme Being who is both immanent and transcendent, both Creator and Unmanifest Reality.*

2. *Hindus believe that the universe undergoes endless cycles of creation, preservation and dissolution.*

3. *Hindus believe that all souls are evolving toward union with God and will ultimately find Moksha: spiritual knowledge and liberation from the cycle of rebirth. Not a single soul will be eternally deprived of this destiny.*

4. *Hindus believe in karma, the law of cause and effect by which each individual creates his own destiny by his thoughts, words and deeds.*

5. *Hindus believe that the soul reincarnates, evolving through many births until all karmas have been resolved.*

6. *Hindus believe that divine beings exist in unseen worlds and that temple worship, rituals, sacraments as well as personal devotionals create a communion with these devas and Gods.*

7. *Hindus believe that a spiritually awakened Master or Satguru is essential to know the Transcendent Absolute, as are personal discipline, good conduct, purification, self-inquiry and meditation.*

8. *Hindus believe that all life is sacred, to be loved and revered, and therefore practice ahimsa or non-violence.*

9. *Hindus believe that no particular religion teaches the only way to salvation above all others, but that all genuine religious paths are facets of God's Pure Love and Light, deserving tolerance and understanding.*

The Beliefs of the Major Sects

Among the four major Hindu streams there are certainly more similarities than there are differences. All ascribe the highest scriptural authority to the Vedas and Agamas, though their Agamas differ somewhat, and the Smarta-Liberal Hindus do not accept the Agamas.

All believe in karma and reincarnation, and in a Supreme Being who both is form and pervades form, who creates, sustains and destroys the universe only to recreate it again in unending cycles. They strongly declare the validity and importance of temple worship, in the three worlds of existence and the myriad Gods and devas residing in them. They concur that there is no intrinsic evil, that the universe was created out of God and is permeated by Him. They each believe in maya (though their definitions differ somewhat), and in the liberation of the soul from rebirth (called Moksha) as the goal of human existence. They believe in dharma and ahimsa (nonviolence), and in the need for a Satguru to lead the soul towards God-Realization. They wear the sacred marks, called tilak, on their foreheads as sacred symbols (though each wears a distinct mark). Finally, they prefer cremation of the body upon death, believing that the soul will inhabit another body in the next life. Here is a brief comparison of the four sects.

On the Nature of God

Saivism:	Personal God and temple Deity is Siva, neither male nor female. Ganesha and Muruga are also worshiped.
Saktism:	Personal God and temple Deity is Sakti—also called Durga or Kali—female, the Divine Mother.
Vaishnavism:	Personal God and temple Deity is Vishnu, male. His incarnations as Rama and Krishna are also worshiped.
Smartaism:	Personal God and temple Deity is Iswara, worshiped as Vishnu, Siva, Sakti, Ganesha and Surya or any Deity of devotee's choice, e.g, Skanda or Krishna.

On the Doctrine of Avatar

Saivism: There are no divine incarnations.

Saktism: The Divine Mother does incarnate in this world.

Vaishnavism: Vishnu has ten or more earthly incarnations.

Smartaism: All Deities may assume earthly incarnations.

On the Nature of Sakti

Saivism: Sakti is God Siva's power and manifest will, energy or mind.

Saktism: Sakti is an active Being separate from a quiescent and remote Siva.

Vaishnavism: No special importance is given to Sakti.

Smartaism: Sakti is a Divine Form of Iswara, His manifesting power.

On Spiritual Practice

Saivism: With bhakti as a base, stress is placed on sadhana, tapas, yoga. Ascetic.

Saktism: Stress is on bhakti and tantric, sometimes occult, practices. Ascetic-occult.

Vaishnavism: Stress is almost entirely on bhakti. Generally non-ascetic.

Smartaism: Preparatory sadhanas are bhakti, karma, raja yoga. Highest path is jnana.

On the Relationship of Man and God

Saivism: God Siva is one with the soul. The soul must realize this advaitic truth by God Siva's grace.

Saktism: The Divine Mother, Sakti, is mediatrix, bestowing advaitic Moksha to those who worship Her.

Vaishnavism: God and soul are eternally distinct. Through Lord Vishnu's grace, the soul's destiny is to worship and enjoy God.

Smartaism: Iswara and man are in reality Absolute Brahman. Within maya, the soul and Iswara appear as two. Jnana dispels the illusion.

On the Personal God

Saivism: God Siva is pure love and compassion, immanent and transcendent, pleased by our purity and sadhana.

Saktism: The Goddess Durga is both compassionate and terrifying, pleasing and wrathful, assuaged by sacrifice and submission.

Vaishnavism: God Vishnu is loving and beautiful, the object of man's devotion, pleased by our service and surrender.

Smartaism: Iswara appears as a human-like Deity according to devotees' loving worship, which is considered a rudimentary self-purifying practice.

Spheres of Influence

Saivism: Geographically widespread, strongest in Sri Lanka and south and north India.

Saktism: Predominantly in north India, especially Bengal and Assam.

Vaishnavism: Widespread throughout India, north and south.

Smartaism: Geographically widespread, most prominent in north and south India.

Scriptures

Saivism: Vedas and Saiva Agamas.
Saktism: Vedas and Sakta Tantras.
Vaishnavism: Vedas and Bhagavad Gita.
Smartaism: Vedas and Smritis—Puranas, Ramayana, Bhagavad Gita, Yoga Sutras, etc.

Ultimate Goals

Saivism: The primary goal of Saivism is Moksha (also called Mukti or Veedu), realizing one's identity with God Siva, in perfect union and non-differentiation, thus gaining Liberation from the cycles of birth and death. This is also termed Nirvikalpa Samadhi and may be attained in this life. A secondary goal is Savikalpa Samadhi, or the experience of Satchidananda, a unitive experience within superconsciousness in which perfect truth, knowledge and bliss are known. The soul's final destiny is to merge with God Siva.

Saktism: The primary goal of Saktism is Moksha, defined as complete identification with God Siva. A secondary goal for the Saktas is to perform good works selflessly so that one may go, on death, to the heaven worlds and thereafter enjoy a good birth on earth (for heaven, too, is a transitory state). For Saktas, God is both the form-less Absolute (Siva) and the manifest Divine (Sakti, Durga or Kali), but emphasis is given to the feminine manifest by which the masculine Unmanifest is ultimately reached.

Vaishnavism: The primary goal of Vaishnavites is termed Videha Mukti, defined as liberation—attainable only after death—when the self realizes union with God's body as a part of Him, yet maintains its pure individual personality. Lord Vishnu—all-pervasive consciousness—is the soul of the universe, distinct from the world and from the jivas which constitute His body. His transcendent Being is a celestial form residing in the city of Vaikuntha, the home of all eternal values and perfection, where the soul joins Him upon Liberation. A secondary goal—the experience of God's Grace—can be reached while yet embodied through taking refuge in God's unbounded love. By loving and serving God and meditating upon Him, our spiritual hunger grows and we experience His Grace flooding our whole being.

Smartaism: The ultimate goal of Smarta-Liberal Hinduism is Mukti, to realize oneself as Brahman—the Absolute and only Reality—and become free from samsara, the cycles of birth and death. For this, one must conquer the state of avidya, or ignorance, which causes the world to appear as real. All illusion has vanished for the realized being (Jivanmukta) even as he lives out life in the physical body. At death, his bodies are extinguished. Brahman alone exists.

Path of Attainment

Saivism: The path for Saivites is divided into four progressive stages of belief and practice, called chariya, kriya, yoga and jnana. The soul evolves through karma and reincarnation from the instinctive-intellectual sphere into virtuous and moral living, then into temple worship and devotion, followed by internalized worship or yoga and its meditative disciplines. Union comes through the grace of the Satguru and culminates in the soul's maturity in the state of jnana or wisdom. Saivism values both bhakti and yoga, devotional and contemplative sadhanas.

Saktism: The spiritual practices in Saktism are similar to those in Saivism, though there is more emphasis in Saktism on God's Power as opposed to Being, on mantras and yantras, and on embracing apparent opposites: male-female, absolute-relative, pleasure-pain, cause-effect, mind-body. A minor sect within Saktism undertakes tantric practices, consciously using the world of form to transmute and eventually transcend that world. The tantric school is somewhat occult in nature; it is considered a path for the few, not the many.

Vaishnavism: Orthodox Vaishnavites believe that religion is the performance of bhakti sadhanas, and that man can communicate with and receive the grace of Lord Vishnu who manifests through the temple Deity, or idol. The path of karma yoga and jnana

yoga leads to bhakti yoga. Neo-Vaish-
navites believe that bhakti sadhanas are
essential, but they do not believe in or
worship the Gods. Among the highest
practices of all Vaishnavites is chanting the
holy names of the Avatars, God's incarnations. Through total self-surrender to
Lord Vishnu, called Prapatti, Liberation
from samsara is attained.

Smartaism: Most Smarta-Liberal Hindus believe that
Mukti is achieved through jnana yoga
alone—defined as an intellectual and
meditative but non-kundalini-yoga path.
Jnana yoga's progressive stages are scriptural study (sravana), reflection (manana)
and continued meditation (dhyana).
Guided by a realized guru and avowed to
the unreality of the world, the initiate
meditates on himself as Brahman to break
through the illusion of maya. Devotees
may also choose from three other paths to
cultivate devotion, accrue good karma and
purify the mind. These are bhakti yoga,
karma yoga and raja yoga, which many
Smartas teach can also bring enlightenment. This non-sectarian sampradaya
follows the Advaita Vedanta philosophy of
Adi Shankara. Their worship is eclectic,
embracing a wide range of Deities.

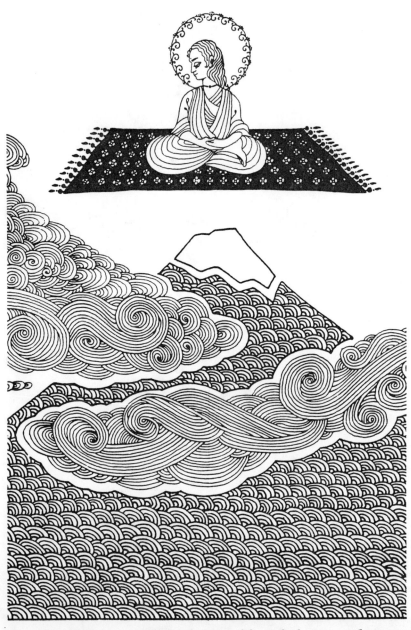

The philosophical mountain can be viewed from the bottom or the top.

Chapter 31

Monistic Theism

A VIEW OF REALITY
FROM THE MOUNTAINTOP,
BEING A DISCUSSION ABOUT
WHETHER GOD AND SOUL ARE
ULTIMATELY ONE OR TWO.

The purpose of this chapter is to further explain the monistic Saiva Siddhanta philosophy—sometimes known as Advaita Siddhanta—which this book embodies, and to juxtapose it briefly with another school of thought, called pluralistic Saiva Siddhanta. This comparison is important because the pluralistic teachings are widespread, so much so that many authoritative texts proclaim Saiva Siddhanta to be wholly pluralistic, and completely overlook the monistic school, which is actually far older.

I first became aware of this ongoing debate in 1948 while living and performing sadhana in Jaffna, Sri Lanka, prior to my initiation from Satguru Siva Yogaswami. I learned that various pluralist adherents in the area were not pleased with Siva Yogaswami's monistic statements and conclusions. At my very first meeting with this extraordinary Natha siddhar, Satguru Yogaswami tested me by asking, "What do you think about monism and pluralism? Explain it to me." He obviously knew I had been exposed to both sides of the debate through village gossip. I said, "Both are true. It is totally dependent upon how one is looking at the mountain. The pluralist looks at the mountain from the foothills and feels separate from the lofty peak. The monist sits in unequivocal oneness on the lofty peak."

In my life, the issue again came into prominence in the

early '80's after my recognition by the world community of Saivites as Guru Mahasannidhanam of Kauai Aadheenam and Jagadachariya of the Natha Sampradaya's Kailasa Paramparai. By that time, our small but dynamic Hindu church had distributed thousands of copies of our *Hindu Catechism,* boldly proclaiming the monistic truths of the Kailasa Paramparai and bravely claiming the term *Saiva Siddhanta* as our own. This did not go unnoticed by pluralist scholars and pundits, who for generations had faced little opposition to their claim that Saiva Siddhanta is pluralistic by definition.

Letters poured into our office at Kauai Aadheenam objecting to our philosophical position and urging us to give up the term *Saiva Siddhanta.* We did not budge, arguing that, indeed, Saiva Siddhanta is the perfect name for our teachings. In response, we reiterated our philosophical position clearly and juxtaposed it with the pluralist views in a technical document called "Monism and Pluralism in Saiva Siddhanta." In an inspired talk distributed throughout the world I asserted, "There can be only one final conclusion, and that is monistic theism." To the pluralists, it appeared we had thrown down the gauntlet. The debate was on.

Once a village affair, this age-old feud quickly escalated into an international conflagration of eight great monasteries in India and Sri Lanka, of sangams in South Africa, Mauritius and Malaysia, and of philosophers, pundits, attorneys, judges and politicians from nearly every continent of the world. But for the first time, perhaps, the issue was faced with the goal of final resolution. Both sides benefited and learned much in the process and now take joy in the fact that a mutual coexistence was attained and devotees of Siva can again work together harmoniously, in a spirit of understanding and mutual recognition, forging an even greater Hindu solidarity, based on a more profound Sivasambandam.

How was the debate resolved?

The debate, rekindled by our statement that there can be
only one final conclusion, was resolved in the understanding
that there are actually two—one final conclusion for pluralists and one final conclusion for monistic theists. This oc-
curred in February of 1984 at the south Indian monastery of
Sri-la-Sri Shanmuga Desika Gnanasambandha Paramacharya
Swamigal, 26th Guru Mahasannidhanam of the Dharmapura Aadheenam, at a meeting of professors, advocates, theologians, academicians and pundits on the issue. The resolution came when His Holiness, presiding over the meeting,
effectively declared that all who follow the Meykandar philosophy are indeed pluralists when he two books written by
the late Saiva Siddhanta scholar, V. K. Palasuntharam—1)
Souls Are Beginningless, and 2) *There Has Always Been Only
a Pluralistic Saiva Siddhanta Philosophy.*

Heretofore, the Meykandar exponents had been equivo-
cal in this area, considering themselves sort of dvaitic and
sort of advaitic, and redefining the word *advaita* (which
means "not two") to allow for two things to exist in the state
of oneness. Through His Holiness, the followers of Meykandar lineage had formally declared themselves pluralists, and
thus acknowledged their disagreement with the monistic
school in Saiva Siddhanta.

We are happy to say that peace, tolerance and forbearance now exist between these two schools. Adherents of each
school also noted that their philosophic disagreement is
small compared to the vast area of belief, culture and practice they hold in common. These are not diametrically opposing denominations. They share more in common than
they hold in difference. In fact, between these two schools
there is 95 percent agreement and only 5 percent dissidence.
Both are committed to the importance of temple worship, to
love of God Siva, both immanent and transcendent, and of
the Gods. They share the same scriptures and saints, a deep

devotion to the sangam of fellow Sivathondar, a belief in
karma and reincarnation, a firm faith in the need to live a
virtuous life and to perform sadhana and yoga, a veneration
of the Satguru and his necessary role in the spiritual illumination of the soul, which, they concur, moves progressively
through the stages of chariya, kriya, yoga and jnana. Both
schools stand together in their disagreement with Sankara's
Vedantic view of maya as mere illusion, insisting that this
world has a divine purpose—the evolution of the soul—and
that, even though it is only relatively real, it is certainly not
unreal. Again and again, on a hundred issues, they find
themselves in harmony. They agree about the importance of
puja and the sanctity of the orthodox Saivite home, where
children are raised for a strong, productive and honest society. They agree about the need for priests well-trained in the
mystical arts, and of meditation, contemplation and samadhi. They are one in their love of Saivite culture and protocol
and their firm faith in the Agamic scriptures. The late A.P.C.
Veerabhagu, an eminent South Indian Siddhantin, entre-
preneur, builder of colleges, schools and libraries, himself a
pluralist, publicly called for our working together and lucid-
ly summarized our essential points of agreement as "Guru,
Linga, Sangam and Valipadu (temple worship)." This, he
said, is the essence of Saiva Siddhanta as found in ancient
Tamil Saiva literature.

    We feel that the foundation for this mutual coexistence
of love and trust was made two years earlier on January 30,
1981, when we met with His Holiness for the first time. I was
on a holy pilgrimage to Saivism's most sacred sites with an
entourage of forty eastern and western devotees when messengers from His Holiness invited us to visit his ancient monastery. Together we sat in the inner chambers of his palatial
spiritual refuge, built by Maharajas in the 16th century. It
was quite a picture—eastern pundits with their guru, and
western mystics with theirs, discussing the philosophical

enigmas that have perplexed the mind of man from the dawn of history. Through our translators we spoke of God, of the soul and the world, and of the dire need for Saivite schools in South India, and around the world, to pass this great knowledge on to the next generation.

After our lively discussion, a special lunch was served. Later, one of our swamis casually inquired of His Holiness about his large golden earrings, wondering where such a pair might be obtained for myself. Without hesitation, the guru summoned an aide and whispered some instructions. Moments later, a pair of earrings identical to those he was wearing were placed in his hands. His Holiness indicated that these were for me. Joyfully shrugging off our objections that he was being too generous, he immediately set about placing them in my ears with his own hands, enlarging the existing holes to accept these massive gold rings which are the traditional insignia of an achariya. Then he presented new orange kavi cloth to me and to the swamis accompanying me.

We gratefully accepted the Sannidhanam's unexpected and generous gift as a gesture of goodwill to help us on our way of spreading the message of Saiva Siddhanta. Perhaps even more importantly, it was to us a sign of cooperative efforts between two great monasteries, one firmly teaching pluralistic Saiva Siddhanta in the East, and the other boldly promulgating monistic Saiva Siddhanta in the West. We thought to ourself that all that transpired after this would be for the best. To the onlooking pundits, this presentation of the achariya earrings meant that all knowledgeable Hindus would know that the Guru Mahasannidhanam of Dharmapura Aadheenam and the Guru Mahasannidhanam of Kauai Aadheenam would work together for the future of Saiva Siddhanta.

Later the same day, Mahasannidhanam asked us to address several thousand people who were seated in the giant

inner hall overlooking the large temple tank. We spoke of
the greatness of Saivism and Saiva Siddhanta and the effects
of its spreading into the Western world. The day culminated
when the His Holiness handed me an ornate silver casket, in
which was kept a precious scroll honoring our work in
spreading Saiva Siddhanta. After being engraved with words
of acknowledgement, the casket was officially presented to
me before ten thousand Saivites in the 1,000-pillared hall at
Chidambaram temple during the sacred Bharata Natyam
dance performance, of the complete 108 Tandava poses, the
first to be held there in 52 years.

Now that you have brought you up to date with this
background of an important debate, we shall proceed. We explore here a view of Reality that is the
oldest of all realizations—monistic theism. It is the essential
teaching of the Hindu faith and, most especially, of the six
sects of Saivism. It finds its fullest expression in the 6,000-
year old Saiva Siddhanta theology (Saivism's major South-
ern school) as scripturally codified in the *Tirumantiram* by
Maharishi Tirumular (a yoga siddhar of the Natha Sampradaya who lived over 2,000 years ago). *Siddhanta* literally
means "ultimate knowledge" or "final conclusion." Monistic
Saiva Siddhanta, which encompasses both Vedic and Agamic traditions, is monistic in that it believes in a one Reality
and in the advaitic or non-dual identity of man with that
Reality. It is theistic in its belief in God as personal Lord who
transcends and yet is also immanent in the world, and in the
Gods or Mahadevas. Thus, monistic Saiva Siddhanta
encompasses the non-dual and the dual, both advaitic
Vedanta and dvaitic Siddhanta.

Monistic theism reconciles certain theological problems
and apparent opposites. A little story offers a parallel in science. Scientists have long been perplexed by the strange

nature of light. In some experiments it behaves like particles, while in others it acts clearly like waves of energy. Arguments flew back and forth. It couldn't be both, so which was it? In jest it was theorized that light behaves like particles on Monday, Wednesday and Friday and like waves during the rest of the week!

In a like manner has the endeavor to fathom the spiritual realities of God and soul led to differing conclusions. It is only by direct cognition, personal experience at the deepest levels, that the mystery of Being can be known. To grasp Reality requires a transcendent point of reference which reconciles the dichotomy of being and becoming, the contradiction of God's eternality and temporal activity, the confusion of good and evil, the paradox of one and two.

For centuries the Kailasa Paramparai of the Natha Sampradaya has taught such a philosophy. Its monistic theism is a progressive path of chariya, kriya, yoga and jnana. Like all Saivite sects, monistic Saiva Siddhanta accepts the existence of *Pati* (God), *pasu* (individual soul) and *pasam* (the bonds that confine the soul to earthly existence).

Monistic Saiva Siddhanta proclaims in simple summary: *God Siva is Creator and Creation.* Pluralistic Saiva Siddhanta, on the other hand, proclaims that *God Siva is Creator, but He is not His creation.* Herein lies the crux of a debate which has simmered for thousands of years and was formally settled in 1983.

The Pluralistic School: A Summary
In the 13th century CE there arose a second school within Saiva Siddhanta which denies monistic theism and takes the Pluralistic Realism of the Meykandar Shastras as its philosophy. While the two schools hold much in common (saints, scripture, temple worship, guru-disciple, etc.), three important theological differences are summarized below:

The pluralist school holds that God, soul and world are

all three eternally coexistent, and therefore Siva did not create soul or world. By creation, they understand that Siva fashions existing maya into various forms. God is the efficient cause of the manifest world, but not the material cause.

Those of the Meykandar Sampradaya teach that world and soul are eternally distinct from God. There is a union of soul in God which preserves the individuality of each—oneness which is not identity. Like salt dissolved in water; it is neither two, nor is it perfectly one.

While monistic theists support the scriptural doctrine that only Siva exists before creation and after the Great Dissolution, pluralists contend that souls and world also survive Mahapralaya.

The Dual and the Non-Dual

Webster defines *monism* as "the doctrine that there is only one ultimate substance or principle, that reality is an organic whole without independent parts." This is the opposite of *dualism*, which is defined as "the theory that the world is ultimately composed of, or explicable in terms of, two basic entities....The doctrine that there are two mutually antagonistic principles in the universe, good and evil." *Pluralism* is defined as "the theory that reality is composed of a multiplicity of ultimate beings, principles or substances."

Stated most simply, the monistic school of Saiva Siddhanta holds that God Siva created (by emanation from Himself) everything, and that each soul is destined to merge in non-dual union with Him, as a river merges into the sea, as as a drop of water loses its individual identity when entering the ocean. As spiritual essence, the soul is always one with Siva; as form, it evolves over time and ultimately merges in Him.

The individual soul—which is a conscious being, a body of light—is created, evolves on the wheel of samsara from incarnation to incarnation, ultimately merging in undifferentiated union with God Siva. This oneness, realized mystics call identity. The essence of the soul (Satchidananda and Parasivam) is eternal and uncreated, does not evolve but is forever perfect. This essence of the soul is not different from Siva. The world and the soul are, in truth, but various forms of Siva Himself, yet He also transcends His creation and is not limited by it. Also, the world and the soul cannot stand independent of God, a fact which makes it clear that they are evolutes and not eternally separate entities, as pluralists would postulate. When world and soul are absorbed in Him at the time of Mahapralaya—the end of the cosmic creational cycle—the three *malas,* or bonds, of ego, karma and illusion (called anava, karma and maya) are annihilated and the soul's individual existence ceases, losing its separateness through union and fulfillment in Siva. After Mahapralaya, Siva alone exists, as Nataraja dancing, until creation issues forth from Him in yet another cosmic cycle.

Siva is All

Saivism places great emphasis on striving, on purification, on sadhana, on the effort to "Know thy Self by thyself." And just what is this Self? It is the knowledge that Siva is the essence of all things, that He alone performs all actions, that He is the Knower as well as the Known. In truth, there is nothing in this universe but Siva; there is not a single place He does not exist. All objects sentient and insentient are Siva. Unity and diversity are Siva. You are Siva. The Self of all is Siva. This world, which appears to be different from Him, is actually created by Him, made of His very being.

Once the seeker has realized himself as Siva, thereafter he sees only Siva wheresoever he looks. This is the highest teaching of Saivism. It is this realization toward which true Saiva Siddhanta leads. It is this attainment toward which all other experiences in life are heading.

Saivism describes three perfections of God Siva. The

highest is Parasivam—timeless, formless, spaceless and causeless. This is Siva's transcendence, His inmost core and Being
for which no description is possible, except to say, "Not this.
Not that."

Satchidananda is Siva's immanent perfection, described
as Pure Consciousness, Cosmic Love, Light and Energy per-
vading all things. It is the Primal Substance of which all else
is made, the "clay" of the cosmos.

Saivism is highly devotional, and Siva is worshiped and
hailed as Lord, as Mother-Father, as Creator, Preserver and
Destroyer. This is His third perfection of Primal Soul or
Mahesvara, a conscious and divine Being, a personal God.
He is the Beginning and the End, the Author of Existence.
He is both material and efficient Cause, and thus His act of
manifestation is likened in scripture to sparks issuing forth
from a fire or a web spun from the body of a spider.

All three perfections of Siva are necessarily inadequate
descriptions of His one, indivisible Reality, which is forever
perfect and complete. Soul and world do exist and are not
equal to Siva any more than a drop of water is equal to the
ocean, though both are of the same essential nature (hydro-
gen and oxygen). Though Siva is His creation (immanent),
He is more than creation (transcendent). Thus, theism and
the devotion and worship associated therewith are an essential part of Saivism.

The Cosmic Creation

Consider the question of creation. Did this world always
exist—therefore requiring no creator to account for it? Or,
did God Siva create the world and the individual soul? Rishi
Tirumular is unequivocal on this point, stating time and
again in his *Tirumantiram* that God Siva has created or
emanated everything from Himself.

Saivites generally use the word *create* in the specific
sense of manifestation, or sometimes as Siva's will, activity

or overflowing radiance. The Sanskrit word for creation is
sristi, meaning "to let loose," which corresponds closely to
the definition of creation as found in the *Tirumantiram*.
Rishi Tirumular uses the Tamil word *padai*. Here are a number of the relevant verses from the *Tirumantiram* which de-
monstrate his doctrine of emanational creation.

> *If the cardinal directions are all Siva, why speak of*
> *someone else, O you men! All smoke emanates*
> *from fire; all creation arises from our Primal Lord.*
>
> VERSE 3010

> *Of yore He created the worlds seven. Of yore He*
> *created celestials countless. Of yore He created*
> *souls without number. Of yore He created all—*
> *Himself, As Primal Param, uncreated.*
>
> VERSE 446

> *When the Creator dances, the worlds*
> *He created dance.*   VERSE 2786

Another view of creation describes God's cosmic creative act
as analogous to a potter who fashions a pot. In this description of creation, God is the potter (called the efficient cause)
who, through the use of a wheel (called the instrumental
cause and thought of as God's power or Sakti), molds from
an already-existing clay (called the material cause and
thought of as a primordial matter or maya), a pot (the effect
of these three causes). This is the pluralistic view. If we hold
such a view of the creative act, then naturally the destructive
act is abhorrent, for it merely is the ruination of the pot, or
its return to formless clay.

    This is unlike the monistic view, which is a more tradi-
tionally Hindu understanding of God Siva's creation. From
this view, the creation of the soul is like a spark issuing from

a fire, like a wave, a bubble or river arising from the ocean, or like the dance of a dancer. The wave or river has a beginning, an evolution and an end. Does something arise out of nothing? No, water arises out of water. Does that water cease to exist when it returns to the vast ocean? No, it merges back into the ocean. It ceases to be a wave or a drop of water and it becomes "ocean-ness." That merging is fulfillment, not destruction. That union in God is the ultimate blessing, the most glorious goal imaginable, the consummate condition of the soul, as it returns to its Source.

The soul body emanates from Siva, evolves in physical and non-physical worlds and ultimately merges back in Him. Is it destroyed in that merging? No, it is made complete and perfect. It becomes Siva. Jiva becomes Siva. This is the conclusion of monistic theism.

Siva Nataraja's dance is perhaps the very best analogy for creation. Unlike other forms of creation, in dance there is no "thing" which is separate from the creator, like the pot is separate from the potter or a painting from the artist.

The soul is Siva's emanated creation, existing within the Divine Mind of Siva. It is not an eternally separate entity. God Siva is the Creator, Preserver and Destroyer, the alpha and omega of existence. As Yogaswami taught, "Everything emanates from the Great Silence. Nothing exists apart from God. It is like the waves and the ocean."

Evil

If God did create, then the question arises: "Why is there evil in the world?" Many people deny the existence of the Divine because they cannot see how a good, compassionate God could have created (or even allowed) an apparently imperfect world. It's certainly true that on the surface this world appears full of sorrow, injustice, evil, disease, death and all manner of imperfection. The soul, too, seems tainted with ignorance and limitation. Does that mean that God could not have created the world? Does it imply that there are forces beyond His control (for a compassionate God would assuredly not permit evil if He had the power to eliminate it)? Or, as Omar Khayyam noted, "Did the hand, then, of the Potter slip?"

The mystic's answer is that this world is, in fact, perfect, though that fact is not apparent to the casual observer. The world and the soul are God Siva's divine and flawless creation. It is superficial to say that sorrow and death are evil, and that only joy and life are good. That is an unenlightened view of the pairs of opposites which, taken together, comprise a perfect whole. Life is precious, indeed possible, because of death. Light depends for its existence on darkness, and joy on sorrow.

The view of Saiva Siddhanta as expounded by Rishi Tirumular, the Saiva Nayanars and Satguru Yogaswami is that this world is, when viewed from superconsciousness, perfect, and that God Siva has purposefully created each thing and its opposite: good and bad, beauty and deformity, light and darkness, joy and sorrow, life and death. Yogaswami taught us that "There is not even one evil thing in the world." He urged us to "See God everywhere," not just in the obviously good. "Sarvam Sivamayam—All is Siva's maya," the Satguru exclaimed.

From our ordinary consciousness, this may be difficult to understand, especially when we personally are confronted with disease, death, violence, poverty and all forms of misery. We may wonder, "Why create the need to mature at all? Siva could just as easily create mature souls who delight in Oneness with Him." It is these very sets of opposites that provide the means for the soul's maturation through the mechanism of karma, that make us to seek beyond the world of duality, that remove the bonds of ignorance and bring each soul to Siva's Holy Feet.

From the enlightened summit reached by the siddhars,

all is seen as necessary and good. All is seen as God Siva Himself, in Him and of Him. A perfect world *has* issued from a perfect Creator.

Final Destiny

What about the soul's ultimate destiny? Is it to be a blessed relationship with God in heaven, unending enjoyment of divine association or the sundering of the joy-enjoyer state and loss of self in Self? Rishi Tirumular teaches of a complete and irrevocable union of the soul in God Siva, a union which is identity. This identity is ever-existent for the essence of the soul. However, with respect to the soul body, identity comes after the soul has completed its sojourn in *samsara* (the cycle of earthly births and deaths) and after further evolution in inner worlds. Rishi Tirumular's conclusions are powerful and compelling. Here are a few verses from the *Tirumantiram* which reflect the siddhar's teachings and the highest monistic doctrine of Saiva Siddhanta:

> *The soul, which in its real condition was of the form of Sivam, was confined and conditioned by its original anava malam. When this malam ceased to obstruct the soul, the soul resumed its original form of Sivam.*

> *None know where the Lord resides; to them who seek Him He resides eternally within; when you see the Lord, He and you become one.*
>
> VERSE 766

> *Even as a shadow disappears with the body, even as a bubble returns into water, even as a flame of camphor leaves no trace, so it is when jiva into Param unites.*
>
> VERSE 2587

You and He are not two separate;
you and He are but one united.
Thus stand, freed of all sectarian shackles;
adore the feet of Paramparai and with Siva one
become—that is the way Siddhanta is fulfilled.

VERSE 1437

Monistic theists accept both Siddhanta (which is highly the-istic) and Vedanta (which is boldly monistic). More precise-ly, they realize that Vedanta is the summit of the vast moun-tain of Siddhanta—Siddhanta is the whole and Vedanta is the part, but the highest part of that whole. Here we speak of Vedanta not as the denial of everything but the Absolute, not as the modern interpretation which makes everything (in-cluding the soul and its evolution) an illusion; rather, we speak of the original and pristine Vedanta of the Upanishads. No awakened Siddhantin will ever deny the Truths of Vedan-ta, for they are the jewels which adorn the Saiva Siddhanta theology.

Satguru Yogaswami taught us, "When the Vedas and Agamas all proclaim that the whole world is filled with God, and that there is nothing else, how can we say that the world exists and the body exists? Is there anything more worthy of reproach than to attribute an independent reality to them? Sages, too, have declared: 'Those who have become Your own are not other than You.' Thus, for several reasons of this kind, there is nothing other than God."

Scriptural Basis

Monistic theism has its roots in the Vedas. Scholars like Max Hunter Harrison, author of *Hindu Monism and Pluralism*, have long noted that the Hindu scriptures are alternately monistic and theistic. It is not a criticism, but a valid obser-vation of a theology that manages to encompass both.

The following quote, taken from page 707 of *The Prin-*

Who is the best devotee of God? It is he who sees,
after the Realization of Brahman, that God alone
has become all living beings, the universe and the
twenty-four cosmic principles.

SRI RAMAKRISHNA (1836–1886)

That all is Brahman is the view of scripture.
Because all is Brahman, there is nothing that
is different from Brahman.

SANKARACHARYA OF KANCHI (1934–)

An Encyclopedic Slant

Below is an excerpt from the *Encyclopedia Britannica* summarizing the discussion from the Upanishadic hymns.

"The Upanishads have, in fact, a variety of themes and emphases, tending generally toward a monistic and mystical philosophy; but on occasion the theistic element is very marked, as in the Katha and the Svetasvatara books of the Upanishads. The absolutist and the theistic views were not always felt to be exclusive...along with the persistence of the monistic strain, the theistic note is sounded much more distinctly, especially in the doctrine and practice of bhakti— devotion to a personal God who bestows grace.

"The Upanishads answer the question 'Who is that one Being?' by establishing the equation Brahman equals atman. Brahman—meaning now that which is the greatest, than which there is nothing greater, and also that which bursts forth into the manifested world, the one Being of which the hymn of creation spoke—is viewed as nothing but atman, identifiable as the innermost self in man but also, in reality, the innermost self in all beings....This final conception of Brahman or atman received many different explications from different teachers in the Upanishads, some of which were negative in character (neti neti, 'not this, not this') while others positively affirmed the all-pervasiveness of Brahman."

Left to right, top to bottom: Tirumular, Rishi, Kadaitswami, Chellap-paswami, Yogaswami, Sivaya Subramuniyaswami.

Chapter 32
The Kailasa Paramparai

THE AUTHENTICITY OF HINDU TEACHINGS IS
PRESERVED BY SPIRITUAL LINEAGES PASSED
FROM GURU TO GURU. HERE WE EXPLORE THE
HISTORICAL SUCCESSION, OR *PARAMPARAI*, OF
SIVAYA SUBRAMUNIYASWAMI.

From time immemorial, the truth of the soul's oneness with God has been propounded by great seers on this planet. One of the foremost traditions perpetuating this knowledge is in the Nandinatha Sampradaya, tracing its guru lineage back over 2,000 years to Maharishi Tirunandi and his eight disciples—Tirumular, Patanjali, Vyagrapadar, Sanatkumar, Sivayogamuni, Sanakar, Sanadanar and Sananthanar—then through Tirumular's disciples. This Saiva Siddhanta succession of siddhars flourishes today in South India, Sri Lanka and elsewhere through the disciples of the disciples of these enlightened rishis. This descent of spiritual awakening and authority has been continued through the preeminent Kailasa Paramparai (also known as the Siva Yogaswami Guru Paramparai). In recent times, the first historically known Satguru of this line was a nameless rishi from the Himalayas (*circa* 1770–1840). From him the mantle of spiritual authority was passed to Kadaitswami of Bangalore, South India (*circa* 1810–1875), then to Chellappaswami (1840–1914), then to Siva Yogaswami (1872–1964) of Sri Lanka, and finally to our beloved Gurudeva, Sivaya Subramuniyaswami (1927–).

Natha Rishi from the Himalayas
Little is known about the "Rishi from the Himalayas." But a few facts are certain. He lived in the late 1700's and he was a

siddhar—an "accomplished or perfected one." Siddhars are the most revered of Saivite yogis, a very special class of God-Realized seers, who may, by virtue of their inner attainment, be adept in various inner powers. But their real magic is their ability to transform the hearts and minds of sincere seekers, to shed light and dispel darkness. That is the most precious wizardry of all.

It is believed that the Rishi received his training and initiation from his Satguru in the Himalayas and was then sent on a spiritual mission to South India to revive and enliven the spirit of Saivism among the people there. For this reason, the paramparai is named after Mount Kailas, the Himalayan abode of Lord Siva.

The Rishi arrived in a village near the city of Bangalore, South India one day, sat down in a tea shop and entered into a deep state of contemplation. Sitting perfectly still with eyes closed, his presence filling the shop with great holiness. He did not move from that spot for seven years, nor did he speak. Within a few weeks of his arrival, more and more people came to pay homage, and the tea shop was transformed into a shrine. The shop owner became the custodian, and later had a railing built around the Rishi to keep visitors from touching him.

People heard about the Rishi even as far away as Europe. There was a constant stream of pilgrims visiting the shrine daily. Many came with problems or questions and found that simply by sitting in his presence, answers would come. Sometimes the Rishi would appear in their dreams at night and talk to them. Often a piece of paper with the answer to an unspoken question would appear in the air and float to the ground. These notes were never addressed to anyone in particular; they were more like general advice, but always solved the problem at hand.

After seven years, the Rishi came out of his inner depths and began to walk around. The villagers gave him a simple thatched hut because they wanted him to stay with them, but he did not seem to want that. He left the village and soon after met his *sishya* (disciple), who later came to be known as Kadaitswami. They were seen walking together near the coast a few miles from Thanjavur. One day, they met a wealthy landlord standing in front of his house. The man greeted them and said he had been waiting for them, because during his morning meditations, he had seen them sitting with him and knew they would arrive that day. He took them to his private temple, where a beautiful image of Lord Siva Nataraja was worshiped in a golden shrine. He told them that they could stay at the temple for as long as they wished, and he would see to their needs. The landlord employed a brahmin family to perform the pujas. Rishi and Kadaitswami stayed for a long time. They spent most of their day in deep meditation together, and often the master would issue forth direction and instruction for his disciple. The last day they were together, Rishi blessed Kadaitswami in a customary way by spreading holy ash on his head and body. That was his initiation. The Rishi sent him on a mission that same day. Rishi stayed on alone at the small temple for a while, then departed. No one knows where he went after that.

Siva Kadaitswami

Kadaitswami was popularly known as Yalpanam Kadaitswami. *Yalpanam* is the Tamil name for Sri Lanka's Jaffna peninsula. He was called Kadaitswami—*Kadai* meaning "market" or "shop"—because he spent most of his time in the vicinity of the town's market. Details of his early life in South India are not known, though it is said that he was a high court judge who was required to pass a death sentence on a man, but refused, left the courtroom and renounced his career at middle age to become a sannyasin. He had heard about the Rishi sitting in the tea shop and pilgrimaged to the village but arrived too late. Rishi had already gone. Kadait-swami pilgrimaged through South India looking for him, asking if anyone knew his whereabouts, until finally they met. During the years they were together, Kadaitswami received constant training and inner instructions from the Rishi, who was preparing him for a mission in Jaffna, where the purest Saivism was still being lived, but was severely threatened by the Christian missionaries and foreign government then in control of the country. Kadaitswami's mission was to go there and revive the spirit of Saivism among the people.

Many siddhis had naturally awakened in Kadaitswami, and the Rishi directed him to "Be a worker of miracles. Display your powers to anyone, but give the gems of wisdom only to a few." After his final diksha, at which he was given the name *Muthianandaswami,* Kadaitswami sailed with fishermen to Vellanai, a small island off the coast, where he performed years of intense yoga before continuing to Jaffna.

He roamed throughout the northern peninsula during his lifetime, but could most often be found in the streets and marketplace of Jaffna town. The presence of this powerful Natha siddhar from South India, who stood nearly six-foot-six, aroused great curiosity and interest among the townspeople. When he gave public talks, large crowds gathered to listen. He taught with fearless authority, and his sakti changed the lives of all who heard him. He inspired great devotion in the people, strengthened their Saivite beliefs and turned their minds from Christian influences. He spoke so often in front of the Siva temple near the Jaffna marketplace that a pavilion was built there for him to address the crowds.

Kadaitswami had several disciples. One was a long-haired, saffron-robed swami, Sadaya Varathar, who founded a Saiva Siddhanta center, called Samaya Achariya Aadheenam, in the village of Erlalai. Another was Mahadevaswami, who founded an Advaita center in Kandy. Two other disciples established Advaita and Sakta organizations. Foremost among the disciples of Kadaitswami was Chellappaswami, the next Satguru in the paramparai.

The stories about Kadaitswami's siddhis are many. It is said that one day while walking, he came across a dead cat by the road. He touched it with his foot and told it to get up. The cat stood up and walked away. There are accounts of his having disappeared and appeared elsewhere, drunk boiling wax, turned iron into gold, turned liquor into honey and honey into liquor. Kadaitswami's siddhis were well-known, but he never made of them a mere performance. He used his powers judiciously to awaken people to greater realities, greater truths.

On one occasion, he entered a shop to beg a few coins for tea. The shopkeeper thought, "I'll have some fun with this old beggar." He took off his diamond ring, hid both hands behind his back and told Kadaitswami that if he could guess which hand the ring was in, he could have it. Of course, the man had no intention of giving him the ring. Kadaitswami surprised him with his answer. "It is in neither hand," he said. The shopkeeper laughed loudly, but when he opened his hands the ring was gone! Kadaitswami left the shop and wandered away. The merchant followed him, not knowing what else to do. A minute later Kadaitswami turned around and spat the ring on the ground. The shopkeeper was transfixed, dumbfounded. Kadaitswami just smiled. "Now you are caught," he said and walked away. Kadaitswami's left the earthly plane in 1875. His mahasamadhi shrine is in Jaffna, built by his disciples according to his instructions.

Siva Chellappaswami

Chellappaswami was born in 1840 in Jaffna town. *Chellappa* means "wealthy father." As a child, he was introverted and spent much of his time alone. He was a young man, about nineteen, when he first met Kadaitswami, who later initiated him as the next Satguru in the line by placing in his hands a large rupee coin wrapped in a betel leaf. Chellappaswami spent most of his time at the Nallur Kandaswami Koyil, a Muruga temple a few miles from Jaffna. In the temple compound is a tall building, called the *theradi,* where the huge wooden chariot used in festival parades is kept. By the steps of the theradi was a shady *bilva* tree. This was Chellappaswami's favorite place. He would stay there for days and months at a time, immersed in contemplation.

After his initiation, the awakening of the chakras and kundalini shakti caused Chellappaswami's behavior to be even more eccentric than before. His profound communion with God made it impossible for him to behave as most men do. He was ablaze with spiritual power, so much so that many feared him. To them, it was like looking directly into the noonday sun. He would not brook the presence of ordinary men and chased them away when they came near, preserving the solitude of his simple compound near the temple.

Chellappaswami wore simple clothing and wandered about as he pleased, taking frequent long walks. Striding powerfully through the countryside or seated by the bilva tree, he would talk aloud to himself as if he were the only person in the world. It was the divine soliloquy of a sage who saw himself as one with Siva, the Self of the whole universe. For him there was no second person, only That which is the Being within all beings. Few people understood the spiritual greatness of this recluse who lived above the din of common life, aloof and detached. He made no concessions to the world, but was ever himself. He was a tall, strong man, and a stranger to fear and desire.

The Western view of the spiritual man is somewhat external, depicting the saint, the man who is outwardly perfected. The Eastern perception tends to be more internalized, caring not so much for appearances as for inner attainment. Thus, the saint is kind, humble and devout on the

outside while he may suffer internally from despair and separation from his God. The sage, on the other hand, may be
common in outer appearance, even unkempt, while inside
he is bathed in pure light and unity. Chellappaswami was
such a sage, the rarest of the rare among human souls, a siddhar, though he did not openly display his powers.

Only a few devotees ever drew close to Chellappaswami.
He was too powerful for most. One who stayed at his side
was Siva Yogaswami, whom he trained for about five years
and then initiated. Chellappaswami attained Mahasamadhi
in March of 1915. The most beautiful descriptions of him by
far are the songs that Siva Yogaswami sang in his later years.

Chellappaswami did not teach by lectures. His was a pragmatic teaching, driven home to his disciple through practical lessons, often on long walks. The few formal teachings he
did offer came in short statements, spoken in the Tamil language, containing the unadorned essence of his awakened
thought. Often he would repeat one of these gems to himself
over and over again, for months at a time, making of it a
sacred mantram. His four most revered statements are known
today as *mahavakiam*, or "great sayings:"

> *There is no intrinsic evil.* ஒரு பொல்லாப்பும் இல்லை
> *It was all finished long ago.* எப்போதோ முடிந்த காரியம்
> *All that is, is Truth.*
> *We know not.* நாம் அறியோம்.

Siva Yogaswami

Siva Yogaswami was born on May 29th, 1872, in Mavidda-
puram, Sri Lanka. His mother died young, and he was raised
by his father's sister in the village of Columbuthurai, near
Jaffna town. As an adult, he worked as a storekeeper in a
government service irrigation project in another village.
During these years, he devoted every available moment to
religious pursuits—meditating, singing devotional hymns

and studying the Saivite scriptures, many of which he knew by heart. His spiritual awakening and burning desire to realize God so consumed him that he finally quit his occupation in his early thirties to devote himself entirely to his spiritual quest.

At about that time he met Chellappaswami at Nallur Temple. Yogaswami later sang many songs about their first meeting. Yogaswami was walking past the temple when Chellappa laughed loudly and yelled, "Do you know who you are?" The question went deep, and in that moment, Yogaswami was filled with light and understanding. He was with Chellappaswami for five years after that and was initiated by him following a forty-day fast and meditation.

After Yogaswami's initiation, he was on a foot pilgrimage around the entire island of Sri Lanka for over a year. He returned to take up residence under an *illupai* (olive) tree in Columbuthurai, across the road from a Ganesha temple. The years that followed were to see him locked in the practice of raja-kundalini yoga. Yogaswami had relinquished all ordinary desire, and his mind was consumed by meditation. For days and weeks on end, even in inclement weather, he could be found seated at the foot of the illupai tree in dispassionate repose. For several years, he followed the regimen of meditating for four days straight, then walking about and eating on the fifth day, before returning to his yogic disciplines.

After repeated requests from villagers concerned with his exposure to the elements, he moved into a simple hut built for him in a corner of the compound of a nearby family. That was around 1914. The next fifty years of his life were to be spent in this humble adobe hut with earthen floor and thatched roof. He was unapproachable at first, but as time passed, a few devotees were permitted near. As the years progressed, it became the popular ashram of one of the greatest spiritual figures to ever grace the tropical expanses of Sri Lanka.

People of all walks of life, all nations, came for his darshan—young and old, peasants and prime ministers, judges,
doctors, politicians, seekers all. One-time pilgrims and daily devotees would sit together at the master's feet, on woven
mats spread for the occasion, generally in the evening. He
would talk about the Saivite path, about the saints and sages
of yore and about his vision of a unified Vedanta-Siddhanta
philosophy. Together, master and devotees sang devotional
hymns, he in his melodious and penetrating voice. He would
discourse on the profound as well as the mundane or sit in
meaningful silence with his visitors. Satguru Yogaswami
stressed the traditional path to all who came, reaffirming the
eternal teachings of the Sanatana Dharma. It was in this
humble hermitage that he initiated an American disciple in
1949—Gurudeva Sivaya Subramuniyaswami. Prescriptions
given to devotees differed, for he offered not a common rem-
edy but precisely what was needed. To one he would give
yoga sadhana, while enjoining another to awaken bhakti and
devotion. "Different medicines for different ailments," he
would say.

Siva Yogaswami wore only the simplest of white cloth,
unsewn and unadorned by even the smallest amount of col-
or. A tall man, robust and full of stamina, he would walk for
twenty or more miles each day, through the paddy fields,
along the village lanes, his white beard and hair glistening in
the tropical sun, which he kept at bay with a black umbrel-
la. Rising before dawn, Yogaswami would perform a guru
puja, honoring the Tiruvadi (holy sandals) of his beloved
master. Like the others in his preceptorial line, Siva Yogaswami was a yogi and Natha siddhar. His years of intense
spiritual practices awakened many inner faculties, though,
unlike Kadaitswami, whose mission it was to display his
powers, Yogaswami would never speak of such things. His
devotees observed, however, that he always knew who was
coming to visit him before they arrived and knew everyone's

thoughts before they were spoken. Nothing was hidden from his inner sight. Whenever tape recordings were made of his singing or speaking, they came out blank. Sometimes this happened with photographs, too. Toward the latter part of his life, he was even more consciously awakened to the inner planes and often saw and spoke to the devas and Mahadevas of the Second and Third Worlds in the presence of devotees.

Satguru Siva Yogaswami sang many beautiful songs in his lifetime. They came to him from within, often when alone or spontaneously as a gift to a devotee whose home he might visit. These inspired verses were later collected together and published by devotees as *Natchintanai*, which means "good thoughts." He constantly encouraged devotees in many kinds of social works in the community, keeping everyone busy. In 1935 he had some of his devotees begin a monthly religious publication, called "Sivathondan Journal." In 1953 he established a spiritual center in Jaffna called the Sivathondan Society. *Sivathondan* means "a devoted servant of Lord Siva." This was a central theme of our Paramaguru—to work for God, selflessly and industriously. Work is worship, he taught.

Siva Yogaswami spoke often of spreading Saivism in the West, of building a bridge between East and West. In 1963 he organized a mission of five of his devotees, charging them with taking the teachings of Saiva Siddhanta to England, saying, "This voice will be heard in America." Siva Yogaswami attained Mahasamadhi on March 24th, 1964, at the age of ninety-one. A few of his central teachings can be found in *Dancing with Siva*.

Gurudeva Sivaya Subramuniyaswami

Gurudeva was twenty-two years old at the time of his initiation into the holy orders of sannyas in 1949. He had surrendered the world for the spirit. His quest for the Self had taken him to India and then Sri Lanka in 1947. There, in the

Caves of Jalani, deep within the central jungles, having renounced all worldly possessions, determined to know the
transcendent Parasivam spoken of in scripture and by his
teachers, he fasted and meditated until his yogic disciplines
brought him into full enlightenment.

Following that transforming experience, the young pil-
grim was taken by a Tamil elder to the Jaffna peninsula,
there to meet Siva Yogaswami in his simple thatched hut in
the village of Columbuthurai on the full moon day in May
of 1949. Gurudeva was twenty-two. Siva Yogaswami, his Satguru, was seventy-seven. Siva Yogaswami instructed him in
the Panchakshara Mantram, gave him powerful directions
for his life's mission and initiated him into the Natha siddhar line with a tremendous slap on the back, saying, "This
will be heard in America! Now go 'round the world and roar
like a lion. You will build palaces and feed thousands." The
local people later called this rare act a "coronation."

Obeying his Guru's instructions, Gurudeva returned to
America. He then spent seven years in continued sadhana
preparing for the work to come. In the wake of his samadhi,
he burst into a series of kundalini experiences which culminated in the profound aphorisms of the book *Raja Yoga*.
Daily sadhana and intense meditation filled the years to follow and brought forth inner faculties of clairvoyance,
clairaudience and other siddhis.

In 1957, at the age of thirty, Gurudeva founded the Himalayan Academy and opened America's first Hindu temple,
in California. There he gave regular weekly inspired talks
and seminars for over twelve years. These were the years of
his public mission and outreach ministry in North America,
of lecture tours throughout the country, of teaching men
and women of all religious persuasions the various yogas and
advaitic precepts of Saiva Siddhanta.

During these early years, Gurudeva established the Saiva
Siddhanta Yoga Order and took into his monastic commu-

nity the first aspirants, training them strictly in the ancient meditative and mystical arts. In 1969 and again in 1972, he pilgrimaged to India and Sri Lanka, taking with him approximately seventy devotees to visit sacred temples and illumined sages. From 1967 to 1983, fourteen such Innersearch Pilgrimages were made to all parts of the world—Satguru and devotees traveling, discussing and meditating together in Japan, Tahiti, India, Sri Lanka, Hawaii, Russia, Switzerland and other parts of Europe.

In 1970 Gurudeva established Kauai Aadheenam, his monastery-temple complex and the international headquarters of Saiva Siddhanta Church on the Hawaiian island of Kauai, midway between the East and the West. Here he founded the Kadavul Hindu Temple and in 1973 installed a six-foot bronze image of Lord Kadavul Nataraja, to whom he had been introduced at the age of ten. This was the first Siva temple built in the United States. Besides establishing his monastery there, Gurudeva brought much to the remote island of Kauai. His monks revived the beekeeping industry, introduced Toggenberg goats and Jersey cows, and gathered from the corners of the world the largest collection of ginger and heliconia plants—over 500 species.

In 1975 Gurudeva had a series of potent visions of Lord Siva that empowered a 10-acre spiritual refuge on Kauai, called the San Marga Sanctuary. Its gardens, groves and temple are open to truth seekers of all paths. In 1979 Gurudeva founded the international newspaper, *Hinduism Today*, which he publishes and his monks design and write to keep Hindus and seekers worldwide informed about mankind's oldest faith. This monthly paper has become Hinduism's most influential English-language journal, published simultaneously in North America, Malaysia, Mauritius, South Africa, Fiji and Europe. Throughout the 1970's Gurudeva worked to help numerous institutions plan and build their temples in North America, providing sacred images, support, inspiration and practical advice in their efforts. Soon Hindu temples began to appear in unprecedented numbers in such diverse communities as Edmonton, Denver, Chicago, Bethesda, Livermore, Fiji, Houston, Fremont, London, Mauritius and elsewhere.

During 1979–1983, Gurudeva was away from the United States for five months, speaking to over 400,000 devotees in Sri Lanka, Malaysia, Mauritius, England, Africa and North and South India and Nepal about the glories of Saivism, the need for brotherhood and solidarity among all Hindus and seekers who have embraced the Hindu path, and the urgency of living a dynamic, fearless spiritual life right here, right now.

In 1983 he was invited to the island nation of Mauritius— where Hindu dharma was dying and being encroached upon by missionaries of other faiths—to establish a monastery-temple complex. The seven-acre facility, with its commercial mango and coconut groves, lies on the banks of a river overlooking the ocean and beaches below. It also serves the people of the French island of Reunion. In that same year he was hosted in South Africa by the Saiva Sithantha Sungum, speaking to Indian communities in a nation perched on the edge of historical changes.

During 1983 and 1984, he organized the largest Sri Lanka Refugee Relief Fund outside of the war-torn nation, providing homes, jobs, medical facilities, food and tools for thousands of needy people.

In 1985 he brought the desktop technology of Apple Macintosh computers into the publishing of Hindu books and journals. His religious publishing institution, Himalayan Academy Publications, was the first to have the largest desktop publishing network in the USA. The work of his monks won awards for professional graphics and typography. Using these tools, he published hundreds of thousands of books, pamphlets, sacred art masterpieces, lessons and scriptural translations on all aspects of Hindu dharma and distributed them in hundreds of communities in thirty nations that are working for the resurgence of their faith.

In August of 1986, the World Religious Parliament in New Delhi honored five Hindu spiritual leaders outside of India who had most dynamically promoted Sanatana Dharma in the past twenty-five years. Gurudeva was one of these noble souls, recognized for their international efforts to lead the Hindu renaissance. He was given the title Jagadachariya, or "World Teacher."

In May of 1987, Gurudeva opened the Palaniswami Sivan Temple in Concord, California, just thirty-five miles northeast of San Francisco, now the cultural center for hundreds of families immigrated from India and Sri Lanka and American Hindus as well.

In August of 1987, he located and brought to Kauai the world's largest, perfectly formed, six-sided crystal, weighing over 700 pounds. This rare Siva Lingam is being worshiped in the Kadavul Hindu Temple, awaiting the completion of the hand-carved, stone Iraivan Temple where it will be installed in the innermost sanctum on the San Marga Sanctuary adjacent to his Hawaii monastery.

In April of that same year, Gurudeva was selected to represent Hinduism at the prestigious Global Forum of Spiritual and Parliamentary Leaders for Human Survival, held in Oxford, England. For five days, two hundred world spiritual and political leaders—of nearly every faith and nation—met in private sessions to discuss ways that mankind's future could be assured. The conference so deeply impressed the Soviets that they offered to sponsor a second Global Forum on Human Survival in Moscow from January 11 to 15, 1990. Again Gurudeva was among those chosen to share the Hindu view of nature and survival to the assembly of 700 spiritual and political leaders from eighty-nine nations, who focused this time more directly on environmental issues. He

brought the eternal Hindu teachings of tolerance and ahimsa, nonviolence, to the world community and spoke on
global education. Mikhail Gorbachev attended the final ses-
sion at the Kremlin, as 2,500 world leaders listened to Swami
Paramananda Bharati intone a Vedic prayer for peace and
joined him in chanting the "Om" three times in unison.

Sivaya Subramuniyaswami lives today at his remote monastery on the sacred Wailua River on Hawaii's northernmost
island with his monastics. He continues to write about the
mystical Saivite teachings and to be outspoken in his support of Hindu revivalism. His discourses, writings and jour-
neys away from the tropical island come, he says, from
"inner orders." He continues to fulfill his Satguru's command
to "roar like a lion, build palaces and feed thousands" with
the nourishment of spirituality. This ends a short biography
of an unfinished life of inner purpose and cosmic vision, a
life given to helping others to "Know thy Self by thyself"
and thus experience Siva's cosmic dance personally.

Glossary

aadheenam: A Hindu monastery-temple complex in the South Indian Saivite tradition. Also referred to by the general terms *madam, math* and *peedam.*

abhishekam: Ritual bathing, ablution of the Deity image (or a person, or other sacred implement) with substances prescribed by Agamic scripture: water, curd, milk, honey, ghee, rosewater, etc. The cascade of substances, each with its own unique chemo-electric and astral properties, serves to channel the divine energies.

Absolute: The ultimate Reality, Parasivam, denoted by the upper case *A.* It is absolute because it is its own source and it is utterly non-relational to all strata of mind consciousness, from Satchidananda to the physical cosmos. It is the undefinable That beyond cause, time, form and space.

Absolute Reality: *Absolute, Absolute Being* and *Absolute Reality* are used synonymously to depict the unmanifest, unchanging and transcendent Parasivam. It is Truth, which is timeless, formless and spaceless, the ultimate essence of man's soul, the Self God.

absolutely real: A term describing God Siva in all three perfections: Parasivam, Satchidananda, Mahesvara. As such, He is uncreated, unchanging, unevolutionary. From Him, all that is relatively real blossoms into manifestation.

absorption: To take in and make part of an existent whole. An alternative term to *destruction* in describing the third of God Siva's five powers: creation, preservation, destruction, revealing grace and veiling grace.

adharma: That which is "not dharma." Thoughts, words and deeds which transgress God's divine laws and the natural conscience of the soul. Adharma creates negative karma and keeps the individual ego-centered, in a low instinctive-intellectual mind state.

advaita: "Not two." Non-duality; monism; philosophical premise that reality is ultimately one. The opposite of dvaita or dualism.

Advaita Siddhanta: "Non-dual final conclusions." Designates an Agamic philosophy that has at its core a non-dual identity of God, soul and world. Same as English term, "monistic theism."

Advaita Vedanta: "Non-dual conclusions of the Vedas." One of several names given to Adi Sankara's *mayavada* (illusion view) philosophy. Distinguishes his school from five other popular interpretations of Vedanta.

affirmation: A positive statement usually consisting of one or several simple sentences repeated over and over again with intense concentration on the meaning and images conveyed by the statement.

Agama: "That which has come down." Joins Vedas in forming *sruti* (revealed scripture) for many Hindu sects. Earliest known Agamas were Saivite, recorded in the first millennium BCE. The Sakta and Vaishnava Agamas came later. While the Vedas express metaphysical principles and are considered general, the Agamas, which detail worship as well as yoga for the attainment of liberation, are considered specific. The Agamas are the source of puja and temple worship, and contain instructions for temple architecture and sculpture.

Agamic: Of or relating to the Agamas, which along with the Vedas are Hinduism's central scriptures, held as revealed scripture by nearly all major denominations.

Aghora: "Non-terrifying"—a name of God Siva meaning light, the absence of darkness or ignorance.

Agni: Fire God; the being of the element fire, invoked through Vedic-Agamic fire ritual known as *homa, havan* or *yagna.*

ahimsa: "Noninjury." *Ahimsa* is refraining from causing harm to others, physically, mentally or emotionally. *Ahimsa* is the first and most important of the ten yamas of ashtanga yoga, the cardinal virtue upon which all others depend.

Aja: "Not born; existing from eternity." A name of Siva. From the Rig Veda, referring to the uncreated First Being.

akasha: "Non-visible." Inner sky, or ether. A broad term referring to the fifth of five elements—earth, air, fire, water and akasha—comprising physical reality. It is perceived as the rarified space or fluid plasma that pervades the universe. Even more subtly, *akasha* names the inner mind or superconscious stratum. It is through psychic penetration into the akasha that great cosmic knowledge is gathered and the entire circle of time—past, present and future—can be known.

ananda: "Bliss." The pure joy of God-consciousness or spiritual experience. Also, a word used to describe all-pervasive Divinity, as in the term *Satchidananda.*

anava: The ego, sense of "I" and "mine," ignorance; separation from God. Denotes a sense of finitude and individuality. Derived from *anu,* meaning an atom or something exceedingly small. One of the three malas or bondages: anava, karma and maya. Anava is the cause of the soul's mistaken sense of separation from God Siva, and is the last bond broken at union, Self-Realization.

anbe: "Love." From *anbu,* a Tamil word for love.

anchorite: "Hermit." A person who lives alone and apart from society for religious meditation, as opposed to serving as a member of a religious order in a monastery or convent.

angel: The Western counterpart of *deva*. Comes from the Greek *angelos*, meaning "messenger."

aniconic: "Without likeness or image." Thus, *aniconic image* denotes a symbolic form which, though it refers to a Deity, does not attempt an anthropomorphic form or representational likeness. An example in the Hindu tradition is the Siva Lingam representing the Absolute God. *Aniconic* can also refer to any religious tradition that does not engage in image worship.

ankusa: Lord Ganesha's goad, symbolizing His power to remove obstacles from our path.

Appar: "Father." Endearing name for Tirunavukkarasu (7th century CE), one of four principle Tamil saints. A convert from Jainism, he led errant Saivites who had embraced Jainism back to Siva. Appar exemplified doing service within the temple, fervently preached and sang the greatness of God Siva in Tamil Nadu.

Aranyakas: "Books of the forest." Third section of each of the four Vedas. Esoteric, mystical knowledge on the inner meanings and functions of the Vedic yajna or fire ceremonies.

arati: Flame, usually ghee, camphor or oil lamps, waved before a holy person or the temple Deity image at the height of a puja as a means of psychically catalyzing the flow of sakti. The lamp is then passed to all devotees present, each one passing his hands through the flame and bringing it to his eyes, thereby receiving the blessings or sakti. Also refers to the performance of such rites. Arati may also constitute an abbreviated form of puja.

archana: A special, abbreviated puja done in the name of an individual devotee or family to invoke guidance and blessings. Archana specifically refers to chanting the names of the Deity during the puja.

Ardhanarisvara: "Half-female Lord." The right half of this murthi is male and the left half is female, esoterically symbolizing the merging of the ida and pingala forces. Ardhanarisvara is Lord Siva as the androgynous God in whom all apparent opposites are reconciled; the murthi representing His perfection of Satchidananda, or Pure Consciousness.

asana: "Seat or posture." Position or posture used in hatha yoga and meditation; the third of Patanjali's eight limbs of yoga. *Padmasana* ("lotus" or cross-legged pose) is a famed example, though many other postures exist which balance the energies of mind and body, promoting both health and serenity. Also refers to the mat or place on which the seeker sits during meditation. An important dimension of Natha sadhana.

ascetic: A person who leads a life of contemplation and rigorous self-denial for religious purposes.

asceticism: The practices of an ascetic, such as self-denial, self-discipline, tapas, fasting, silence, etc. Also, the religious doctrine that one can reach a higher spiritual state by such practices.

ash: Whitish, finely powdered ash integral to Saivite worship and used for sectarian marks worn on the forehead. (Often "holy ash.")

ashram: "A place of striving." Holy sanctuary; abode or residence of a sadhu, saint, ascetic or guru engaged in religious instruction.

ashrama: Any of the four stages into which a person's life is divided according to Vedic teachings.

ashrama dharma: That dharma (way of righteousness) which expresses the natural unfoldment of the body, mind and emotions through four stages of life: student, householder, elder advisor and religious solitaire.

ashtanga yoga: "Eight-limbed union." The classical raja yoga system of eight progressive stages or steps as described in numerous Hindu scriptures including various Upanishads, the *Tirumantiram* by Saint Tirumular and the *Yoga Sutras* of Sage Patanjali. The eight limbs are: restraints (*yama*), observances (*niyama*), postures (*asana*), breath control (*pranayama*), sense withdrawal (*pratyahara*), concentration (*dharana*), meditation (*dhyana*) and contemplation (*samadhi*).

astral body: "Body of the stars." A subtle, non-physical sheath sometimes known as the emotional body. The astral body is the third most dense of the five interpenetrating bodies or sheaths (known in Sanskrit as *koshas),* through which the soul functions in various planes or strata of consciousness.

astral plane: The subtle, non-physical plane in the Second World where souls function in their astral bodies.

astral: "Of the stars." Belonging to the subtle, non-physical dimension of the Second World. "Astral forces" exist in the Second World but can be felt psychically in the First.

asura: "Not spiritual." A Second World being living on the lower astral plane, sometimes called a "demon." Such beings are capable of interacting with the First World Earth consciousness, causing both major and minor problems in people's lives. However, asuras evolve too and are not permanently in this state.

asuric: Of the nature of an asura, "not spiritual."

Atharva Veda: "Wisdom of Atharva"—name of the individual mythically held to be most responsible for the composition of this fourth Veda. Also a name of Siva. Considered the last Veda recorded, the Atharva consists of 20 books with 720 hymns.

atma: "Breath." The soul, including the individual soul body and its essence, Satchidananda and Parasivam, in contrast with the outer self of individuality and personality with which a person commonly identifies.

atmartha puja: Personal Hindu ritual and worship performed by a devotee in the home shrine to invoke God and the Gods. Communal worship is called parartha puja.

Aum Tat Sat: "Aum, That is Truth." A phrase which appears in Hindu sacerdotal chants, often at the finale. A famous Vedic *mahavakiam,* or "great saying."

Aum: Mystic syllable of Hinduism, identified in the Upanishads as standing for the whole world and its parts, including past, present and future, as well as for *Paramatma,* the Self of all things. "Aum" is the seed sound, the one undifferentiated primal vibration from which all manifestation issues forth. Associated with Lord Ganesha. Pronounced: "ah," "oo," "mm."

aura: A subtle, luminous energy field radiating within and around the human body as far as three to seven feet.

auspicious: Favorable, of good omen, boding well for the future. Hindu astrology defines a sacred calendar, noting times that are favorable for various human endeavors. Much of daily Hindu life and religious practice revolves around the concept of auspiciousness.

avatar: "He who descends." A divine incarnation of God; a central theological belief of the Vaishnavite denominations, though not accepted in Saivism.

Ayurveda: Hindu medical system that prevents or cures ill-health and disease through adjustment of subtle and gross body physiology by using herbs and minerals.

Being: When capitalized, *Being* is equivalent to God, or to God Siva in all three perfections as a one single totality. Sometimes refers to all that exists as a divine totality.

bhajan: Spiritual song. Individual or group singing of devotional songs, hymns and chants.

bhakta: A devotee, also *bhaktar.*

bhakti: Devotion; the expression of love for and surrender to God.

bhakti yoga: "Union through devotion." Bhakti yoga is the practice of devotional disciplines, worship, prayer, chanting and singing with the aim of awakening love in the heart. Bhakti may be directed toward God, Gods or one's spiritual preceptor.

Bhuloka: "Earth (bhur) world (loka)." The physical world perceived through the five senses. Also called the First World, as it is the first and least subtle of the three worlds, the other two being the De-valoka (Second World or subtle plane) and the Sivaloka (Third World or causal plane).

bilva: Bael; species of tree sacred to Lord Siva.

birthstar: The nakshatra (asterism) the moon is in line with at the time of a one's birth.

Brahma: God Siva in the aspect of Creator of the Universe; one of the Hindu Trinity.

brahmachari: An unmarried, male spiritual aspirant who prac-tices continence, observes religious disciplines, including sadhana, devotion, service and teaching, and who may be under simple vows.

brahmacharini: An unmarried, female spiritual aspirant who practices continence, observes religious disciplines, often relating to devotion, service and teaching, and who may be under simple vows.

brahmachariya: "Godly conduct." Brahmachariya, among the ethical restraints known as the *yamas*, means sexual purity—the re-straint of lust and other aspects of the instinctive nature.

Brahman: A name for God or Supreme Deity in the *Vedas*. De-scriptions of Brahman include the Transcendent Absolute, the All-Pervading energy, as well as the Supreme Lord or Primal Soul.

Brahmanas: One of three parts of the ritual section of a Veda; con-cerned with details of sacrificial fire worship (see *homa*) and with spe-cific duties and rules of conduct.

brahmin: First and highest of the four main castes of the ancient Vedic social system of India, which still persists today, even though caste discrimination is prohibited in India. Vedic scripture and certain Hindu dharma shastras invest the brahmin caste with the responsibil-ity of religious leadership, including teaching and priestly duties.

breath: Scriptural metaphor used extensively in the *Upanishads* to convey God's creative impulse, as in, "He created the worlds; He breathed out the Vedas."

Buddhism: The religion based on the teachings of Siddhartha Gautama, known as Buddha. He refuted the idea of man's having an immortal soul and did not preach of any Supreme Deity. Instead he taught that man should seek freedom from greed, hatred and delu-sion, and enlightenment through realizing the Four Noble Truths and following the Eightfold Path.

caste: A hierarchical social system established in India in ancient times by Vedic brahmin priests, now unconstitutional in India, though still extant. One's caste was determined by heredity and occupation.

causal body: "Body which causes." The innermost body (or being) of man—a self-effulgent body of light known in Sanskrit as the *anan-*

damaya kosha. The source of all other bodies or sheaths of the soul. Same as soul body.

causal plane: Highest plane of existence, from which all other planes emanate. The Third World or Sivaloka.

chakra: "Wheel." *Chakra* names any of the centers of force and consciousness located within the inner bodies of man. Nerve plexes, ganglia and glands corresponding to principle chakras are located in the physical body. Situated along the spinal cord from its base to the cranial chamber are the seven principle chakras, psychically seen as colorful, multi-petalled lotuses. Many more exist in humans, including seven chakras located below the base of the spine which give rise to instinctive consciousness. This makes fourteen major chakras in all, which are listed below, beginning from the very lowest, each with its corresponding location and major quality.

chakra	location	attribute
patala	soles of feet	malice
mahatala	feet	consciencelessness
rasatala	ankles	selfishness
talatala	calves	confused thinking
sutala	knees	jealousy
vitala	thighs	anger
atala	hips	fear
muladhara	base of spine	memory
svadhisthana	below navel	reason
manipura	solar plexus	willpower
anahata	heart center	cognition
vishuddha	throat	divine love
ajna	third eye	divine sight
sahasrara	crown of head	illumination

chariya: "Good conduct." Service; living life according to traditional codes of ethical conduct.

chariya marga: "Path of service." First of the four successive stages (margas) of spiritual unfoldment and practice in Saiva Siddhanta— chariya, kriya, yoga and jnana. In chariya the devotee serves God through selfless service, known as *karma yoga* or *Sivathondu.* Traditional acts of chariya include cleaning the temple, lighting lamps and collecting flowers for worship.

Chellappaswami: "Wealthy father." Reclusive siddhar who was Satguru of Siva Yogaswami. Lived 1840–1915 on the Jaffna peninsula of Sri Lanka, dwelling in a small hut near the Nallur Kandaswamy (Muruga) Temple.

Chit: Consciousness, knowing or pure knowledge. In Saiva Siddhanta, used to describe God Siva's Divine Mind. Not to be confused with *chitta,* the subconscious mind.

church: A structured religious organization whose members believe and worship alike, forming a congregation. Also names a place of worship. Under the guidance of a ministry, church members pursue their spiritual, social, cultural, educational and economic goals, both individually and collectively.

concealing grace: An alternative term for God Siva's veiling grace, or *Tirodhana Sakti.*

conscious mind: The everyday, thinking state of mind. We function in the conscious mind during most of our waking hours. One of the five states of mind: conscious, subconscious, sub-subconscious, subsuperconscious and superconscious.

consciousness: Perception, awareness, apprehension. There are many layers or levels of consciousness, ranging from the ordinary, everyday consciousness of our body and mind to omniscient states of superconsciousness. Consciousness aware only of itself is Pure Consciousness.

contemplation: Superconsciousness. Profoundly deep state beyond meditation where consciousness is functioning in the superconscious mind state with zero awareness of the physical, astral or mental bodies. Natural mind state of the soul.

creation: The act of creating, especially the act of bringing the world into ordered existence. First of the five powers of God Siva: creation, preservation, destruction, veiling grace and revealing grace. God Siva creates out of Himself, through emanation. *Creation* also refers to all of created existence, the cosmos.

Creator: He who brings about creation. Term for God Siva in His aspect of *Brahma.* Siva using the first of His five powers: creation, preservation, destruction, veiling grace and revealing grace.

crown chakra: The seventh chakra, or psychic nerve plexus, located at the top of the head. Called *sahasrara* in Sanskrit, this 1,008-petalled chakra is the seat of transcendental consciousness.

darshan: "Auspicious sight;" vision of the divine—physically or psychically. Can refer to the seeing of a temple image (murthi), a holy person or place, or to a psychic vision of a God. Also a "point of view" or philosophical position.

Deepavali: "Festival of Lights" (also known as "Divali"). During this very popular home-community festival, Hindus of all denominations light oil or electric lights and set off fireworks in a joyful celebration of the victory of goodness over evil, light over darkness.

Destroyer: He who brings about destruction. Term for God Siva in His aspect of *Rudra*. Siva using the third of His five powers: creation, preservation, destruction, veiling grace and revealing grace.

destruction: Process of breaking down into lesser or constituent or fundamental parts. Third of the five powers of God Siva: creation, preservation, destruction, veiling grace and revealing grace. Such destruction is better understood as transformation, the constant resolution of forms into their composite elements, and ultimately the absorption of worlds and souls in Siva, likened to rivers merging into their source, the ocean.

deva: "Shining one." A Second World being living in the higher astral plane in a subtle body.

Devaloka: "The world (loka) of light-beings (devas)." The higher region of the subtle plane, where souls live in their astral or mental bodies. It exists within (rather than above or beyond) the physical world, known as the First World or the Bhuloka.

devonic: Happening in association with or under the influences of the devas in the higher Second World. Implies that something is divinely guided.

devotee: A person strongly dedicated to something or someone, such as to a God or a guru. Often used interchangeably with *disciple,* though the latter term generally implies a deeper commitment.

dharma: Divine law; the law of being; defined broadly as the way of righteousness or "that which holds one's true nature." The fulfillment of an inherent nature or destiny. To "follow dharma" means to act in accordance with divine law.

dissolution: Dissolving or breaking up into parts. An alternative term for *destruction*, third of God Siva's five powers: creation, preservation, destruction, revealing grace and veiling grace.

Divali: See: *Deepavali.*

Dravidian: A sub-group of the Caucasoid race, primarily found in South India and Northern Sri Lanka. Also refers to the family of languages spoken by this group, including Tamil, Malayalam, Telegu, Kannada, etc.

dualism: See: *dualistic, dvaita.*

dualistic: Anything based on dualism, from the word *dual* meaning "of two," "composed of two parts." The term *dualistic* can apply to thoughts, concepts, writings, theories, philosophies or religions which postulate that existence is ultimately composed of, or explicable in terms of, two basic entities such as God and world, mind and matter. Opposite of monism. Also, doctrines which hold that there are two opposite principles in the universe, e.g., good and evil.

duality: Something having or composed of two parts or kinds.

Durga: "The Incomprehensible One." Sakti, the Universal Mother. God Siva seen in feminine form. Usually depicted as ten-armed and riding a lion. Prayers are offered to Durga evoking strength, health and eradication of impurities.

dvaita: Dualism; any philosophy which posits two fundamental realities. God and man are considered to be eternally separate from each other in dvaita philosophies.

ego: The external personality or sense of "I" and "mine." Broadly, the individual's identity as outwardly perceived. In Saiva Siddhanta, the ego is equated with the *anava mala,* or that which limits man's consciousness, giving a feeling of individuality and separateness from God.

eight-limbed yoga: See: *ashtanga yoga.*

emanation: To "flow out from." In Saiva Siddhanta philosophy, God Siva creates and *is* His creation. Siva's creation of the world from Himself is described in scripture as being similar to "sparks issuing forth from fire" or "a web from a spider." This vision of cosmic creation contrasts with other views such as "creation out of nothing" (Judeo-Christian), or non-creation—a view in which reality is permanent and always existing (Meykandar Saiva Siddhanta and other dualist and pluralist schools).

enlightenment: Self-Realization or God-Realization, samadhi without seed (Nirvikalpa Samadhi); the ultimate attainment. The realization or non-experience of That which exists beyond space, time and form as Parasivam.

ether: Used most often to translate *akasha.* Most subtle of the five elements (earth, air, water, fire and ether) which make up the physical universe.

etheric body: A general term for the inner being of man, excluding the physical body or sheath, but including all other bodies in which the soul is functioning.

fate: The power or agency supposed to determine the outcome of events before they occur. From the Latin: *fatum,* "prophetic declaration, oracle." According to Hindu thought, man is not ruled by fate, but he is impelled by the laws of the universe (dharma), and by the impetus of his own past actions (karma).

First World: The physical universe of gross or material substance in which phenomena are perceived by the five senses.

formless: Without outer configuration; beyond form (not the same as *amorphous,* which implies a form that is vague or changing), transcending the realm in which all things conform to the laws of form. Used in attempting to describe the indescribable Absolute which is "timeless, formless and spaceless."

Ganapati: "Leader of the ganas." A name of the elephant-faced Deity, Lord Ganesha.

ganas: A troop of devas, especially used in reference to Lord Siva's attendants under the special superintendence of Lord Ganesha.

Ganesha: "Chief of the ganas." The elephant-faced Patron of Art and Science, first Son of Siva, Remover of Obstacles. A Mahadeva, or great God, created by Lord Siva to assist souls in their evolution.

garbagriha: The innermost chamber, or *sanctum sanctorum,* of a Hindu temple, wherein the primary Deity image is installed and through which the God's power is most centrally channeled.

Gayatri Mantram: Most famous Vedic mantram, used in puja and personal chanting. Transliteration: *Om bhur bhuvah suvah, tatsavitur varenyam, bhargo devasya dhimahi, dhiyo yo nah pracodayat.* Translation: "Oh Divine Beings of all three worlds, let us contemplate the resplendent form of our Divine Creator, the Primal One, Who, like the radiant sun, has the power to burn away all ignorance. May He grant us His grace and guide our intellects."

ghee: Clarified butter. The liquid butter remaining when butter from cow's milk or buffalo milk is melted, boiled and strained. An important item in homa rites.

God-Realization: A general term describing the direct and personal experience of identity in and with God Siva, ultimately realizing God Siva as Satchidananda and Parasivam. It is used loosely, and inaccurately, to describe a multiplicity of religious experiences including, but not limited to: seeing the inner light within oneself, seeing a vision of God or any of the Gods.

Godhead: God; Divinity. A term describing the essence of the Supreme Being.

Gods: Mahadevas, "Great Beings of Light." Extremely advanced beings existing in their self-effulgent soul bodies in the Sivaloka. Originally created by Siva, as all souls are, Gods have evolved to a constant superconsciousness as they govern, advance and assist all worlds. Gods are genderless, neither male nor female, but pure kundalini-energy beings.

gopuram: Temple entrance tower. Often several stories tall and adorned with ornate carvings and figures.

Gorakhnath Saivism: One of the six schools of Saivism; also referred to as *Siddha Siddhanta.* Extols Siva as immanent and transcendent. Path of Siva yoga for Siva identity. Strong emphasis on control over body and senses.

gotra: Family lineage; usually designated by the name of the family's patron rishi or preceptor.

grace: "Benevolence, love." Central religious concept denoting God's innate quality of giving and caring for creation.

grihastha: Householder; family man or woman. The period of human life following brahmachariya, or studentship, a phase of life when the individual establishes a career, home and family.

gross plane: The "First World" or physical universe.

gunas: "Qualities." Metaphysically, the gunas are fundamental cosmic qualities of nature. The three gunas are *tamas* (inertia, density, the force of contraction, resistance and dissolution), *rajas* (stimulation, restlessness, activity; the expansive energy of growth and movement) and *sattva* (quiescence; rarified, translucent, pervasive, reflecting the light of pure consciousness).

guru: "Remover of darkness;" guide. A teacher. Though it can connote a teacher of any subject, *guru* usually denotes a spiritual teacher or master.

Guru Purnima: "Full moon day of the guru"—name of the annual festival honoring the presence of one's personal guru and all true Satgurus. Occurs during the full moon in July/August.

guru paramparai: A line of spiritual gurus in authentic succession of initiation.

gurubhakti: A noun meaning the expression of devotion to the guru. Also, one who exhibits dedication to his spiritual master.

gurudeva: "The shining spiritual being who is the destroyer of darkness or ignorance." An affectionate, yet respectful term used to address the guru or spiritual master.

gurukulam: *Guru* means teacher. *Kulam* means family. *Gurukulam* usually refers to a training center where young boys come to live and learn in residence with their teacher.

hatha yoga: "Sun-moon yoga." The manipulation of the physical-astral bodies through specific asanas (postures) and mudras (hand positions).

heart chakra: The fourth chakra or psychic nerve plexus, governing cognition or understanding, located near the physical heart. In Sanskrit it is called *anahata.*

heaven: The celestial spheres, the Devaloka and the Sivaloka. The spiritual area of the inner worlds where souls rest and learn between births, and mature souls continue to evolve after completing their earthly incarnation cycle. The heaven world is also entered by incarnate souls during sleep and deep meditation for briefer periods.

hell: Narakaloka. An unhappy, mentally and emotionally congested, distressful area of consciousness.

Hindu: A follower of Hinduism. A term originally coined by the

Persians to describe the people of the Indus Valley and, by extension, the religions of these people.

Hinduism: Traditionally known as the Sanatana Dharma, "eternal faith," or the Vaidika Dharma, "religion of the Vedas." The world's most ancient religion, the only religion not founded by man, Hinduism encompasses a broad spectrum of philosophies ranging from pluralistic theism to absolute monism. There are three main sects: Saivism, Vaishnavism, Saktism—and liberal, non-sectarian forms, such as the Smarta Sampradaya.

Holi: Spring festival celebrated in the home and community during the month of Maasi (February-March). It is a time of expressing spontaneous feelings during which youth often playfully throw colorful powders on friends. Holi is also known as *Kamadahan,* mythologically the day on which Lord Siva burned Kama, the God of Love and Desire.

holy feet: "Tiruvadi." Respectful reference to the feet of the Satguru or any holy person. Also refers to the feet of Siva as the Primal Soul, Mahesvara. The guru's feet are especially sacred as they represent the point of contact of the divine and the physical spheres.

homa: A ceremony dating from Vedic times in which oblations are offered into a fire built according to scriptural injunctions; a ritual to communicate with God, Gods and devas. Also called *yajna* or *havan.*

human dharma: The natural expression and growth of the body, mind and emotions through four stages of life: student, householder, elder advisor and religious solitaire; also called *ashrama dharma.*

Iccha Sakti: Desire. One of Siva's three primary saktis or energies along with *Kriya* (action) and *Jnana* (wisdom), by which He administers His divine laws of dharma in all three worlds. These three are represented in the three prongs of Siva's Trisula or trident, the royal scepter of the Saiva Dharma.

ida: Inner body *nadi* current, pink in color, that flows downward, ending on the left side of the body. This current is feminine in nature, it is the essential physical-emotional energy.

immanent: Inherent. Living, remaining or operating within. In religion, *immanent* means present throughout the universe, said of God Siva. Easily confused with three other words: *imminent* (meaning about to happen or impending); *emanate* (meaning to come forth from); and *eminent,* (meaning high in rank).

incarnation: Endowment with a human body; appearance in human form. Usually refers to the soul taking a human birth. Also used in the term "Divine Incarnation" or *avatar,* meaning the taking of human birth by the Supreme Being to save mankind, a concept which is central to Vaishnavite philosophy but not accepted in Saivism.

Indra: Vedic God of rain and thunder, occasionally hailed as the warrior king of the devas.

inner bodies: The subtle bodies of man within the physical body. Specifically, the pranic, astral, mental and causal (or innermost soul) bodies. Conceived of as sheaths, one inside or interpenetrating the other.

instinctive: In a religious context, *instinctive* and *instinctiveness* are used to describe the lower animal instincts of human nature—for example: greed, hatred, anger, fear, lust, and jealousy.

intrinsic evil: Evil that is a real and innate part of the universe, such as the Christian notion of "original sin." In Saiva Siddhanta, there is no intrinsic evil. Rather, everything in the entire universe is essentially good. We only perceive certain things as intrinsically evil when we do not have a complete understanding.

intuition: Direct understanding, without the use of reason. The ability to perceive or know things without conscious reasoning but by direct cognition.

Isa: "Lord, master of all, superior, supremely powerful, commanding, reigning." *Isa* and its derivative *Isana* are very old names for God Siva found in the Rig Veda.

Jainism: An ancient religion of India based on the teachings of Mahavira (Great Hero), *circa* 500 BCE. The Jain Agamas teach great reverence for all life forms and strict codes of vegetarianism and renunciation for ascetics. Jainism's goal is to achieve realization of highest perfection of man, which in its original purity is free from all pain and bondage of birth and death.

japa: "Recitation." Japa is the spiritual practice of devotedly repeating a mantram (sacred syllables), often while counting the repetitions on a mala, or rosary. Japa may be done silently or aloud. Sometimes known as mantram yoga, it is one of the ten niyamas (practices) of ashtanga yoga, serving to quiet the mind prior to meditation.

Jayanthi: "Birthday." Generally refers to the birthday of the guru, a time of celebration for all disciples, of renewed commitments to one's preceptor.

jiva: The individual soul, or embodied atma; the soul identified with its outer sheaths—the physical, pranic, astral and mental bodies.

Jivanmukta: "Liberated soul," one who is free from the cycle of birth and death (samsara) while yet living. A great soul who has realized the Self God and is liberated before death from all liability to future births. *Jiva* refers to the embodied soul and *Mukti* to freedom or emancipation.

Jivanmukti: Liberation while yet living in a physical body; the attainment of freedom from future births.

jnana: Wisdom, yogic experiential knowledge of the highest order, including realization that God and soul are one. Last of the four successive stages (margas) of spiritual unfoldment and practice in Saiva Siddhanta—chariya, kriya, yoga and jnana.

Jnana Sakti: "Power of Wisdom." One of Siva's three primary Saktis or energies along with *Iccha* (desire or love) and *Kriya* (action), by which He administers His divine laws of dharma in all three worlds.

jnana marga: "Path, or stage, of wisdom or knowledge." Last of the four successive stages (margas) of spiritual unfoldment and practice in Saiva Siddhanta—chariya, kriya, yoga and jnana.

jnana yoga: "Union of knowledge." *Jnana yoga* describes the esoteric spiritual practices of the fully enlightened being, or jnani, who strives for repeated experiences of the Self God. An alternative meaning, put forward by Swami Vivekananda, is the quest for cognition through intellectual study, as one of four alternate paths along with bhakti yoga, karma yoga and raja yoga.

jnani: One who possesses *jnana*—"knowledge" or "wisdom." In its highest meaning, a knower of Parasivam, the Absolute Reality, realized through Nirvikalpa Samadhi, the culmination of the yoga marga (path of yoga).

Kadaitswami: "Marketplace swami." A Satguru in the Siva Yogaswami Guru Paramparai. Birthdate is unknown; died 1875. Believed to have renounced his career as a judge in South India, Kadaitswami became a sannyasin and trained under the nameless "Rishi from the Himalayas." He performed severe tapas on an island off the coast of Jaffna, Sri Lanka, attaining Sivajnana and awakening many siddhis. For decades he spurred the Sri Lankan Saivites to greater spirituality through his inspired talks and demonstration of siddhis. Initiated Chellappaswami as the next Satguru in the paramparai.

Kadavul: "Beyond-Within." An ancient Tamil name for Lord Siva; "He who is both immanent and transcendent, within and beyond."

Kailas: "Crystalline." The four-faced mountain peak of the Himalayan range, located in western Tibet, presently Chinese territory. Mount Kailas is sacred to Lord Siva and is the ultimate pilgrimage destination for both Saivite Hindus and Tibetan Buddhists. Kailas is understood as the symbol of the Third-World abode of Lord Siva as Mahesvara, the Primal Soul at the center of existence in the Sivaloka. It is also associated with Mount Meru.

Kailasa Paramparai: See: *Siva Yogaswami Paramparai.*

kalasa: A pot of water on which a husked coconut is nested on five mango leaves; integral to certain Hindu rites.

Kali Yuga: "Dark Age." The Kali Yuga is the fourth age in the repetitive cycle of four phases of time the universe passes through. It is comparable to the darkest part of the night, as the forces of ignorance are in full power and many of the subtle faculties of the soul are obscured.

kama: Love, sensory enjoyment. One of the four legitimate goals of life along with *artha* (wealth), *dharma* (righteous conduct) and *Moksha* (realization). *Kama* (upper case) also names the God of Love and Desire.

karma: "Deed or act." *Karma* more broadly describes the principle of cause and effect, as well as the totality of one's actions and their concomitant reactions in this and all previous lives.

karma yoga: "Union through action." Karma yoga is selfless service, work for work's sake, performing one's actions as an offering to God, neither seeking praise or recognition nor shunning criticism or correction.

Kartikkeya: Lord Muruga worshiped as the six-headed, lance-wielding God of War, celestial general, the most common image (along with Skanda) of Muruga in North India.

Kashmir Saivism: One of six schools of Saivism. Mildly theistic, intensely monistic. Siva is immanent and transcendent. God-Realization relies on the grace of the Satguru. Strong emphasis on purification and yoga to realize Siva as Self.

Kauai: The northernmost of the eight-island chain known as Hawaii, the 50th State of the United States of America. Kauai is located in the middle of the Pacific Ocean, approximately 3,000 miles due west of Mexico City. Site of Kauai Aadheenam, the International Headquarters of Saiva Siddhanta Church, and the site of the San Marga Sanctuary.

kavi: Orange robes worn by the sannyasin. Literally "a reddish clay soil," referring to the color taken on by white robes worn by sadhus who meditate frequently on such grounds.

Kriya Sakti: "Power of Action." One of Siva's three primary saktis or energies along with *Iccha* (desire or love) and *Jnana* (wisdom), by which He administers His divine laws of dharma in all three worlds.

kriya: "Religious action; worship." The regular practice of temple worship, both internal and external, through which one's understanding, closeness and love for God and the Gods deepens through worship, devotional singing and scriptural study.

kriya marga: "Path of religious action; path of worship." Second of the four successive stages (margas) of spiritual unfoldment and attainment in Saiva Siddhanta. chariya, kriya, yoga and jnana. The central focus of the kriya marga is the awakening of bhakti, love, through external worship, called *bhakti yoga.*

kumkum: Literally, "red red." Specifically, the red powder worn by Hindus as the "pottu," or dot, at the point of the third eye on the forehead.

kundalini: "Serpent power," the primordial cosmic energy in every individual which lies coiled like a serpent at the base of the spine and rises up the sushumna nadi. Through yoga it is awakened and made to rise up the chakras to the crown or sahasrara chakra.

kuthuvillaku: A standing lamp found in the temple, shrine room or home. Often kept burning constantly to keep the inner atmosphere pure and serene.

Lakshmi: Sakti, the Universal Mother as Goddess of Wealth. God Siva seen in feminine form. Usually depicted on a lotus flower. Prayers are offered to Lakshmi for wealth, beauty and peace.

liberal Hinduism: Non-sectarian Hinduism; an extension of Smarta Sampradaya teachings. Contemporary form of Hinduism that encourages a Hindu to follow any combination of theological, scriptural, sadhana and worship patterns regardless of their sectarian or religious origins. Thus, each liberal Hindu constructs his own spiritual pattern, drawing not only from Hindu teachings and spiritual personages, but non-Hindu ones as well. Stresses the Smarta Sampradaya teachings that: 1) the Deities are man-generated symbols of an impersonal Divinity, 2) the cosmos is ultimately illusion, 3) realization of God may be achieved through a choice of bhakti, karma, raja or jnana yogas, 4) the highest form of Hinduism bridges all sects, and 5) sectarian paths are inferior in understanding and practice.

Liberation: *Moksha;* release from samsara (the round of births and deaths).

linga: See: *Siva Lingam.*

loka: Habitat, region or plane of existence. A place of a particular level of vibration and associated beings, Gods, devas or humans. Three primary lokas (*Bhuloka, Devaloka* and *Sivaloka*) and fourteen sub-classifications of the cosmos are designated in Hindu scripture.

lotus asana: The most famous of hatha yoga poses and the optimum position for meditation. It is known as the *padmasana* (lotus pose), as the legs are crossed, turning the soles of the feet up resembling a lotus flower.

macrocosm: "Great world or universe." Esoterically, the universe in which one is consciously functioning, in contrast to the microcosm, or world within. For example, the Second World is the microcosm to a soul living in his macrocosm of the First World.

madams: Stages of life, or *ashramas.* Literally, "a storied house," in Tamil. A term used by Siva Yogaswami to refer to the natural periods that an individual passes through from studenthood to old-age, each with its duties, responsibilities, lessons and benefits to the unfolding individual.

maha: Prefix meaning "great."

Maha Sivaratri: "Siva's Great Night." The most profound and sacred of all Saivite holy days, honoring Lord Siva on the new moon of February/March.

Mahadeva: "Great Deva" or "Great Shining One." A name of Siva. Also used to denote any of the multitude of Gods—Ganesha, Muruga, etc.

Mahapralaya: "Great Dissolution." Periodic universal dissolution at which all three worlds—including time and space—dissolve into God Siva, as all souls (their evolution perfect and complete) lose individuality and become one with Him.

Mahasamadhi: "The great samadhi." Dropping off of the physical body at the point of death by an illumined soul. This transition process usually catalyzes a powerful sakti as the soul departs the body.

mahavakiam: "Great saying." A terse, profound aphorism taken from and summarizing the teachings of a Hindu scripture or holy person. The most famous mahavakiams are the four from the Upanishads: *Prajnanam Brahma* ("Pure Consciousness is Brahman"), from the *Aitareya Upanishad; Aham Brahmasmi* ("I am Brahman"), from the *Brihadaranyaka Upanishad; Tat tvam asi* ("Thou art That") from the *Chandogya Upanishad; Ayam Atma Brahma* ("The Soul is Brahman"), from the *Mandukya Upanishad.*

Mahesvara: "Great Ruler." Lord Siva as the Primal Soul and Personal Lord, Creator, Preserver and Destroyer of all that exists.

mala: 1) Rosary for performing japa, recitation of holy names; 2) A general term used in conjunction with the three bonds: anava, karma and maya, e.g., anava mala.

mantra: A sacred mystic syllable, word or verse used in puja to invoke God and Gods. In the repetitive recitation called japa, a mantra quiets the mind, balances the inner bodies and helps attain other desired aims. Often chanted repeatedly to create and sustain a vibration.

marga: "Path" or "way." Spiritual path.

mature soul: An old soul, one who has experienced many lives on earth. Such souls may be recognized by their love, compassion, selflessness and deep understanding.

maya: According to Saiva Siddhanta, this world—and, indeed, all of existence—is maya, the principle of matter, that which is subject to change. Maya is that which is in the continuous process of creation, preservation and destruction, performed by God and man.

mayil: "Peacock." The vahana or mount of Lord Muruga.

meditate: To think deeply and continuously. In yoga, *meditation* describes a quiet, alert, powerfully concentrated state wherein new knowledge and insights are awakened from within as awareness focuses one-pointedly on an object or specific line of thought.

mental body: The body of mind, in Sanskrit known as the *vijnamaya kosha* (wisdom sheath), which forms a subtle vehicle for each individual soul.

Meykandar: "Truth seer." The renowned 13th century theologian of South India. He was either the author or the Tamil translator (from the *Raurava Agama*) of the *Sivajnanabotham*. The Meykandar Sampradaya, which promulgates pluralistic Saiva Siddhanta, began with Meykandar.

microcosm: "Little world" or "miniature universe." Esoterically, the inside of the macrocosm; the inside of one's present plane of consciousness. The Second World is the microcosm of the First World; the Third World is the microcosm of the Second World.

mind: Faculty of memory, thought, reason, logic, perception and sensation. It is universal consciousness, the substratum or primal substance flowing in and through all things and the totality of all things. In truth, there is but one mind.

modaka: A round, sweet goody made of rice, coconut, sugar, etc. It is a favorite treat of Ganesha. Esoterically, it corresponds to *siddhi* (attainment or fulfillment), the gladdening contentment of pure joy, the sweetest of all things sweet.

Moksha: Liberation from samsara, the round of births and deaths. Same as *Mukti.*

monism: Doctrine of oneness. As a world-view, the belief that reality is of one kind or substance (contrasted with dualism and pluralism). Monism holds that the material and the spiritual, the physical and the mental are all aspects of one being or substance. Monistic Saiva Siddhanta teaches that this one being or substance is God Siva.

monistic theism: Monism is the doctrine that Reality is a one whole or existence without independent parts and that the soul is ultimately one with Reality in non-dual identity. Theism is the belief that God exists as a real, conscious, personal Supreme Being. These are often regarded as opposing points of view. The combined theological perspective of monistic theism (also called *panentheism*) simultaneously accepts that God has a personal form, that He creates, pervades and *is* all that exists, that He ultimately transcends all existence, and that the soul is one with God (and thus one with all existence) in His essential states. Thus, it encompasses the non-dual and the dual, both advaitic Vedanta and dvaitic Siddhanta. This unified doctrine is also known as *Suddha Saiva Siddhanta* or *Advaita Siddhanta.*

monotheism: The doctrine or belief that there is only one Supreme God. *Polytheism* means belief in many Gods. These philosophical positions are not necessarily mutually exclusive. For example, Hinduism is polytheistic in having many Gods, but it is monotheistic in that each sect considers only one God as the Supreme God.

mudras: Symbolic hand gestures used in puja and the practice of yoga. Also has the broader meaning of "bodily position," such as the poses of dance or hatha yoga.

Mukti: The soul's liberation from samsara, the round of births and deaths. Same as *Moksha.*

muni: A sage or sadhu vowed to complete silence or who speaks but rarely and seeks stillness of mind, known as *summa* in Tamil. Often lives in seclusion.

murthi: "Image." Sculpted, carved or painted image of God or a God used in worship.

Muruga: "Beautiful one." A Mahadeva, Ganesha's younger brother, created by God Siva to assist souls in their evolution, especially through the practice of yoga.

Mushika: "Mouse," from the root *mush*, meaning "to steal." Lord Ganesha's vahana, the mouse, traditionally associated with abundance. Symbolically, the mouse carries Lord Ganesha's grace into every nook and cranny of the mind.

mysticism: Spirituality; the pursuit of direct spiritual or religious experience. Spiritual discipline aimed at direct union or communion with Ultimate Reality or God through deep meditation, or trance-like contemplation. From the Greek *mystikos,* "of mysteries." Characterized by the belief that ultimate Truth transcends intellectual processes and must be directly intuited.

nada: "Sound," "vibration." Mystic sound of the Eternal; the Primal Sound or first vibration from which all creation emanates. Also the psychic sounds heard during deep meditation.

nadi: Psychic nerve channel; the network of subtle energy fibers (traditionally said to number 72,000) that form the nervous system of the inner body. These nadis interconnect the chakras. The *sushumna, ida* and *pingala* are the three main nadis.

naga: "Snake," often the cobra; symbol of the kundalini coiled on the petals of the muladhara chakra.

nagasvaram: "Snake note." A temple musical instrument common in South India. A double-reed woodwind about three feet long, similar to the oboe, but its sound is more piercing and shrill.

nakshatra: "Star cluster." The nakshatras are 27 star-clusters, or constellations which lie along the ecliptic of the moon, the path of the moon as it rises and crosses the sky. The moon's orbit intersects them, one approximately each day of the moon's orbital period. The nakshatra is an important factor in determining the characteristics of an individual, or the nature of a given day.

nama diksha: "Name-giving initiation." Also known as *namakarana samskara.* A temple or home ceremony held to name a newborn Hindu baby and re-connect it with his or her guardian devas. It is also held for anyone entering the religion converting from another religion or having no prior religion.

namakarana samskara: Hindu name-giving ceremony. Same as nama diksha.

Namasivaya: "Adoration (or homage) to Siva." The supreme mantra of Saivism, known as the *Panchakshara* or "five letters." Embodying the essence of Saiva Siddhanta, it is found in the center of the central Veda (the Yajur) of the original three Vedas (Rig, Yajur and Sama). *Na* is the Lord's veiling grace; *Ma* is the world; *Si* is Siva; *Va* is His revealing grace; *Ya* is the soul. Namasivaya is a mystic chant which should be given by an authorized teacher.

namaskaram: Traditional Hindu greeting of respect. Hands are raised, palms together in a mudra gesture which honors the Divine in others. Also used in devotion before a temple Deity or great master.

Nandi: "The joyful." Lord Siva's vahana. A white bull with a black tail. Symbolizes the ideal devotee, in constant communion with God Siva.

Nandinatha: "Lord of Nandi," a name of Siva. Also names a siddhar, the Satguru (*circa* 2nd century BCE) of Sundaranatha (Tirumular), the famed Sivajnani who wrote the *Tirumantiram.*

Narakaloka: "Demon place." Hindu concept of hell; lower realm of the Second World in which souls temporarily experience self-created hellish states of mind.

Nataraja: God Siva as "King of Dance." His tandava dance represents His five powers: creation, preservation, destruction, veiling grace and revealing grace. One foot (representing veiling grace) stands upon and subdues the demon Muyalaka, symbol of ignorance and worldliness. The other foot, raised upward, represents His revealing grace. One hand is raised in blessing (preservation), another points to the foot of grace, the third hand shakes the drum of creation and the fourth holds the fire of destruction.

Natha Sampradaya: "Lineage of Masters." *Natha* means lord or master, one who has mastered the intricacies of his inner and outer bodies and realized Parasivam. *Sampradaya* means an established oral teaching tradition or lineage. The Natha Sampradaya is the oldest Saivite sampradaya existing today, currently consisting of two lineages: the Nandinatha lineage and the Adinatha lineage.

Nayanars: Sixty-three canonized saints of South India. All but a few were householders, recognized as outstanding exemplars of devotion to Siva.

Neti neti: "Not this, not this." Upanishadic formula connoting, through a negative description, the undefinable and inconceivable nature of the Absolute. It is a contemplative process in which the seeker encounters various levels of his being, even the innermost core of Satchidananda, and applies "Neti neti," "It is not this, not this." Ultimately, he exits all "thisness" to realize the Absolute.

Nirguna Brahman: Brahman "without qualities." Refers to the Absolute Reality, Parasivam or Parabrahman. It is totally transcendent of guna (quality), manifest existence and even Satchidananda, all of which exhibit perceivable qualities.

Nirvikalpa Samadhi: "Samadhi without seed;" Self-Realization. The ultimate attainment. The experience, or "non-experience" of Parasivam, That which exists beyond space, time and form.

niyama: "To unleash." The niyamas are ethical and religious practices. These observances comprise the third limb of the ashtanga ("eight-limbed") yoga system codified in numerous Saivite scriptures including the *Sandilya* and *Varuha Upanishads, Hatha Yoga Pradipika* by Sri Gorakhnath, the *Tirumantiram* (200 BCE) by Saint Tirumular and the *Yoga Sutras* (200 BCE) of sage Patanjali. There are ten yamas and ten niyamas in all, though Patanjali listed only five yamas and five niyamas in his classic work, and these have become widely known. Along with the yamas (restraints), the niyamas provide guidelines for ethical, moral life and lay the foundation for yoga. The ten niyamas are:

1) *hri* (remorse)
2) *santosha* (contentment)
3) *dana* (giving)
4) *astikya* (faith)
5) *Isvarapujana* (worship)
6) *Siddhantasravana* (study)
7) *mati* (cognition)
8) *vrata* (sacred vows)
9) *japa* (recitation)
10) *tapas* (austerity)

Note: Patanjali's niyamas are *saucha* (purity), *santosha, tapaha, svadhaya* (scriptural study) and *Isvarapranidhana* (worship).

Obscuring Grace: An alternative term for God Siva's veiling grace, or *Tirodhana Sakti.* See: veiling grace.

ontology: "Knowledge of Being." The branch of metaphysics dealing with the nature of being, reality or ultimate substance.

original sin: The Christian notion that a tendency toward sin and depravity is inherent in mankind as a direct result of Adam's rebellion in the Garden of Eden. Sometimes mistakenly related to the Saiva Siddhanta concept of the three malas or bondages: anava, karma and maya, especially anava.

padapuja: Ceremonial worship of the holy feet of the guru (spiritual preceptor) with the aim of worshipping the Divine Self which the guru embodies and helps disciples to know.

pancha nitya karmas: "Five constant duties." A traditional regimen of religious practice for all Hindus: 1) *dharma* (virtuous living), 2) *upasana* (worship), 3) *utsava* (observance of holy days), 4) *tirthayatrai* (pilgrimage) and 5) *samskaras* (observance of sacraments, known as *samskaras,* such as rites of birth, first feeding, marriage, etc.). While dharma and upasana are daily obligations, utsava, tirthayatrai and samskaras are periodic.

Panchakshara Mantram: "Five-lettered chant." See *Namasivaya.*

pandaram: "Custodian or caretaker." One who has taken up priestly duties without necessarily having had formal training or diksha.

pandit: A learned brahmin, usually married, who teaches and advises on questions of conduct within the community. Same as *pundit.*

panentheism: "All in God." The view that the universe is part of the being of God, as distinguished from *pantheism,* which identifies God with the total reality. *Panentheism* is a philosophical term that describes God as immanent and transcendent, relative and Absolute.

pantheism: The doctrine that God is not a personality, and that all laws, forces and manifestations of the universe are God.

para: A Sanskrit prefix meaning, "supreme" or "beyond," referring to the highest dimension of whatever it precedes—as in *Parasivam,* the transcendent perfection of Siva.

Parabrahman: "Supreme Brahman." A Sanskrit term for Absolute Reality, That which is beyond the manifest Being of Brahman.

Param: Sanskrit prefix meaning "Supreme, Beyond." Name of Siva, denoting his Absolute Reality—beyond time, form and space.

Paramaguru: The guru of a disciple's guru.

Paramatma: "Supreme Soul or Self." The Upanishadic universal Self or Primal Reality, Parabrahman or Parasivam.

paramparai: "Uninterrupted succession." A traditional line of gurus, each guru passing on the power of the lineage to his successors.

Parasakti: "Supreme Sakti." God Siva as the universal Mother.

Used interchangeably with *Sakti*. Also used to mean the supreme state of Sakti, that is, Parasivam.

Parasivam: "Transcendent Siva." Siva's Absolute Reality. That which transcends time, form and space and defies description; the Self God.

Parvati: One of many names for the Universal Mother, the conception of God as feminine. Mythologically, Parvati is wedded to Siva. In reality, Sakti is Siva's own manifesting power.

pasa: Same as *pasam;* world.

pasam: "Rope" or "tether." In Saiva Siddhanta, *pasam* means the fetters or bondages of the soul: *anava, karma* and *maya.* Pasam exists for the sake of the soul's spiritual growth toward God-Realization.

pasu: "Cow." In Saiva Siddhanta, *pasu* refers to the soul.

Pasupata Saivism: One of six schools of Saivism. Simultaneously monistic and theistic. Siva is supreme cause and personal Ruler of soul and world. Primarily an ascetic's path emphasizing sadhana to seek "internal kundalini grace."

Pasupati: "Lord of Animals." An ancient name for God Siva describing Him as the shepherd of souls, the protector of life in all its forms. This earliest known iconographic depiction of Siva occurs in the "Pasupati" seal from the 6,000-year old Indus Valley civilization.

Patanjali: A Saivite siddhar who codified the ancient practice of ashtanga yoga into the pithy and potent aphorisms of the *Yoga Sutras.* Lived around the 2nd century BCE.

Pati: "Lord" or "master." In Saiva Siddhanta, *Pati* refers to God Siva in the formulation: "Pati, pasu, pasam," which literally means "master," "cow" and "tethering rope" and esoterically connotes God, the soul and the world that binds the soul.

perfections: Describes a quality, nature or dimension that is infinitely perfect. Used to describe God Siva's three perfections of Parasivam, Satchidananda and Mahesvara. Though spoken of as three perfections for our understanding, Siva is a one transcendent-immanent Being.

personal dharma: The individual pattern of societal and spiritual conduct that most advances a soul in a given lifetime, thus positively affecting future lifetimes. Also known as *svadharma.*

Peruman: "Great One." Highly venerative term for God Siva, expressing the devotee's overwhelming awe of God.

Pillaiyar: "Noble child." Form of Lord Ganesha as a child-like Deity.

pingala: Inner-body nadi current, blue in color, that flows upward, ending on the right side of the body. This current is masculine in nature, radiating an intellectual, mental energy.

pluralistic: Any theology that perceives God, soul and world as separate realities.

polytheism: Belief in or worship of many Gods, or more than one God.

pottu: Small dot of red powder (kumkum) placed between and just above the eyebrows. This mark symbolizes the opening of the third eye, seeing with the superconscious vision of the soul.

pradakshina: "Right-facing." Sacred act of worshipful circumambulation, walking clockwise around the temple sanctum or other holy place. This act shifts the mind from worldly concerns to a heightened awareness of God.

prana: Vital energy or life principle; literally, "vital air," from the root *an,* "to breathe." Prana in the human body manifests further in five primary modifications, known as *vayus,* "vital airs or winds:" *prana, apana, samana, udana* and *vyana,* each governing crucial bodily functions, and five auxiliary vayus: *naga, kurma, krikara, devadatta* and *dhananjaya.* Usually, *prana* refers to the life principle, but it sometimes refers, in a broader sense, to energy, power or the animating force of the cosmos.

Pranava Aum: The symbol and mantram denoting God and the Primal Sound. *Pranava* is a Sanskrit adjective meaning "wondrous" and "ever-new."

pranayama: "Life force restraining." Science of controlling prana (life force or vital energy) through breathing techniques which dictate the lengths of inhalation, retention and exhalation; prepares the mind for deep meditation and develops psychic abilities. Fourth stage of ashtanga yoga.

pranic: Adjective form of *prana,* the vital energy which permeates the universe. Living forms are most charged with prana, but inanimate forms have their own low-level prana energies as well.

pranic body: The subtle physical sheath known in Sanskrit as the *pranamaya kosha,* the vital force of the physical body of man. It is second of five bodies, or vehicles, through which the soul functions in various planes or strata of consciousness. The pranic body is of the sphere of physical energy, and is the source of health and vitality. This body co-exists with, and disintegrates at the death of, the physical body.

prarabdha karma: Karma "that has been unleashed or aroused." Karma that is actively manifesting in the present experiences of the individual; karmas generated in the past which have caused one's present birth and circumstances.

prasadam: Food and other offerings that are presented to the Deity during puja or to a holy person in ritual or ordinary circumstances. Thus blessed, the offerings are distributed to devotees.

pratyahara: "Drawing back." Withdrawal of the senses. Fifth process in the ashtanga yoga system. Individual consciousness is withdrawn or shifted from the sensorial input of the physical body, from the emotion-network of the astral body and intellectual energies of the mental body. This leads to loss of body consciousness and awakening into higher states.

Primal Soul: The uncreated, original, perfect Soul—Siva—who emanates from Himself all universes and an infinite plurality of individual souls whose essence is identical with His essence.

Primal Substance: The material form from which the manifest world in its infinite diversity is derived. The substance is Pure Consciousness, God Siva's Divine Mind.

psychic: "Of the soul or psyche." Non-physical, pertaining to the soul. Also the quality of being attuned to or adept at the more subtle psychic, or soul, faculties and energies. Psychic faculties include such extra-sensory perceptions as clairvoyance, clairaudience, precognition and psychometry.

puja: Agamic rite of worship performed to the murthi (home or temple image) to invoke and establish a psychic connection with the God in the inner worlds. During puja, the officiant (pujari) recites various chants praising the God and beseeching divine blessings, while making numerous offerings in accordance with established traditions.

pujari: Hindu temple priest. One who performs a puja.

pundit: Hindu scholar and teacher of the scriptures. Literally, "learned." (Sanskrit equivalent of the Hindi word *pandit*.) Usually a married man, a pundit is one who teaches and decides questions of conduct within the community.

Purana: Hindu mythological literature which contain ethical and cosmological teachings and explain Gods, man and the world through stories.

Pure Consciousness: Satchidananda; Siva's Divine Mind. The ground state of Being which contains and underlies all form, time and space.

purusha: Male person in mundane usage, as in *purusha dharma*. When used metaphysically, however, *purusha* refers to the soul, neither male nor female.

purusha dharma: Man's proper pattern of conduct; observances, vocational and spiritual options that will most advance him in a given lifetime. The pattern for a woman is known as *sthree dharma.*

rajasic: *Rajas* is the second of the three *gunas,* or fundamental cosmic qualities of nature, as described in the Samkhya system—*tamas* (inertia), *rajas* (activity) and *sattva* (illumination, purity).

relatively real: Describes the Three-World existence manifested from Lord Siva as being subject to evolution, change and time. The world is real, not an illusion or form of mistaken reality. However, its reality undergoes creation, transformation and dissolution (ceasing to exist at Mahapralaya). Thus, it is "relative," whereas Siva's reality is "absolute," eternal and unchanging and continues to exist even at Mahapralaya.

religion: "To bind back," describing the process of becoming and living God-consciousness. It is a structured vehicle for soul advancement which includes theology, scripture, spiritual and moral practices, a priesthood and liturgy.

revealing grace: God Siva's unveiling power. One of Siva's five potent acts—creation, preservation, destruction, veiling grace and revealing grace—which animate the universe and guide souls to maturity. Siva's grace in Saiva Siddhanta is in two forms: veiling grace (*Tirodhana Sakti*) and revealing grace (*Anugraha Sakti*). Anava, karma and maya constitute His concealing grace, providing the matrix for experience and evolution. As the soul matures, it is through the power of revealing grace that it ultimately transcends the bonds of anava, karma and maya and realizes its identity with Siva.

Rig Veda: Oldest of the four Veda Samhitas (collections): *Rig, Sama, Yajur* and *Atharva.*

rishi: An old and venerated sage or seer, often a visionary who sees beyond the present time.

rita dharma: The inherent order of the physical cosmos; universal dharma. The laws of being and nature that govern all forms, functions and processes of the universe from nuclear particles to galaxy clusters to the power of mental thought and perception.

Rudra: A name for Siva in His aspect of Absorber or Destroyer.

rudraksha: "Eye of Siva." Marble-sized, multi-faced, reddish-brown seeds from the species *Eleocarpus ganitrus,* commonly called the blue marble tree. Rudraksha beads are sacred to Siva and worn as a rosary or mala around the neck or wrist. Used to perform japa, or mantra repetition.

Sabdhabrahman: The word or sound of Brahman; the primal vibration of Satchidananda.

sacrament: A rite that conveys a spiritual blessing. Used to translate *samskara,* any of the various temple or home ceremonies performed by a priest, such as name-giving, first-feeding, beginning of formal study, marriage, death, etc. *Sacrament* also names the various sacred items passed out after a puja, such as holy ash, kumkum and holy water.

sadhana: "Effective; leading straight to the goal." The practice of spiritual disciplines such as meditation, japa, fasting, austerity, yoga and humble service.

sadhu: A pious seeker or holy man, usually an ascetic or mendicant who lives simply and wanders homeless.

Saguna Brahman: Brahman "with qualities." Describes Siva's perfections of Mahesvara and Satchidananda, "the Primal Soul and His Divine Mind"—that part of God which is superconscious, all-knowing, all-loving, all-powerful and omnipresent.

sahasrara: "Thousand-petals." Seventh chakra, located in the cranial chamber of the soul body. It is composed of 1,008 petals indicative of the God-powers of the Satchidananda state in which this chakra is awakened and fully functions.

Saiva Agamas: Agama is "that which has come down or been received," referring to a body of knowledge divinely authored. The 28 primary Saiva Agamas are specific to Saivism. The Saiva Agamas are detailed manuals on the four margas or paths of Saivism—chariya, kriya, yoga and jnana.

Saiva Siddhanta: "Final conclusions of Saivism." The name of the most widespread and influential Saivite school today. It is predominant especially among the Tamils in Sri Lanka and South India. *Siddhanta* means the final conclusions in a field of knowledge. Saiva Siddhanta constitutes the final theological and metaphysical conclusions of Saivism.

Saivism: The name of the religion followed by those who worship the Hindu God, Siva. One of the three primary sects of Hinduism, Saivism (the oldest of the three), is in turn divided into a number of distinct sects with diverse theologies. Six major schools of philosophy exist today out of many now extinct. They are: Siva Advaita, Virasaivism, Kashmir Saivism, Pasupata Saivism, Saiva Siddhanta and Gorakhnath Saivism.

Saivite: Of or relating to Saivism, the religion of those who worship Siva as the Supreme God. Also names the adherents of Saivism. There are approximately 400 million Saivites in the world.

Sakti: "Power, energy." Refers to the active power of Siva (or other Deities), popularly envisioned in the feminine form as a Goddess or Devi—such as Parvati or Lakshmi. *Sakti* also refers to specific forces or powers, such as *Iccha* (desire or love), *Kriya* (action) and *Jnana* (wisdom), three Saktis wielded by Siva. The divine energy experienced in the temple during puja, in deep meditation or in the presence of a holy person is also called *sakti* (lower case).

Saktism: Religion followed by those who worship the Goddess Sakti as the Supreme Being. One of the three primary sects of Hinduism, Saktism is in turn divided into a number of distinct sects with diverse theologies. The primary goal of Saktism is Moksha, and the spiritual practices in Saktism are similar to those of Saivism, though there is perhaps more emphasis in Saktism on God's power as opposed to being. In the Sakta sect of Hinduism, Sakti is worshiped as the Supreme Being exclusively, as the dynamic aspect of Divinity, while Siva is considered solely transcendent.

Sama Veda: "Wisdom of the melodious song." Third of the four Vedas, its 1,875 stanzas are entirely derived (with exception of 104) from the Rig Veda. It is essentially a collection of hymns that are to be melodically sung with a distinctive cadence during yajna (fire ceremony) performance, augmenting the chanting of stanzas from the Yajur Veda.

samadhi: "Sameness," "union." Merging with the point of concentration—deep contemplation. Principally refers to the eighth step in the practice of ashtanga yoga. Total contemplative absorption of individual awareness. There are two stages. 1) Savikalpa, "with seed," is a spiritual state including a wide range of superconscious experiences wherein the mind is motionless and the meditator and the object of meditation are one, and 2) Nirvikalpa, "without seed," is the simple yet ultimate non-dual state, or Self-Realization, wherein the meditator is absorbed in the Self—Parasivam—God's unspeakable Absolute Being beyond time, form and space.

samaya diksha: "Religion initiation." The most fundamental initiation in Saivism, also known as mantram diksha, in which the disciple receives the blessings and instruction of the guru to chant the Panchakshara Mantram ("Namasivaya").

Samhitas: One of three parts of the ritual section of a Veda, a collection of mantrams and hymns to Vedic Gods.

sampradaya: "Tradition." *Sampradaya* can be understood in two ways. First, it refers to an oral tradition of teaching, such as a Guru of an established lineage verbally passing on eternal truths to his sishya. Second, it refers to an established historical lineage, a living stream of tradition or theology within Hinduism.

samsara: The cycle of birth, death and rebirth; the total pattern of successive lives experienced by a soul.

samskara: "Impression." The imprint or traces left in the mind after an experience, whether in this or previous lives. Root impressions, especially from profound events, which mold character and guide actions. Also denotes ceremonial purification, one of a number of religious ceremonies performed at psychological moments, such as first-feeding, marriage, death rites, etc. Also various ceremonies performed to restore something to its original purity.

Sanat Kumar: "Eternally beautiful and youthful prince." Name of Lord Muruga as the Prince Son of Lord Siva, Sovereign of all Three Worlds. It also conveys the matured qualities of all individual soul bodies: luminous, ageless beauty.

Sanatana Dharma: "Eternal religion" or the "eternal path." It is the oldest name for the Hindu religion.

sanctum sanctorum: "Holy of Holies." Originally the innermost part of the Jewish Temple in ancient Jerusalem. Now used for the innermost chamber or center of any sacred place, such as the main sanctum (garbagriha) of a Hindu temple.

sankalpa: "Will, volition, desire, purpose, intention, determination." A solemn vow or declaration of purpose to perform any ritual observance. Most commonly sankalpa names the mental and verbal preparation made by a temple priest as he begins rites of worship.

Sankara: Also *Samkara* or *Shankara.* A name for Siva meaning "causing prosperity, auspicious, beneficent." Also the name of the 9th century monk, Adi Sankara, preeminent Guru of the Smarta Sampradaya. He is most noted for his non-dualistic Vedanta, for establishing four monastic centers, ratifying 10 orders of sannyasins and writing prolific scriptural commentary.

sannidhya: "Divine Presence." The radiance and blessed presence of superconscious sakti that accumulates within and around a temple or a holy person.

sannyas dharma: "The way of renunciation." The path of the renunciate monk or sannyasin; often simply *sannyas. Sannyas* means to "throw down" or "abandon" the duties and obligations of the householder path in favor of the monastic quest for divine awakening and God-Realization.

sannyas diksha: "Renunciate initiation." Initiation into the renunciate path of Hindu monkhood; marks the complete and irrevocable abdication of the householder dharma in favor of the monastic path in the quest for Self-Realization.

sannyasin: "One who throws down or abandons." A Hindu monk; a single man who has renounced the world for God-Realization and service to humanity, and who has received sannyas diksha (initiation) from a qualified sannyasin, thus entering him into the world brotherhood (or holy order) of sannyasins. Diksha is usually given only after years of disciplined training.

Sanskrit: "Well-made, perfected." The classical sacerdotal, or religious, language of ancient India, considered a pure vehicle of divine communication. Employed today as a religious, literary and scholarly language, but no longer used as a spoken language.

Sarasvati: Sakti, the Universal Mother; Siva seen in feminine form as Goddess of the arts and learning. Sarasvati is usually depicted wearing a white sari and holding a veena, sitting upon a swan or lotus flower. Prayers are offered to Sarasvati for refinements of beauty, culture and knowledge.

Sat: Pure being or existence.

Satguru: "True remover of darkness." A spiritual preceptor of the highest attainment; one who has realized the ultimate Truth and is able to lead others securely along the spiritual path.

Satchidananda: "Truth-consciousness-bliss." Lord Siva's Divine Mind and simultaneously the superconscious mind of each individual soul. It is perfect love and omniscient, omnipotent consciousness, the fountainhead of all existence, yet containing and permeating all existence.

sattvic: "Of illumination, purity, truth." *Sattva* is the most subtle of the three gunas, or fundamental cosmic qualities of nature described in the Samkhya system—*tamas* (inertia), *rajas* (activity) and *sattva* (illumination, purity). The *sattvaguna* is rarified, translucent, pervasive, reflecting the light of pure consciousness.

Second World: Exists within the dimensions of the First World or physical plane; the astral or mental plane of existence wherein the soul continues its activities in the astral body during sleep and after the physical body dies. Includes the Devaloka and the Narakaloka.

Self: Same as *Self God* or *Parasivam*. The term *self* in lower case denotes the personal ego, one's individual identity or personality in contrast with the Divine Self.

Self God: The soul's ultimate attainment, the timeless, formless, spaceless Absolute Reality: Parasivam.

Self-Realization: Direct knowing of the Self God; samadhi without seed (Nirvikalpa Samadhi); the ultimate attainment. The realization or non-experience of That which exists beyond space, time and form as Parasivam. *Self-Realization* is also often used as a non-religious term in contemporary society to describe optimizing one's abilities and human potential.

seval: The large, red, fighting rooster that adorns Lord Muruga's battle flag, heralding the dawn of wisdom and the conquest of the forces of ignorance.

shadkonam: "Six-pointed star." Found in Lord Muruga's yantra, formed by two interlocking triangles. The upper one stands for Siva and the lower for Sakti.

Shanmukha: "Six-faced." A name for Lord Muruga, denoting the multiplicity of His divine functions.

shastra: Religious manual. Also, any scientific or legal treatise. Shastras belong to the class of scripture called *smriti*, "that which is remembered." Shastras are not considered revealed scripture (*sruti*, "that which is heard") as are the Vedas and Agamas.

sheaths: The bodies of man—physical (*annamaya kosha*), pranic (*pranamaya kosha*), astral (*manomaya kosha*) and mental (*vijnamaya kosha*)—surrounding the innermost soul, or causal, body (*anandamaya kosha*).

Siddhanta: "Final attainments" or "final conclusions." *Siddhanta* represents ultimate understanding arrived at in any given field of knowledge.

siddhar: A "perfected one" or accomplished yogi, a person of great spiritual attainment or powers.

siddhis: "Powers" or "accomplishments." Natural powers of the soul, awakened through spiritual maturity and yogic sadhana designed to unfold the chakra-nadi network of the inner and outer bodies. Siddhis unfold as a result of certain esoteric yoga practices, through yogically pursuing Self-Realization and as a result of repeated Self-Realization.

sin: Transgression of divine law, especially willfully or intentional violation. Akin to the Latin *sons,* meaning "guilty."

sishya: "To be taught." A pupil or disciple, especially one who has proven himself and has formally accepted a Satguru as his guide in spiritual instruction.

Siva: "The auspicious one; the kind one, the friendly one; the pure one." Supreme Being of the Saivite religion. God Siva is All and in all, simultaneously the Creator and the creation, both immanent and transcendent. As personal Deity he is creator, preserver and transformer-absorber of all forms, forces and beings. Cognized as a one Being consisting of three perfections: Primal Soul, Satchidananda, Absolute Reality.

Siva Lingam: "Mark, or symbol, of Siva." A rounded, elliptical, aniconic image representing God Siva, usually set on a circular base, or *yoni.* The Siva Lingam is the simplest and most ancient symbol of Siva, especially of Parasivam, God beyond all forms and qualities. Lingams are usually of stone (either carved or naturally existing, *svayambu*), but may also be made of metal, precious gems, crystal, wood, ice or any natural substance.

Siva Yogaswami Guru Paramparai: Spiritual teaching lineage named after Siva Yogaswami (1872–1964), Natha Siddhar and Satguru of Jaffna, Sri Lanka, who ordained Gurudeva Sivaya Subramuniyaswami (1927–) as his successor in 1949. Yogaswami's guru was Chellappaswami (1840–1915), whose guru was Kadaitswami (*circa* 1810–1875). Kadaitswami was preceded by the nameless Rishi from the Himalayas. The paramparai finds its roots in the Nandinatha Sampradaya, tracing its guru lineage back to Tirunandi and his eight disciples—Tirumular, Patanjali, Vyagrapadar, Sanatkumar, Sivayogamuni, Sanakar, Sanadanar and Sananthanar—then through Tirumular's disciples. This Natha line flourishes today and is the spiritual heritage of Saiva Siddhanta Church and its members. This spiritual lineage propounds a Vedic-Agamic monistic Saiva Siddhanta and fosters South Indian traditions of worship and culture. Also known as the *Kailasa Paramparai.*

Siva-Sakti: Father-Mother God, both imminent and transcendent. A name for God Siva encompassing His unmanifest Being and generative power.

Sivachariya: A traditional temple priest of the South Indian Saivite tradition.

Sivajnanabotham: "Treatise on Siva Wisdom." A work, either authored or translated by Meykandar in the 13th century CE, consisting of twelve terse verses describing the relationship of God, soul and world. Regarded by the Meykandar Sampradaya as a pluralistic exposition. However, some view it as monistic in character with pluralism being introduced by commentators. Some say it is derived from the *Raurava Agama.* Others claim it to be an original work by Meykandar.

Sivajnanam: "Siva wisdom." The result of repeated samadhi experiences of Satchidananda and Parasivam. It is the state of being one with Siva's Divine Mind.

Sivaloka: "World or cosmos of Siva." Siva's habitat, region or level of existence. Known as the causal plane or Third World, the Sivaloka is the superconscious universe of God Siva, the Mahadevas and highly advanced souls. It exists deep within, and transcends, the Second World.

Sivamayam: "Siva is all." Denotes the totality of manifestation—the forms, forces and beings of all three worlds. A monistic term describing Siva as being All, and All as being Siva.

Sivanadiyar: "Slave of Siva." Conveys a mystic relationship between the devotee and Siva in which all spiritual, mental and physical actions are perceived as fulfilling the will and design of Siva.

Sivathondan: "Servant of Siva." Conveys the same mystic meaning as Sivanadiyar, denoting a devotee who regularly performs actions dedicated to God Siva; selfless work in service to others.

Sivathondu: "Service to Siva." Akin to the concept of karma yoga.

Sivayanama: Form of the sacred Panchakshara Mantram recommended for drawing the energies inward toward Self-Realization. One of five ways this mantram can be chanted, each for a specific purpose, each taught and empowered by a Satguru.

sloka: A Sanskrit couplet, usually composed in a specified meter.

Smarta Sampradaya: A widespread Hindu lineage whose adherents principally follow the smritis, the body of man-developed scripture (*Manu Dharma Shastras, Ramayana, Mahabharata, Bhagavad Gita, etc.*). The Smartas accept the Vedas, but reject the Agamas.

smriti: "Remembered." Second great category of Hindu texts—sruti is first—produced by man's own inquiry into the exterior and interior universes and his communication of those findings. Smriti are man-made, whereas sruti are God-given. Smriti discusses both the secular—science, law, society—and the spiritual, ranging from day-to-day subjects to the extraordinary superconscious knowledge embodied in works such as the *Tirumantiram*.

soul: The soul is an immortal and spiritual body of light, the essence of which is Satchidananda and Parasivam, eternal, uncreated and identical with God Siva. The soul animates life and reincarnates again and again until all necessary karmas are created and resolved and its essential unity with God Siva is realized. The soul is the *atman* of the Vedas.

soul body: The being of the soul. Natural, unshrouded body of light. Term used to name the soul's manifest nature as an individual being, the uncreated essence of which—Satchidananda (Pure Consciousness) and Parasivam (Absolute Reality)—is eternally identical with God Siva. Also known as the causal body, or anandamaya kosha, "bliss body"—around which are formed mental, astral, pranic and physical bodies, as required to function in various planes of consciousness.

spiritualism: The cosmological view that the spiritual, or inner psychic, planes are a prime element of reality, and that communication between our physical world and the astral and superconscious worlds is not only possible but part of the process of religion.

Sri Rudram: The preeminent Vedic hymn to Lord Siva, located in the Yajur Veda (precisely in the middle of the first three Vedas), and chanted daily in Siva temples throughout India. It is here that the preeminent Saivite mantra Namasivaya first appears.

sruti: "That which is heard." A term for Hinduism's central scriptures, the Vedas and Agamas, which were revealed in superconscious contemplation by God and Gods to rishis and yogis who communicated this visionary knowledge for the benefit of mankind. Eventually it was recorded in writing.

sthree dharma: Conduct, observances, vocational and spiritual patterns that will most advance a woman in a given lifetime. The parallel pattern for a man is known as purusha dharma.

subsuperconscious mind: Insight, creativity. A state of mind in which the superconscious mind works through the conscious and subconscious, bringing intuition, perfect timing, creative breakthroughs, extrasensory perception. In a creative or awakened individual, the subsuperconscious is vibrant and alive.

subconscious mind: The phase of mind beneath ordinary consciousness. Known as *chitta* in Sanskrit, the subconscious is the storehouse, the reflection of all previous experiences. All the past experiences of the soul (whether remembered consciously or not), unresolved karma and involuntary physiological processes lie in the subconscious mind.

Subramuniya: Composite Sanskrit name that means the *muni* (silent sage) who teaches from *subra,* superconscious knowledge and light. It is the name that was given to Gurudeva, Sivaya Subramuniyaswami, founder of Saiva Siddhanta Church, by his Satguru, Siva Yogaswami, of Jaffna, Sri Lanka, just prior to being initiated by the illustrious sage.

suddha: Sanskrit adjective meaning "pure, unadulterated."

Suddha Saiva Siddhanta: "Pure Saiva Siddhanta." Term found in *Tirumantiram.* A Siddhanta that contains both advaita identity and a theistic evolution towards merger into Siva. Serves to distinguish monistic Saiva Siddhanta from pluralistic Saiva Siddhanta, the core of which is dvaita, non-identity.

Sundaranatha: Original name of Natha siddhar Tirumular before he trekked to South India from the Himalayas and transferred his inner bodies into a Tamil physical body.

superconscious mind: Satchidananda, the Divine Mind of God Siva and of all souls, for "there is only one mind." The superconscious mind is "the mind of light," of omniscient knowing, omnipresent awareness, pure consciousness, truth and love.

supernatural: Beyond or transcendent or controlling the natural laws of our physical cosmos. Of or relating to an order of existence beyond the visible universe and to all events or agencies or knowledge that supersede or mystically explain the expected laws of nature.

Surapadman: Legendary demon, leader of the forces of darkness,

selfishness and ego, whom Lord Muruga vanquished in battle. In
metaphysical reality, this demon is a vast, congested cloud of negative
astral force generated by humanity. Skanda Shasti, a primary Muruga festival, honors the annihilation of this force.

sushumna: The major nerve current that passes through the
spinal column from the muladhara chakra at the base to the sahasrara
at the crown of the head. Through yoga the kundalini energy laying
dormant in the muladhara is awakened and made to rise up via this
channel through each chakra to the sahasrara.

svadharma: "One's own way." One's perfect individual pattern
through life, by which one can best resolve the sum of accumulated
seed karmas inherited from this and past lives as they relate to the collective effect of universal dharma, human dharma and social dharma.

svayambhu lingam: "Self-existent, self-born, self-formed mark."
Names a Siva Lingam discovered in nature and not carved or crafted
by human hands; often a smooth cylindrical stone such as found in
the River Narmada in India.

swami: "He who knows himself." Title for a Hindu holy man, usually a sannyasin.

swastika: The ancient Hindu symbol of auspiciousness and good
fortune. Literally, "It is well." The right-angled arms of the swastika
denote the indirect way in which Divinity is reached— through intuition and not by intellect.

tamasic: "Of darkness or inertia." Tamas is the densest of the three
gunas or fundamental cosmic qualities of nature as described in the
Samkhya system—*tamas* (inertia), *rajas* (activity) and *sattva* (illumination, purity). The *tamaguna* is the quality of denseness, inertia,
contraction, resistance and dissolution.

Tamil: The Dravidian language of the Tamils, a Caucasoid people
of South India and Northern Sri Lanka. Spoken by approximately 50
million people.

Tamil Agama: A respectful, endearing term for the scripture *Tirumantiram* by Saint Tirumular. The term derives from the fact that the
Tirumantiram is in the Tamil language and contains many of the essential teachings of the Saiva Agamas and Vedas, two earlier bodies of
scripture written in Sanskrit.

Tamil Nadu: State in South India where the principle language is
Tamil. Population: 50 million.

tandava: An energetic style of dance—as opposed to the *lasya*,
softer style. One of the principal "cosmic dances" of Lord Siva, having 108 poses. His dance of terrifying destruction, a potent (some call
it violent) dance Siva performs after the cosmos is absorbed and He

alone exists.

tantra: "Loom," "methodology." A class of Hindu scripture providing detailed instruction on all aspects of religion, mystic knowledge and science. The tantras are associated with the Agamic Saiva and Sakta traditions.

tapas: "Heat" or "fire." The performance of purificatory spiritual disciplines, sadhana, penance and sacrifice. One of the niyamas in the ashtanga yoga system. Tapas indicates the inner fire of transformation kindled by ascetic practices.

tapasvin: "One who performs tapas." An ascetic who seeks purification through yoga, austerities, penance and rigorous disciplines.

Tat Purusha: "That Soul." One of a series of five special names of Siva used in Vedic mantras. Implies supreme soul or spirit.

tattva: "Essential nature." In Hindu cosmology tattvas are the primary principles, states, categories or divisions of existence, e.g., omnipotent energy, sound, light, time, prana energy, the individual soul, ego, mind, five senses, five physical elements, and so forth.

temple: A place of worship of God or Gods. An ancient Jewish term, later adopted by various religions, used to translate Indian language words like koyil, madam, etc.

theism: Theological perspective that God exists as a real, conscious, personal Supreme Being. In Saiva Siddhanta, God is wholly immanent and active in the universal environment and in the affairs and unfoldment of the soul.

Third World: The causal plane or Sivaloka: Siva's "loka"—habitat, region or level of existence; the abode of Siva, the Mahadevas and highly advanced souls. It exists deep within and transcends the Second World.

three worlds: In Hindu theology, these are the three levels, or planes, of existence. The First World is the physical universe. The Second World is the astral universe. The Third World is the superconscious or causal universe.

Tirukural: "Holy couplets." The ethical and moral scripture written by Saint Tiruvalluvar on dried palm leaves over 2,000 years ago near present-day Madras, South India. It embodies a treasury of knowledge on conduct, human experience and Hindu Dharma.

Tirumantiram: "Holy mantras." The Natha Sampradaya's oldest Tamil scripture; written *circa* 200 BCE. Earliest of the *Tirumurai*. It is considered an illumined compendium of the Saiva Agamas.

Tirumular: Siddhar, sage and yogi of the Natha Sampradaya who came from the Himalayas (*circa* 200 BCE) to Tamil Nadu where he composed the more than 3,000 hymns of the *Tirumantiram*.

Tirumurai: "Holy book." A twelve-book collection of hymns and writings of Saivite saints of South India.

Tiruvacagam: "Holy utterances." Saiva scripture written by Saint Manikkavasagar in the 9th century CE. Considered the most lyrically beautiful of Tamil devotional literature.

Tiruvalluvar: Tamil weaver and householder saint who wrote the major Saivite ethical scripture, *Tirukural (circa* 200 BCE).

Transcendent Absolute: Denotes God as beyond time, form and space; known as *Parasivam* in Saivism and as *Parabrahman* in the Vedas; identical with the Self (*Paramatma*); beyond concepts and description and realizable only through Nirvikalpa Samadhi.

trikonam: A triangle; symbol of God Siva's Absolute Reality; also represents the element fire.

triple bondage: The three primal forces which bind the soul, also known as "pasam"—*anava* (ignorance), *karma* (the law of cause and effect) and *maya* (the principle of matter). Though termed bondages in Saiva Siddhanta, the three malas provide the soul with the experience it needs to realize its identity with Siva and evolve to its full potential.

tripundra: "Three lines." Sect mark of Saivites, worn on the forehead. Consists of three horizontal lines of vibhuti (holy ash), often with a red dot, or *pottu,* at the point of the third eye. The three lines represent the consumption (as in burning to ash) of the soul's three bonds—anava, karma and maya.

Trisula: A three-pronged spear or trident wielded by Lord Siva and some Saivite ascetics; symbolizes his Iccha, Kriya and Jnana Saktis (powers)—volition, action and wisdom.

Umapati: "Lord of Uma." Name for Siva meaning He who is the Lord of Uma, or Sakti. Used to address Siva's merciful, compassionate, mother-like nature. Also connotes the divine cosmic Mother-Father God.

unevolutionary: Perfect, complete, not undergoing change. In the same form at the beginning, the middle and end of all evolution. Used in describing God Siva.

unfoldment: A making known or laying open to view, especially in stages or little by little. Often used in the phrase "spiritual unfoldment" to mean the gradual uncovering of our soulful, spiritual qualities and abilities through consistent religious practice, meditation and grace.

universal dharma: See: *rita dharma.*

universal dissolution: See: *Mahapralaya.*

upadesha: "Advice, religious instruction." Often given in question-

and-answer form from guru to disciple. The Satguru's spiritual discourses.

Upanishads: "Sitting near devotedly." The final portion of the *Vedas*. Philosophical chronicles of rishis who expounded the inner and outer natures of God, soul and cosmos. The loftiest and most recent portion of the *Vedas*.

upasana: "Sitting near." Worship or contemplation of God. One of the pancha nitya karmas, *or* "five constant duties," of Hindus. Upasana is to be performed daily without fail.

utsava: "Festivity." The Sanskrit word for *religious festival* or *holy day*. It also names the observance of holy days—including festivals in the home and temple—as part of one's yearly religious pattern. Utsava is one of the pancha nitya karmas, or five duties.

vahana: "Bearing, carrying or conveying." Each Hindu God is depicted as riding an animal-bird vahana, which is symbolic of a function of the God. For example, Siva rides the bull, Lord Muruga rides the peacock and Lord Ganesha rides the mouse.

Vaikasi: The Tamil name of the second month of the year in the Hindu system (in which the new year begins in mid-April). Vaikasi extends from mid-May to mid-June on the Gregorian calendar.

Vaishnavism: The religion followed by those who worship Vishnu as Supreme Being or any of that God's professed incarnations, most especially the incarnations of Krishna and Rama. One of the three main sects of Hinduism. The Hindu epics *Mahabharata* and *Ramayana* are important scriptures of this religion. Vaishnavism incorporated the Saiva Agamic worship and temple building system, formulating their own Agamas. Vaishnavism is divided into a number of distinct sects with diverse theologies and hundreds of scriptures and is exemplified by many saints. The goal of Vaishnavism is the attainment of Mukti, defined as blissful union with God's body, the loving recognition that the soul is a part of Him. Orthodox Vaishnavites believe that religion is the performance of bhakti sadhanas, that man can communicate with and receive the grace of Lord Vishnu who manifests through the temple image. Through chanting the holy names of Lord Vishnu's incarnations, and total self-surrender to Him, liberation is attained.

Vaishnavite: A follower of the Vaishnavite religion. Also an adjective meaning "of Vaishnavism."

Vama: "Lovely, dear, pleasant." One of a series of five special names of Siva from Vedic mantras.

vanaprastha: "Forest dweller." Third ashrama or stage of human life. The period, roughly after the age of fifty, when the individual

lvi   DANCING WITH SIVA

dedicates a large percentage of his time to religious sadhana and, utilizing his lifelong experience, acts as an advisor and counselor to the grihastha community.

varnashrama dharma: Social dharma; the duties and responsibilities an individual must fulfill as a member of his or her nation, community and family.

vata: Banyan tree, an ancient symbol of Saivism, or Sanatana Dharma, chosen because of its nature of branching out in many directions both above and below the ground. It is also associated with Lord Siva as Dakshinamurthi, the Silent Sage who sits beneath the banyan tree and teaches the ancient wisdom.

Vedanta: "Ultimate wisdom" or "final conclusions of the Vedas." The philosophy embodied in the Upanishads, the realized knowledge portion of the Vedas.

Vedas: "Wisdom." Composed 4,000–500 BCE, four companion scriptures—*Rig, Yajur, Sama, Atharva*—consisting of roughly 20,000 Sanskrit verses that form Hinduism's primary scripture (along with the Agamas).

veiling grace: God's obscuring power. A purposeful limiting of the faculties of consciousness (such as cognition or memory). Siva's grace in Saiva Siddhanta is in two forms: revealing grace (*Anugraha Sakti*) and veiling grace (*Tirodhana Sakti*).

Vel: "Spear, lance." The symbol of Lord Muruga's divine authority as Lord of Yoga and Commander of the devas.

vibhuti: "Resplendent." Holy ash, prepared by burning dried cow dung cakes into a whitish ash. Vibhuti connotes purity. Saivites apply the ash as the tripundra, or three horizontal lines drawn across the full width of the forehead, signifying the burning away of the three bonds of pasam: anava, karma and maya.

Vighnesvara: "Lord of Obstacles." A name for Lord Ganesha describing His power to both remove and create obstacles to guide souls along the right path. Hindus supplicate Lord Ganesha in this form before undertaking a task, planning a change in life or worshiping the other Gods.

Vinayaga: "He who takes away" (implying the removal of obstacles). A name for Lord Ganesha. The name *Vighna* (obstacle) *Vinayaga* (remover) even more fully conveys the meaning of "Remover of Obstacles."

Virasaivism: "Hero Saivism." One of six living schools of Saivism, founded by Basanava in the 12th century CE. Also called "Lingayat Saivism." Approximately 15 million followers, mostly located along the western coast of Karnataka state in India.

Vishnu: Supreme Deity of the Vaishnavite religion, depicted as the great Preserver God and worshiped for prosperity in hundreds of temples in India and elsewhere.

vrata: "Vow." A religious oath. Vratas are personal promises to perform certain disciplines over a period of time, such as penance, fasting, specific japa repetitions, worship or meditation.

Vyagrapadar: "Tiger Feet." Famous Natha Sampradaya siddhar who trained under Nandinatha and was a brother disciple of Tirumular and Patanjali. Probably lived around the 2nd century BCE. He pilgrimaged south from Kashmir, settling at the Chidambaram Siva Temple (Tamil Nadu, South India) to practice yoga. Legend says that he developed tiger claws so he could scale trees to pick the choicest flowers for his daily Siva worship.

yajna: Hindu fire ceremony. A sacrificial rite of the Vedas and Agamas, performed to establish communication between the physical world and the astral and superconscious universes.

Yajur Veda: "Wisdom of sacrifice." Second great Veda that contains, both in poetry and prose, the hymns and formulas chanted during ritual. This work is divided into 40 chapters of 1,975 stanzas, about 30 percent of which are repetitions of the *Rig Veda.*

Yama: "Rein or restrain." Hindu God of Death; oversees the processes of death transition, guiding the soul out of the present physical body.

yama: "To rein, or restrain." The *yamas* are ethical restraints that check or curb the base, instinctive nature. The ten yamas are:

1) *ahimsa* (noninjury)
2) *satya* (truthfulness)
3) *asteya* (nonstealing)
4) *brahmachariya* (sexual purity)
5) *kshama* (patience)
6) *dhriti* (steadfastness)
7) *daya* (compassion)
8) *arjava* (honesty)
9) *mitahara* (moderate appetite)
10) *saucha* (purity).

yantra: "Vessel, container." A mystic diagram composed of geometric and alphabetic figures—often etched in gold, silver or copper—which focuses spiritual energies. A yantra is generally installed with each temple Deity. Psychically, the temple yantra is a three-dimensional edifice of light and sound that is much larger than the temple itself. The devas of the temple work within it.

yoga: "To yoke or unite." Connotes the process of yoking or fusing individual consciousness with the Divine and the method followed to achieve this union. One of the six *darshanas* (systems of orthodox Hindu philosophy), according to the *Yoga Sutras* of Patanjali.

Yogaswami: "Master of yoga." Sri Lanka's most renowned spiritual master (1872–1964), Siva Yogaswami was a Sivajnani and Natha siddhar lauded by both Hindus and Buddhists. He was trained in and practiced deep kundalini yoga under the guidance of his Satguru, Chellappaswami, who eventually gave him guru diksha. Yogaswami was in turn the Satguru of Sivaya Subramuniyaswami, current Satguru of the Kailasa Paramparai.

   yogi: One who practices yoga, especially kundalini or raja yoga.

   yoni: "Origin, nest, lap, womb." Term for the base of the Siva Lingam, representing Siva's manifest Sakti.

   yuga: "Period, age." One of four ages which chart the duration of the world according to Hindu thought. They are: Sat, Treta, Dvapara and Kali. In the first period dharma reigns supreme, but as time progresses virtue diminishes and wickedness increases. At the end of the Kali yuga, which we are in now, the cycle begins again with a new Sat yuga.

Colophon

These teachings of the world's oldest spiritual tradition have been gathered, edited, designed and illustrated by the swamis of the Saiva Siddhanta Yoga Order at Kauai's Hindu Monastery on Hawaii's Garden Island. *Dancing with Siva* was assembled on a network of Macintosh computers using QuarkXpress, Microsoft Word and Adobe Illustrator. The text was laser set in 11.5-point Minion. The color cover was ported to a Scitex for output on a high-resolution color plotter. The book was printed by Banta Company on a Cameron Belt Press on 55# Butte des Morts, a predominantly recycled paper. The cover art is an 18th century painting, Chamba School, of Siva and Parvati witnessing a dance, displayed in the National Museum, New Delhi. The back cover photo of His Holiness Sivaya Subramuniyaswami was taken by Rohini Kumar in Kuala Lumpur, Malaysia.

Publications from Himalayan Academy

HINDUISM TODAY INTERNATIONAL NEWSPAPER

"Affirming the dharma and recording the modern history of nearly a billion Hindus" is the bold motto of this graphically rich monthly newspaper which promotes Hindu solidarity among all sects of the world's oldest faith.

This extraordinary monthly paper is the best way there is to keep in touch with Hindu happenings on a global scale, the leaders, the institutions, the trends; but more than that, it provides a continuous flow of spiritual teaching and insight that will help your whole family apply the timeless truths to each day's experience. Published in five countries by Gurudeva Sivaya Subramuniyaswami and assembled and edited by the monks of the Saiva Siddhanta Yoga Order in Hawaii. $20 for one year, $30 for two, $40 for three, $50 for four, $60 for five years, $300 for a lifetime. Individual, collector's-item back issues—$5.00 each. A complete set of 11 years of back issues in a massive, library quality hardbound volume is available in limited quantities for $300.

THE MASTER COURSE

The Master Course is a profound spiritual study. It is the cream of forty years of teaching by Gurudeva Sivaya Subramuniyaswami, spanning the entire gamut of Saivite religious life.

Book One: Hindu Catechism

This is an expanded edition of *Dancing with Siva*, designed as a study text with 63 daily lessons, multiple-choice tests and more. 9th ed., 1987, 200 pgs., 8.5"x11", $29.95 (ISBN 0-945497-04-0)

Book Two: Hindu Sadhana

In 63 daily lessons, Book Two focuses on regular performance of spiritual disciplines, meditation, introspection. 8th ed., 1983, 90 pgs., 8.5"x11", $15.00 (ISBN 0-945497-34-2)

Book Three: Hindu Metaphysics

Book Three deals with the seven chakras, the human aura, color meditations and karma. A preliminary edition, 1989, 130 pages, 8.5"x11", $15.00 (ISBN 0-945497-35-0)

GURUDEVA'S TAPED DISCOURSES

Gurudeva's Recorded Talks on the Telephone
This could be the most important phone call you will ever make. For what you need to know when you need to know it, call 808/822-SIVA (7482) and enjoy listening to Gurudeva's enlightened thoughts on a wide variety of topics. The tapes are changed daily, so call often.

The 1970 Master Course Tapes
In twelve one-hour recordings, Gurudeva describes the path to God-Realization; the mind, reincarnation, yoga, sadhana, auras, chakras and superconsciousness. The story of his own path and spiritual encounters is on the second tape. $108 for set of 12, or choose from the following titles. Single tapes are $10.00. (ISBN 0-945497-35-0)

- The Great Story of Awareness
- The Making of a Master
- Life the Great Experience
- The River of Life
- The Donkey and the Carrot
- The Faithful Computer
- The Illumination of Man
- The Mind of Light
- Cultivating Willpower
- Chakras, Energies, Death and Reincarnation
- The Two Paths
- The Language of Meditation

THE SAIVITE SERIES

Special pre-publication limited editions of Gurudeva's most current works that comprise a supplementary study to The Master Course. *Plastic ring binding, photocopy printing, 8.5"x11", glossy paper cover.*

Saivite Names: A Practical Manual for Entering Hinduism
Brief synopsis of each of the world religions and philosophies, and steps to formally becoming a Saivite Hindu. 1st ed., 1989, 161 pgs., $20.00 (ISBN 0-945497-10-5)

Saivite Calendar: The Kadavul Hindu Panchangam
Tamil Hindu Vedic calendar for auspicious planning of daily activities, business and important changes in life, complete with instructions and glossary. Computer-generated specifically for your region. Send city and time zone with order. 100 pgs., $20.00 (ISBN 0-945497-12-1)

Saivite Dictionary: A Collection of Hindu Philosophical Terms
Definitions of 900 words from the monistic Saiva Siddhanta of the
Natha Sampradaya's Kailasa Paramparai. 2nd ed., 1987, 50 pgs.,
$9.00 (ISBN 0-945497-11-3)

Saivite Virtue: A Seven-Week Course on the Power of Celibacy
Frank discourses on the metaphysics of sex to help young Hindus
understand, harness and transmute their energies, instincts and
desires into higher expression for a fulfilling life. 100 pages, $15.00
(ISBN 0-945497-25-3)

Saivite Astrology: Your Hindu Horoscope
Includes interpretations and disciplines to help you face particular karmic challenges indicated in your chart. Send birth star,
place, time and date of birth. 25 pages, $21 (ISBN 0-945497-32-6)

THE POCKETBOOK SERIES

Lord Ganesha: Benevolent Deity for the Modern Hindu World
His symbols and forms, nature and functions. Richly illustrated,
includes mantrams, esoteric explanations of the Gods, 108 names
in Sanskrit and English and more. 2nd ed., 1989, 190 pgs., 5.5"x
7.5", $6.00 (ISBN 0-945497-08-3)

God's Money
The origins, means and benefits of tithing, called *dasamamsha* by
Hindus, who have practiced giving to religion for 6,000 years. Useful tool for institutions seeking to raise funds. 1st ed., 1987, 5.5"x
7.5", 170 pgs., $6.00 (ISBN 0-945497-05-0)

THE RISHI COLLECTION

Raja Yoga: A Manual on Spiritual Consciousness
In 35 compellingly simple aphorisms and commentary upon
them, Gurudeva challenges us to seek nothing less than the Ultimate Being of ourselves. 1st ed., 1973, 8.5" square, 193 pgs., hand-
set type, gold embossed white cloth hardcover and jacket, $25.00,
(ISBN 0-87516-348-3)

Gems of Wisdom: 108 Classical Hindu Meditations
Meditations to inspire the seeker to look deeper into the wondrous mysteries of life and consciousness, with 108 photos from
pilgrimages in the Orient. 5th ed., 1973, 234 pgs., 8.5" square, gold

embossed white cloth hardcover and artistic jacket, $25.00 (ISBN 0-87516-346-7)

Dancing with Siva: A Hindu Catechism
A comprehensive, illustrated presentation of Saivite Hinduism. This is a slightly abridged edition of *Hindu Catechism,* Book One of *The Master Course,* without that edition's daily lesson format. 3rd ed., 1990, 320 pgs., $9.95 (ISBN 0-87516-346-7)

PATHFINDER'S LIBRARY

A six-book collection of inspired talks by Gurudeva given in the late 50's and early 70's, printed in 1973 on recycled "oatmeal" paper. Paperbound, 48 pages, illustrated with photos of nature. $1.00 each.

The Fine Art of Meditation
How to breathe, what to eat, what to concentrate on; questions and answers for meditators. $1.00 (ISBN 0-87516-356-4)

I'm All Right, Right Now
On quieting the external, nomadic ramblings of the mind, seeking within and centering ourselves in the now. $1.00 (ISBN 0-87516-355-6)

The Power of Affirmation
Nine affirmations with instructions on how to use them to awaken unrealized potential. $1.00 (ISBN 0-87516-357-2)

Everything is Within You
We create of our own life happenings; everything resides deep in our own consciousness. $1.00 (ISBN 0-87516-358-0)

On the Brink of the Absolute
Reminding us what it's like to live in cosmic consciousness, at the "apex of creation." $1.00 (ISBN 0-87516-359-9)

The River of Life
Seven daily meditations to help us go with the flow of life in affectionate detachment. $1.00 (ISBN 0-87516-354-8)

ON THE PATH SERIES

Six talks by Gurudeva on enlightenment, printed in 1972–73, paperbound, embossed cover, heavy, white classic-laid paper, 5"x5", 72 pages.

The Self God
The best concise summary of Gurudeva's teachings of the timeless, causeless, formless Self. $2.00 (ISBN 0-87516-353-X)

The Clear White Light
A seeker's guide to the many varieties of superconscious experience one encounters on the path. $2.00 (ISBN 0-87516-350-5)

The Lotus of the Heart
Everyday experiences that reveal we are indeed the master of our own consciousness. $2.00 (ISBN 0-87516-352-1)

The Search is Within
Simple guidelines for spiritual living, with thirty-six basic principles.$2.00 (ISBN 0-87516-349-1)

The Meditator
"Meditation is a disciplined art, a pilgrimage into the mind itself." Gurudeva teaches how to achieve superconscious states of awareness. $2.00 (ISBN 0-87516-351-3)

Reflections
Pithy and profound sayings centering around the quest for enlightenment, each verse a crystal of insight. With photos. $2.00 (ISBN 0-87516-354-8)

OTHER FINE BOOKS

The Saiva Dharma Shastras:
Book of Discipline of Saiva Siddhanta Church
A complete overview of Church history, membership and doctrine. Talks by Church founder, Gurudeva Sivaya Subramuniyaswami. 6th ed., hardbound, 1986, 8.5"x11", 360 pgs., $51.00 (ISBN 0-945497-03-2)

My Hindu Color Book
Forty pages of line drawings for children, with Hindu themes that include saints, temples and cultural images. Printed on quality paper, 11"x17", $6.00 (ISBN 0-945497-01-6)

Atmartha Puja for the Hindu Home
Presents and explains in step-by-step detail the traditional Hindu ceremony for the Saivite home shrine. 1st ed., 1986, 100 pages, cassette included, $10.00 (ISBN 0-945497-22-9)

Praying to the Gods: A Modern Tantra on Writing
Prayers for the Sacred Temple Fire
Gurudeva unveils his wonderful Tyaf script, designed for writing prayers to be sent to the inner worlds through the temple fire. A rich treasure of instruction and insight on prayer, states of mind, karma and the Divine. 150 pages, 5.5"x 8.5", plastic GBC binding, $12.00 (ISBN 0-945497-38-5). Apple Macintosh disk with Tyaf Postscript Font: $15.00.

VIDEOS

Kauai's Siva Temple
A 45-minute VHS of Hawaii's Siva Nataraja temple's 1985 Kumbhabhishekam celebration. $33.00 (ISBN 0-945497-02-4)

The Story of Hinduism Today
A slideshow video of the inside story of *Hinduism Today*—the award-winning international newspaper—showing the Hawaii editorial offices and staff and journalists and franchisees worldwide. 17 min. VHS and PAL. $25.00

COLORFUL POSTERS

Siva's Saints
Elegant, full-color calligraphic masterpiece of the 63 Saivite saints penned in holy mantrams in Tamil and English. It took the artist four years to complete this extraordinary bija mantra art in Tamil and English. Brief biographies included on back side, 17" x 22". $10.00

Siva's Cosmic Dance
Lord Siva, the Cosmic Dancer portrayed in the 108 Tandava poses. 17" x 22". $10.00

POSTCARDS

Exquisite new collector's-item cards printed on hard glossy stock in rich colors. 25¢ each, 10 for $2.50, 25 for $6.00, 50 for $11.75, 100 for $23.00

Choose from the following selection:
Ganesha, Nandi, Muruga, Yogaswami, Gurudeva, Samadhi, Bhajan, Darshan, Crystal Lingam, Ganapati (16 forms).

Order Form

All prices are listed in U.S. currency. When ordering, specify name of item, quantity and unit prices. Add 5% for postage and handling in USA and 10% foreign. Foreign orders are shipped sea mail unless otherwise specified and additional postage is provided. (Add 50% for foreign airmail postage.) Make check or money order payable to Himalayan Academy Bookshelf. VISA and Master Card are accepted.

We highly recommend that you subscribe to Hinduism's foremost international newspaper, *Hinduism Today*—with news, features, teaching sections and editorials on the vast array of Hindu traditions, events and people. It's the best way there is to keep in touch with Hindu happenings on a global scale. Founded and published by Sivaya Subramuniyaswami, printed in five nations. USA subscription for one year: $20. In Malaysia: M$32; in Mauritius: Rs 85; in Africa: R30.

☐ *Yes, I would like to receive a free literature packet.*
☐ *Yes, I would like to subscribe to Hinduism Today.*
☐ 1-year subscription $20   ☐ 2-year subscription $30
I would also like to order the following items: *Cost*

_____

_____

_____

_____

☐ My payment is enclosed.   Charge to: ☐ Master Card   ☐ Visa

Card number: _____

Expiration date: _____   Total of purchase: _____

Signature: _____

_____
First and Last Name (Please Print)   Telephone

_____
Address

_____

Mail orders to:

USA: Himalayan Academy Publications,
P.O. Box 157, Hanamaulu, HI 96715 USA
MALAYSIA: Siddhanta Publications, P.O. Box 301,
46730 Petaling Jaya, Selangor, MALAYSIA